INDUSTRIAL SECURITY
Second Edition

Industrial Security

Second Edition

David L. Berger

With Chapters By
Guest Authors

Charles A. Sennewald

Steve Kaufer

Jurg W. Mattman

Dr. Sanford Sherizan

Boston   Oxford   Auckland   Johannesburg   Melbourne   New Delhi

Butterworth–Heinemann supports the efforts of American Forests and the Global ReLeaf program in its campaign for the betterment of trees, forests, and our environment.

Library of Congress Cataloging-in-Publication Data
Berger, David L., 1929–
    Industrial security/ David L. Berger ; with chapters by guest authors, Charles A. Sennewald . . . [et al.]. — 2nd ed.
       p.   cm.
    Includes bibliographical references and index.
    ISBN 0-7506-7139-4 (hc. : alk. paper)
    1. Industries—Security measures.   I. Sennewald, Charles A., 1931– . II. Title.
HD61.5.B47   1999   98-48867
658.4′7—dc21   CIP

British Library Cataloguing-in-Publication Data
A catalogue record for this book is available from the British Library.

To Mildred and Greb

Contents

Foreword

I have known David Berger for well over 30 years, having first met him during my tenure as chief of the Los Angeles Police Department. Following my retirement from that agency, I became involved in the purchase of his investigation agency and security guard company, International Investigation Systems. That company had been established for almost 20 years and had enjoyed both an impressive list of quality individual and commercial clients, along with an excellent reputation with high-ranking law enforcement officials and the general public. He and his company had, in fact, pioneered many of the security techniques, equipment, and procedures now considered standard in the industry. At the time he sold the company, Mr. Berger had decided to accept a position as a peace officer with the Los Angeles County District Attorney's Bureau of Investigation.

Industrial Security, first published in 1979, is still one of the definitive texts on the subject of security. It has been of immense value to anyone—beginner, professional, or teacher—interested in the subject. I personally have always found it useful and practical and am delighted that David has prepared a second edition of the book for a new generation of security practitioners.

The revisions and additions to this already "standard" work will make it more valuable than ever to every serious student of security. It is a work of great value to both the beginner and the professional.

Thomas Reddin
Chief, Los Angeles Police Department, retired

Preface

Industrial Security was originally published in 1979 after three long years of preparation. In 1975 and 1976, security was still an emerging discipline and the term *industrial security* was still an all-encompassing term meaning "private" security, as opposed to a government function. The specialties were only beginning to be recognized as full categories through the efforts of mass communication within the industry's organizational newsletters, magazines such as *Security World,* books published by Security World Publishing Company, which was later purchased by Butterworth-Heinemann, and, of course, the annual International Security Conference, along with other industry-initiated conferences and seminars.

It wasn't until the early to mid-1970s that industry pioneers began addressing the specialty concept in texts devoted to those areas. Ed San Luis's *Office and Office Building Security,* Russell L. Colling's *Hospital Security,* and Walter J. Buzby II and David Paine's *Hotel and Motel Security Management* are just a few examples of the emergence of the specialty areas within the security field. Around the same time "Security" began to be offered as an elective course within the then-developing Police Science programs in colleges and universities; and Ray Farber, then owner of Security World Publishing Company, decided to reenter the world of academia with a beginning text to be titled *Industrial Security.* Ray had already authored *Introduction to Security.* As he explained, that title would be better understood by the law enforcement students who would be taking the course and who would be familiar with that term in defining "private security." He felt that *Industrial Security* would present the industry in a more dignified manner.

It was only then that he approached me with an offer to author the book. I had written, or ghost written, some articles for *Security World* magazine and helped develop the first International Security Conference at the Ambassador Hotel in Los Angeles. His only directive to me was that the book be extremely basic in its concept.

I made the decision to present my ideas by means of a mythical company that manufactured widgets and to show how the security concept and methods of protecting people and assets develops throughout the growth of that small mom-and-pop operation up to, and including, its maturation as a multinational corporation. Along the way, of course, the company increases its workforce and expands its building facilities, and experiences all of the other problems generally manifested by continued expansion.

Industrial Security has been used in colleges continuously since its publication in 1979. I am aware of the criticism regarding the book's title when, in fact, it is not about "industrial" security, because in today's world "industrial" is assumed to pertain to "manufacturing." Who, the critics ask, is this guy Berger, whose CV does not indicate one hint of experience within an "industrial" environment as a director of security, much less as a posted guard? Sadly, my critics are correct. They are absolutely accurate—within the limited scope of their ability to perceive our discipline in its totality.

Allow me, if you will, the privilege granted authors within the context of the "preface." I began my career in 1954 as a private investigator in the state of California. Shortly thereafter I expanded my business to include a contract security guard service; then, in 1960 began designing total integrated systems and consulting with large businesses, industry, and retail and commercial complexes, evaluating their existing security and presenting new concepts such as CCTV, having previously come from the broadcasting industry. During that period, *Kline vs. 1500 Massachusetts Ave.* arrived on the scene and the totally new field of forensic security consultants was born. I became engaged in my first forensic assignment shortly after the *Kline* case and worked in that field part time for the next few years. In 1980, I entered that arena full time. In the interim, I spent time as a peace officer in California, director of security at the corporate level for a couple of large concerns, and finally devoted myself to my forensic practice in Las Vegas. I have had a great many varied assignments and experiences during the past 44 years, but my work in the forensic field has really opened my eyes to the problems and shortcomings of our industry.

For those of you who are not familiar with the functions of a forensic security consultant, allow me to briefly define the job. *Forensic* means legally arguable or publicly debatable. It is a subject that is commonly argued or debated in court, with "subject" being defined as a "branch of knowledge." That "subject," therefore, could be medicine, accounting, plumbing, or security. Thus, if you are a physician, CPA, plumber, or security consultant with the word *forensic* preceding your title, you are qualified to present an expert opinion in a court of law.

A forensic security consultant is retained when security is a relevant issue in civil litigation and that issue must be defined by an expert, along with that expert's opinion relative to the case, enabling (theoretically) the court, or jury, to arrive at a just decision based partially on their newly acquired knowledge of those security issues and how they relate to the case at bar. When the security consultant prepares a case, he or she reviews, very carefully, all of the discovery materials: depositions, interrogatories, police reports, security manuals, and any other documentation relative to the case, such as security logs and incident reports, security officer personnel files, security officer training procedures, technical aspects of alarm installations, closed-circuit television applications, and so on. Then, when there is a "foreseeability" issue (determining the potential of criminal activity occurring at some specific location), crime statistics prepared by the local law enforcement agency are examined and calculations in the form of crime statistical summaries must be prepared, which evaluate the potential of criminal activity. Finally, site inspections are conducted during which every physical aspect of the environment where the incident occurred is examined.

The forensic security consultant thus examines every conceivable aspect of the security issues under a microscope. Comparisons are made by researching past case histories, volumes of texts, academic studies published in journals, volumes from the U.S. Department of Justice, and Bureau of Justice Statistics. Research, research,

research. Finally, all of the mistakes, errors in judgment, deliberate falsifications of reports, examples of poor training, obvious lack of proper selection of security personnel, lax background investigations (if any) . . . everything . . . becomes apparent to the examiner, the forensic security consultant. The forensic consultant, in time, begins to see patterns evolving in the behavior of some security officers. He recognizes a loss prevention officer whose prejudice or ego takes control of good judgment and professional conduct. Signs of alcohol or drug addiction become apparent to the forensic examiner, usually early in an evaluation. A forensic consultant's experience, over time, alerts him to subtleties that may have been overlooked by other, less experienced, reviewers of the case history. There is no doubt in my mind at all that the forensic practitioner develops an awareness of the problems with the industry that continue to manifest themselves repeatedly in case after case over long periods of time. This is possible only because of her or his unique position of reviewing those case histories, knowing the results of inadequate or improper security procedures or conduct as they are ultimately adjudicated in a court of law. The forensic practitioner understands the consequences of a legal precedent and how it can affect the security industry . . . like it or not.

The author has been examining security conduct and procedures, as a forensic consultant, for more than 25 years. Over the years, he has seen which issues involving inadequate and improper security conduct and procedures are the primary issues in security-related litigation. Although those issues are numerous and extremely specific, only two have, in the author's mind, been significant enough to guide the direction of this, the second edition of *Industrial Security.* The first significant issue is the level of *training* provided to security personnel, especially in the uniformed officer category. The so-called "basic" training, sometimes referred to as the Powers to Arrest course, is sorely lacking in those elements necessary to prepare new security officers for performing their assignments and being responsible for the lives of the people with whom they will come in contact or the protection of the property and assets under their control. Some of the firearms courses I have evaluated make me fear for the officers' lives as well as any others within the range of their weapons (and I won't even mention those new officers who have hidden priorities for that weapon, undisclosed by a background investigation of any kind).

The second factor developed through years of reviewing cases involving poor security conduct and strategies is, in fact, the surge of technological development. I first became aware of the danger of the "technology revolution" when I was the director of security for a major Southern California bank in the 1970s. At that time, we were installing, and I was helping to develop, one of the very early computerized access control systems. It was the first computer that actually controlled door-locking hardware and the fire, burglary, and robbery alarm systems at all of the branches, from one control center. The computer also maintained surveillance over all employees by virtue of their sensitized ID badges. You know what I'm talking about—all of those functions that are now considered ancient history, but which were, in those days, the first of their kind; the prototype for the future. That was also the time when ATMs were first being installed and I and other directors in the banking industry turned our thumbs down saying, "Surely, someone will be killed at one of those infernal machines."

The problem with all of this wonderful technology is that when an officer's computer is not functioning, many officers don't have the basic knowledge needed to enable them to function independently of that computer. Oh, it's true, the company "security manual' undoubtedly may be referred to in some instances, but the time consumed could be disastrous. It is, after all, those "disasters" that have led to the litigation that in recent years has been a significant disaster in itself, particularly within the security industry. For that reason alone, even though *Industrial Security* is no longer primarily a college text, I have decided to retain the work as a "basic" volume, emphasizing the theory and philosophy of security strategies.

This basic approach is not intended to insult the professional, nor is it intended to degrade the journeyman security officer; rather it is designed to provide the industry with a source for helping to educate the new practitioners entering our field. It is they, after all, who will become the security directors of the future. It also serves as a reference for those interested in learning why they do what they do, enabling them to arrive at intelligent procedural options when emergencies arise and their usual resources become unavailable.

I do not feel comfortable entering into a subject requiring the unique skills of an individual, practicing in a highly specialized area of security. Even though I am qualified to evaluate those areas of expertise, I prefer that the "specialist" handle the in-depth subtleties of the teaching process. I do, on numerous occasions, refer forensic clients to other consultants in the field more qualified than I to address those particular highly specialized areas of security. Some chapters of this work will, therefore, be presented by some very special invited guests. These are individuals with whom I have worked closely in the past; skilled professionals who are well known in their field and respected for their work, writing, and involvement in the educational process. Forty-four years ago, when I first entered the security arena, the "job" was handled mostly by older men who were retired or unable to find other employment; after all "guards" and "night watchmen" only earned about $1.25 an hour and, believe it or not, many of them had to kick back a portion of their weekly salary to the supervisor who hired them. "Store detectives" and the hotel "house dick" would often bust a poor kid who picked up an item at the counter, then made the mistake of walking ten feet in the direction of the door . . . or the intoxicated person who inadvertently got off the hotel elevator on the wrong floor. Burns and Pinkertons were all over the place along with a very few other guard services. most of whom were "bodyshops." Over the past years, the "job" progressed to a "security position," and now, in modern times, to a "discipline." Hopefully, some day, the term "professional" will be applied to many in our ranks.

The history of security is fascinating—going all the way back to the stone age when early man built fires and posted men at the entrances of caves to protect the tribe from wild animals and marauding enemies. The pyramids of Egypt were probably the first security structures, penetrated only because of the building materials they had to work with. The Chinese military theorist, Sun Tzu, whose five point treatise established modern intelligence techniques; his writings appeared some time around the fourth or sixth century B.C. The reader may believe that none of that really has any value in determining today's strategies but the development of our industry has, in fact, been guided by *history* and some of those lessons of the past are extremely significant. The architect Imhotep, along with Sun Tzu, developed their projects because of conditions which required those skills relating to *security* issues. It should be mentioned that they did not have the "computer" to guide the development of their work. It should also be mentioned that their work has remained a constant focus of study for thousands of years . . . along with the constant reoccurrence of those same security issues for each generation to cope with. Each generation, in turn, has looked to history to consider the theory, successes, and failures that have taken them to their point in time; if they do not, they are only going to repeat the mistakes of the past and waste the most valuable of all gifts—*time.*

The history of our security industry is interwoven with the development of law enforcement, the military, architecture, and a host of other disciplines. Imhotep and Sun Tzu are now joined by Sir Robert Peel, Wilson, Healy, Farber, and others. With the exception of that first caveman, all have learned from the others and maybe that is why we remember them today. Each of them are fascinating stories in themselves . . . but that's another book.

Acknowledgments

This revision of *Industrial Security* was not only a true labor of love, it also heralded my entry into the world of computers. Had it not been for my family, the project probably would have failed along with my ending up in a loony bin. My wife *Greb,* undoubtedly suffered the most, becoming a "computer widow" and not liking it one bit; but through it all, she provided me with the encouragement, food, and vitamin pills necessary for my survival.

Between us, we have a lot of daughters, three wonderful sons-in-law and, obviously, grandkids. They were all fantastic. Naia (Sarah) purchased the computer and initiated its programming. Julie spent literally hours on the telephone talking me through the operation of this monster and getting me to a point where I could really work the damn thing. Then, at various times when I got "stuck," Katherine and Alexandra exhibited extraordinary patience, both on the phone and here at my home in Las Vegas, explaining to the "old man" what every child of seven knows. Bobby, Mike, and Lawrence also took their turns getting me out of one jam after another. Then there were the grandkids, Mary, Nick, and Katie, who kept the computer from rusting, through lack of use, by playing with it during their visits to our home. Watching them was embarrassing. They didn't need any help at all.

Then there were the contributors to the text, who never once questioned their participation, but furnished time, talent, and extraordinary expertise unhesitatingly. I introduce each contributor individually at the beginning of their chapters later in this text, but I do want to add here that working with them makes me proud to be in this business.

To all of the above, thank you!

Part I

INTRODUCTION

Chapter 1

The Evolution of Security

Sooner or later all businesses, large and small, will require some degree of protection. Problems begin to materialize that may impair the company's ability to produce its products in a safe, efficient, and profitable manner. Risk factors manifest themselves that affect almost every area of product development, technical procedures, mechanical operations, and personnel activity. To many company executives, untrained and unfamiliar with security methods and procedures, the "problems" may appear insurmountable: fire risks, safety hazards, criminal activity, theft, burglary, embezzlement, sabotage, competitive industrial espionage, first-aid emergencies, disaster planning, alarm systems, communications, simple traffic control, and so on.

Initially, the basic security strategies are consistent, regardless of whether the business is a service provider such as an advertising agency, an architectural firm, an industrial or manufacturing company, hotel, residential complex, hospital, retail store, shopping center, and so forth. The basic protection for structures, parking areas, personnel selection, etc., is ultimately modified only due to the unique qualities of a particular business.

For the purpose of this examination of the basic security techniques and applications, we will follow the growth of a mythical industrial company that manufactures widgets.

THE EARLY YEARS

In the early years of company growth the business was different. The "Old Man" burned the midnight oil, struggling over books and composing letters to a potential customer. He could be found prowling through the back room on occasion to check the quality of the product or offer fatherly advice to one of the dozen or so faithful old servants comprising "our little family." These first employees were a loyal and faithful crew, laboring not so much for their meager salaries as for their pride in their craftsmanship and in the excellent quality of the finished product. Even the "Old Man's" wife was a familiar presence, bringing in hot coffee and sandwiches, passing the time of day, and coming to know everyone's children by their first names.

During these early years, the basic security needs just seem to happen in the form of measures so taken for granted that they are not even thought of as a conscious effort toward security planning. These measures include such simple devices and practices as placing a good lock on the front door, securing the windows against penetration by a burglar, placing a couple of extra fire extinguishers near obviously combustible materials, and keeping a first-aid kit at a convenient location. Usually, too, the company's insurance carrier will establish minimum criteria regarding safety measures as provisions of the policy.

The "Old Man's" constant presence during this time is in effect a successful guard and patrol force, successful not only because the work area and employees are under continual surveillance but, more importantly, because the employees do not feel that they are being "watched." They work in an environment of trust, and morale is high—a vitally important factor in an efficient operation. Even the Old Man's wife's concern, and her intimate knowledge of each and every employee, serve as a competent personnel clearance procedure that is continuously updated.

GROWTH AND PROBLEMS

The successful small business does not remain static. It grows and changes. With growth there is an increase of on-premise stock, equipment, and other assets that, by the mere nature of their dollar value, are subject to considerable loss, either through accident, negligence, or willful intent. As the company's manufacturing process becomes more sophisticated, experience and technology lead to more efficient methods of production. Products may improve to the extent that the company's competitors become concerned enough to attempt to learn of the rival processes affecting their own sales picture. This can lead to a full-scale attempt at penetrating the company through various espionage techniques in an effort to glean not only design and production methods but also sales and customer lists and bidding information.

In an effort to meet the demand for increased production, the labor force grows over a period of time. Ten, twenty, fifty, even a hundred workers are hired—and now, statistically and inevitably, the dishonest employee begins to surface occasionally, engaging in various activities such as stealing company property, such as stock, tools, parts, or even finished products. Now, too, can be found the employee who is actually an undercover agent for a competitor's intelligence-gathering agency, or one who creates internal friction among employees, seriously affecting morale and contributing to the disruption of the total production effort.

Eventually, it seems, a monster has been created. Now there are three shifts around the clock. Instead of the small band of loyal employees, there are hundreds of nameless faces, executives, sales forces, secretaries, accountants, skilled and unskilled labor, and maintenance men. There is valuable new machinery, equipment, and even computers. There is more space, less time . . . and more problems.

THE TURNING POINT

The essential point, of course, is this: When does the need for a formal security program arise? At what point during a company's development from a small business to a large one, or even a major industry, is it necessary to consider professional protective mechanisms?

The nature of the particular business will make this decision a different one for each company. Ultimately, however, this point will be reached when management begins to notice a rising increase of losses or other incidents that indicates a need to establish certain measures designed to eliminate, or at least to minimize, those incidents.

The incidents will be many and varied. Inventories may develop stock shortages. Tools may vanish from production areas. Several industrial accidents may occur. A couple of break-ins at the plant will indicate a need for more adequate perimeter control. A gasoline-spill fire near the assembly line may spread and cause considerable damage when an untrained employee uses the only extinguisher available and unnecessarily spreads the fire by using water flow. The latter incident would certainly indicate a need not only for adequate fire equipment but also a fire-control training program for the employees.

Then too, consideration must be given to the potential of a lawsuit being filed as a result of someone being injured during a security-related incident. The defense of that litigation, especially if the company is held liable or is forced to negotiate a settlement, could potentially be extremely costly. A more practical and cost-effective strategy would be to establish programs to anticipate potential litigation, thus eliminating or, at least, minimizing the ability of the person initiating the litigation to claim the company was "negligent" in its security program.

The pattern described here is typical throughout industry. With growth and success come increased risks, a rising incidence of losses, and more complex security and safety problems. No longer are these controllable through casual or stopgap measures or through the personal influence of management. When losses continue uncontrolled and security incidents proliferate, profits are eroded and the well-being of the company is threatened.

At this stage the conscious need for a security program is apparent. But it is less obvious how this need should be met. For a small business, of 100 or fewer employees, it may not be economically feasible to justify an in-house staff of trained security personnel. Such companies must turn to the logical alternative: contract security services.

FIRST-STAGE PROTECTION: CONTRACT SERVICES

There are available to industry various private security services which provide protection by furnishing personnel and related hardware or electronic equipment on a contract basis. Although these services are discussed individually here, many contract agencies offer several, or all, of the various types of protection services.

Security Consultants

The security consultant, as the name would imply, is a specialist experienced in all aspects of protection and loss prevention. Some may have particular expertise in specific areas of security, such as alarm systems planning or industrial espionage, or in security problems affecting particular types of business or industry. Most competent consultants offer general security counseling, backed by a depth and range of experience that qualifies them to design a total program.

The security consultant is the expert who should be consulted initially by the businessperson contemplating a security program for the first time; or by those businesses whose working security programs are not functioning effectively and require a trained, objective analysis to bring them up to maximum efficiency.

After considerable study, analysis, and research of the company's past, current, and *potential* problem areas, the consultant will submit a report indicating what measures should be instigated to solve any identified problems.

If alarms are called for, the consultant will not only specify what alarms (contacts, ultrasonic, motion detection, etc.), but also diagram and place each contact point at each specific location on the premises.

Uniformed guards may be suggested. The consultant will also program the guards, outlining their patrol procedures, post locations, and methods of reporting, and establish criteria for their total performance.

The consultant will study the procedural aspects of the company and design methods to combat or detect internal theft, embezzlement, espionage, and sabotage. He will carefully analyze personnel clearance procedures and, if necessary, design new application forms and provide instruction on clearance methods.

Closed-circuit television and communication systems will be considered where appropriate, and the consultant will designate the careful placement of cameras and monitors, as well as frequencies that are efficient considering the physical structure of the premises. She will point out the possible savings and cost effectiveness of electronics under certain conditions, where the areas to be placed under surveillance are too numerous to be covered effectively by a guard force.

Key control systems will be designed along with access and traffic control. Computerized systems, when justified, are highly effective, not only in the operation of the system, but also in the saving of man-hours. The consultant will also enter into the areas of safety and fire prevention, designing alarms and sprinkler systems and placing specialized fire extinguishers in areas where water is not only inadequate but could pose extreme hazards. He will point out areas of unsafe conditions and suggest methods of eliminating or minimizing those dangers.

In all, the competent security consultant should design a total program of security covering all areas of potential loss, even going to the extent of preparing a disaster plan in case of a major emergency. She will also take into consideration the potential of litigation resulting from charges of "inadequate security" by designing the total program to be consistent with current statutory and case law effecting the adequacy of the security program. Areas such as determining the level of security based on the perceived "risk" factors of existing environmental criminal activity must be addressed and the proper legal balance met. The consultant is trained to recognize all areas of potential loss through incidents of criminal behavior, natural disaster, accidents, poor training and preparation, etc.

The final report submitted by the consultant will cover every aspect of the business and suggest remedies varying from minimum to maximum measures to be established. Management can then install whatever programs the current budget will justify. The consultant's report can be referred to at a later time to see where protection might be increased as the company grows or other circumstances dictate.

The consultant can also negotiate, on the company's behalf, with other security service or hardware concerns, contracting for their services at discounted rates, and oversee the installation of equipment. He should remain with the project until the entire security program is functioning to his and the company's satisfaction. The security consultant is, in effect, the company's contract chief of security.

Contract Guard Services

Uniformed security officers, both stationary and in patrol cars, have in the past 20 years become a major industry. Together, proprietary and contract guards provide nearly twice the manpower available in all of the public law enforcement agencies put together.[1] A number of studies, including the Rand Report, indicate that about one-fourth of all private security personnel are contract guards and investigators, and approximately one-half of the estimated $6 billion spent on private security annually in the United States is for contract services.[2]

The rapid growth of the security guard industry has not permitted time for the government to establish competent regulations or other criteria designed to protect the consumer, although some movement has been made in this direction at both the national and state levels. As of the writing of this text, 32 states have some regulations and license some aspect of the industry—and many of these agencies are understaffed and underfunded. In the vast majority of states the regulations are perfunctory—and the regulating even more so. Only in a few states, such as in California, have comprehensive regulations and training programs been established governing the hiring and training practices of contract guard service agencies.

Private patrols offer a service in which, for a monthly fee, a uniformed, armed patrolman will drive a patrol car to the customer's premises a designated number of times each day, usually during the night hours, and check the premises for indications of unlawful entry. Many companies also utilize this service to perform other tasks, such as entering the premises to check for fires or to see that lights, machinery, air conditioning units, etc., are turned off or on. The fees charged by the patrol company depend on the number of patrols effected each night and the tasks to be performed by the patrolman. Usually the patrolman leaves a card each time he visits the premises to indicate to the company that he has in fact been there.

Obviously this system is not as effective as having a guard on the property at all times; however, it does provide a certain level of deterrence. The patrol service posts signs on the premises indicating that the property is covered by a roving patrol and, if the patrols are efficiently programmed, *no regular schedule* is followed. The potential burglar seeking a target and "casing" the company may be deterred because he never knows when the patrolman will arrive. It would be safer to select a target where there is no chance that he might be discovered by a patrol that could show up at any moment.

The contract guard service, on the other hand, furnishes uniformed or plainclothes, armed or unarmed security officers assigned to permanent locations. The service may provide a single officer either to maintain a fixed post for the purpose of limiting access to authorized personnel, or to walk a patrol area to check for various hazardous conditions, unauthorized personnel, etc. The service may also furnish a complete force of security officers on a 24-hour basis, along with the necessary permanently assigned supervisors (sergeants, lieutenants, etc.).

The contract guard service is designed to furnish security manpower where it is not economically feasible for a company to maintain their own in-house staff. Over and above the hourly cost factor, the in-house staff poses additional problems; for example, the extra cost incurred when an officer calls in sick and the lack of relief personnel necessitates overtime; the cost of furnishing uniforms and equipment; the additional problems of training, recruiting, managing, and supervising scheduling; and, last but not least, the benefit package, payroll taxes, and additional liability insurance, which accrues to about 35 percent over and above the basic pay scale. All of these factors are assumed by the contract guard service.

The major problem with this kind of service is the quality of performance the contract guard companies are capable of delivering. In order to sell the service, the guard companies must necessarily keep their charges to the customer at a rate below the cost of an in-house security force, thus saving the customer money and making it practical for them to hire the guard service. In addition, the guard service must remain competitive with other guard companies, which are bidding on and anxious to obtain the same account. Thus, with their low bids and the necessity of meeting the overhead costs mentioned earlier, the salaries these contract services pay their guards are far below the compensation adequate to recruit and retain the caliber of individual needed to accept the heavy obligation placed on them. Much of the time minimum wages are paid.

For all of these reasons, guard companies often make promises that they are unable to keep. Training is an example. The guard company may advertise a complete training program for its guards, including firearms, self-defense, laws of arrest, first aid, fire control, and so on; however, training is not only expensive but also time consuming. And the low pay scale inevitably evokes a heavy turnover. Guards are hired too quickly, without proper background checking, and there is usually insufficient time to put the new employee through a training program before assigning her to a post.

This situation is not entirely the fault of the guard company; the consumer must share the blame. The consumer company, seeking a less expensive source of manpower, is many times only willing to pay the lowest rate, forcing the guard company to operate within this given budget, thus compelling it to cut corners in an effort to make a profit.

Most contract guard companies are capable of providing an excellent service, given adequate funds with which to operate. An ethical guard service company will explain this very carefully to the consumer company so that the company is aware of the risks and can reconsider a budget that may be too low in an effort to increase the competency and efficiency of the security force.

The solution to hiring a competent contract guard service, therefore, is twofold: First, negotiate the contract at a reasonable price, incorporating both budget considerations and the quality of manpower that will be assigned to the company; second, stay on top of the guard force operation by constantly reviewing its performance and insisting on changes where necessary. The hiring company should assign a staff member to supervise the contract personnel on a daily basis.

The company hiring a contract guard service should check out that service very carefully. Review and carefully check all references, making certain that the service has in the past lived up to all its promises and obligations. If the customer resides in an area where guard services must be licensed, either at a state or local level, check with the licensing agency, verify the license, and inquire as to whether any complaints have been filed by other customers.

Visit the guard service's offices and make certain that the company is professionally oriented, with qualified management and normal business practices. Review and observe the training program to make certain that it is as advertised and utilized in the training of *all* security personnel. Ask to see the personnel applications and records of the individual guards to be assigned to the company's premises.

Finally, specifically emphasize to the guard service's management what is required of the guards. Explain the duties and the kind of personnel to be assigned, and—most importantly—how the guards are to conduct themselves with regard to their appearance, manners, and relations with the company's staff and visitors. The management of both the hiring company and the guard service should, together, compose a set of written "post orders" to be maintained at the station where the guard is to perform his job. The "post orders" should carefully specify the guard's function; thus when a replacement officer is assigned, he will have a reference to support his on-the-job training by a supervisor.

A contract security guard represents the company to which she is assigned and usually provides visitors with their first impressions of that company. The visitor does not take into consideration the fact that the guard comes from a contract service.

Central Alarm Companies

Central alarm service companies should not be confused with alarm service manufacturers or suppliers whose alarm systems are installed for in-house use with only local (on-premise) notification. Those types of systems are discussed in another chapter.

Central alarm companies, for an installation fee plus monthly charge, will install an alarm system, connected by an outside source (usually telephone company line equipment), to a central location, where 24-hour personnel are retained to monitor the system and notify the proper authorities should the alarm on the customer's premises be triggered, indicating a source of trouble such as fire, burglary, or armed robbery.

Planning for the specific alarms should be effected by either a competent security consultant or the alarm company's representative who is experienced in the installation of proper alarm equipment. The consultant or representative should determine which type of alarm (and there are many) would best suit the needs of the particular environment under consideration. This will involve determining, for example, which fire alarm type would be most effective, a smoke or heat detector. Or, in the case of burglar alarms, whether door contacts, motion detection, or ultrasonic units would be more efficient.

Credit Reporting and Personnel Clearance Agencies

The four categories of private agencies that conduct credit and background investigations are (1) credit reporting agencies, (2) private investigation firms and detective agencies, (3) polygraph examiners specializing in personnel matters, and (4) companies that conduct psychological personnel testing and evaluation.

The advantage of retaining an agency specializing in personnel investigation is that such agencies have access not only to normal channels of information, but also to numerous confidential sources, which, when added to regular procedures of verifying former employers, residences, education, etc., may help to develop an accurate appraisal of the new or potential employee. Many of the agencies specializing in personnel clearance will design special application forms specifically for the client company.

Regular credit reporting agencies are also available to company personnel or accounting departments on a subscription basis, charging a small minimal fee per report solely to report financial histories. These credit agencies are computerized, and many are tied into national organizations, extending the areas of coverage for their reports on a national scale. This can be an important factor, considering the extreme mobility of persons in contemporary society. Nationwide reporting agencies make it a great deal easier to check a new employee's background in New York if she just recently moved from Ohio.

Shopping Services and Undercover Agencies

Shopping services primarily provide trained personnel to conduct test purchases at retail establishments for the purpose of discovering internal theft by salespersons. The same system can also be applied to other situations, such as service counters or parts departments in industrial manufacturing concerns.

The basic method of the mathematical investigative procedure is simple but effective. The shopper first enters the establishment and selects a salesperson, either at random or by prior arrangement, in the latter case from a description provided or the employee's identification-name badge. The shopper then engages the salesperson, acting as a normal customer. He makes a purchase for, let us assume, $3.95. The agent gives the salesperson a $5.00 bill, requiring the clerk to go to a cash register for change. The agent-shopper notes the ring on the register immediately preceding the $3.95 sale—in our example, let us assume the amount was for $8.30. Then, just prior to leaving with his purchase, the shopper has second thoughts and decides to buy two additional items, one for $1.00 and the second for $2.50. He pays for these items in cash, giving the sales clerk the exact amount of $3.71, constituting the total of both purchases plus tax, and walks out of the store.

This additional "test" purchase gives the salesperson the opportunity to do one of three things: He may honestly ring up the entire purchase; ring up only one purchase, pocketing the difference; or pocket the total of both purchases. In any event it is a simple matter for the store manager to check on the clerk's honesty. All she must do at the end of the day, after receiving the shopper's report of purchases, is check the register tape for the two identifying purchases ($8.30 and $3.95), then see if the test buy of $3.71 follows on the tape within a reasonable interval. Should a discrepancy appear and the test buy not be registered, the shopping service is notified and the shoppers will return to recheck the suspect salesperson by means of additional test purchases using various techniques in an attempt to verify the tendency to steal. One apparent theft might be attributable to error; a repeated pattern of theft constitutes evidence of guilt.

Shoppers are not limited to making purchases in a store. They can test employees under other circumstances ordered by the customer. One service sends shoppers to a large apartment house complex once a month simply to test the attitude and conduct of the apartment house manager. The service offers many possibilities for employee testing.

Shopping services also provide "undercover agents" to industrial facilities. These agents are trained investigators who work within a plant in a normal personnel assignment, such as a secretary, shipping clerk, or assembly line worker. The agent's role as an undercover security investigator is not known to the other employees. She normally submits daily reports to the agency director, who in turn reports to the client company.

The undercover method of investigative surveillance can be extremely successful in developing evidence of internal theft and espionage. Reports by undercover agents have also exposed sources of employee unrest and poor morale, as well as developing other intelligence of great value to management.

Undercover personnel are also furnished by detective agencies and some guard services.

Private Detective or Investigation Agencies

Most of the services just described are provided by private investigation agencies, which have developed a specialty in a particular field. The "pure" private investigator, although capable of providing all of the services discussed so far, tends to generalize. He conducts investigations in most civil, criminal, and industrial matters. His services are also available should the client company suffer a loss or suspected loss where, for one reason or another, the authorities have not been called in and no formal complaint has been filed.

The private investigator has facilities and techniques for surveillance operations. They can openly conduct interviews or other methods of interrogation or investigation in an effort to obtain sufficient evidence of wrongdoing to be turned over to a law enforcement agency or to justify the termination of an employee. Private investigation agencies are also called in frequently to determine if a company's competitor is conducting espionage activities on the premises.

CONTRACT SERVICES: AN OVERVIEW

During the 1960s the contract security industry began to grow at an enormously accelerated pace. Crime—white collar and industrial crime in particular—jumped to unprecedented levels. Public law enforcement agencies, already overtaxed in trying to keep up with the increase in major crimes, simply could not cope with business and industrial crime.

The original version of *Industrial Security* reported that, "The number of private security firms doubled in the 9 year period from 1963 to 1972, and the industry has continued to grow at a rate of more than 10 percent annually through the 1970s." Attempting to update those figures as of this writing in 1998 has been a little more difficult, due to the extraordinary expansion of the industry. One "online" source, Westergaard/Mallon Security2001, viewing the industry from an investment perspective, along with excellent background and research, states that "Security/Crime Control is a $100 billion growth industry that continues to expand faster than the overall economy."[3] This source states that in the security guard field alone, "experts assess industry size at about $1 billion in revenue and growth at 5 percent to 8 percent annually."[4]

On the other hand, two American Society for Industrial Security reports on their "online" Security News and Information page, both obtained on September 28, 1998, differ in their assessment. One report titled, "The US Security Market" shows "Growth rates for security products and services are relatively high varying from just over 4 percent to over 17 percent."[5] The second report, "General Security Industry Facts" states, "Security is 7th fastest growing service industry with an annual growth rate of 15 percent for the 90s."[6] Returning to the Westergaard/Mallon Security2001 market analysis, they report "the sector [security/crime control] as a whole has outperformed the broad market averages during much of the 1990s."[7]

Regardless of the difference in the numbers, it is reasonably clear that our industry is here, it's healthy, and it's here to stay.

In any event, in the early developmental days of the security industry, only a brief thirty years ago, it was easy to obtain a guard company or detective agency license. Most states in the United States, until recent years did not even have licensing facilities. Few, if any, requirements were necessary. Certainly there were no educational or professional experience criteria of any real significance. Anyone could go into the security services business—and with very little capital.

Industry, feeling the bite of the increase in crime, soon turned more and more often to the private security companies for protection. The major industrial complexes increased their proprietary security forces and, because of their ability to pay better wages to their security officers, the contract agencies were left with less qualified personnel.

As the profit potential grew within the expanding security industry, major conglomerates entered the picture, buying up guard and security companies throughout the nation. Mergers, acquisitions, and stock manipulations all contributed toward nonprofessional ownership and management within the industry. There simply were not enough security professionals available to staff the management positions that rapidly became available.

Many retired law enforcement personnel from all levels of government entered the newly prominent private security field, and many found the transition from civil service to private industry difficult, at best. Most of them eventually sought and obtained staff positions with in-house security departments, finding that their experience made them better qualified to maintain an enforcement program than to have to cope with the complex business aspects and competitiveness of the security services industry.

During that period there were few educational programs at the college and university level in security. Most of the education was provided by a few far-sighted individuals who formed security organizations, published security magazines and other literature, and sponsored study groups and seminars in security. These media disseminated the knowledge of those professionals in the field who sincerely strove to elevate the quality of service, which could be offered to the general public, industry, and ultimately the economy.

The great increase in the number of private security firms created an unbelievable rush to obtain clientele. The competitive atmosphere was hectic. The older, established firms attempting to maintain a level of quality service found themselves repeatedly underbid on projects by large, conglomerate-owned companies with sufficient capital to operate at ridiculously narrow margins of profit. Too often, false and misleading advertising, poorly qualified and underpaid guards, and insufficient supervision came to be expected; but industry had no alternative if a contract service was all they could afford.

The author remembers talking to a friend who managed one of the country's major guard companies about a large contract recently lost to another major service. "Don't worry," the manager said, "we just picked up one of theirs—and we'll trade again in a few months." That was the environment. And it was contagious.

It has only been in recent years that the general quality of contract security services has begun to improve. This has come about through more extensive educational programs, better communication among members of the industry, continuing development of qualified personnel, and the knowledge that the security business is here to stay. However, the residual effects of the recent past remain. For this reason it is incumbent on the client business concern to select a contract security service very carefully, making certain that it is dealing with professionals who are properly educated, fully experienced, and, most importantly, have a good track record of successful operation.

REVIEW QUESTIONS

1. Under what circumstances should a business firm seek the services of a security consultant? What are some of the aspects of a total security program that should be covered in the security consultant's report?
2. Describe the services provided by a private patrol. Why should the patrols not follow a regular time schedule?

3. Explain why it is important to negotiate a contract for guard service "at a reasonable price incorporating both budget considerations and the quality of manpower that will be assigned to the company."
4. How can the company hiring a contract guard service go about checking out that service?
5. Describe the service offered by a central alarm company.
6. What is the advantage to an employer of retaining an agency specializing in personnel investigation?
7. How does a "shopper" from a shopping service test the honesty of salespersons?

NOTES

1. National Advisory Committee on Criminal Justice Standards and Goals, *Private Security: Report of the Task Force on Private Security* (Washington, DC, 1976), p. 1.
2. *Ibid.*, pp. 34–35.
3. Westergaard/Mallon Security2001, "Industry Overview," http://www.security2001.com
4. Westergaard/Mallon Security2001, "Guards," http://www.security2001.com
5. American Society for Industrial Security, "The US Security Market," http://www.asisonline.org.
6. American Society for Industrial Security, "General Security Industry Facts," http://www.asisonline.org.
7. Westergaard/Mallon Security2001, "Industry Overview," http://www.security2001.com

Chapter 2

Developing a Proprietary Security Program

As a company continues to grow and to experience increasingly complex security problems, consideration must eventually be given to the advisability of developing a proprietary (in-house) security program, complete with staff security personnel, alarms, communications, and other electronic and computerized controls that are maintained and monitored on the premises, and more sophisticated procedures designed to contribute to a more efficient program of total protective services.

The primary determining factor in the decision to develop a proprietary security program is growth of the company. Growth may be accomplished in a number of ways: the slow process of increasing production due to increased demand for the product; the sudden acquisition of a large private or government contract; possibly a merger with another company. The results of growth—larger quarters and facilities, additional manpower, an increase in production capacity, larger quantities of stock maintained on the premises, an extension of the working day to two or possibly three shifts, requiring 24-hour operation—all seem to indicate that additional security is needed.

COST AND CONTROL

As the security and protective problems that arise every day require an increase in services, two facts become apparent:

1. The cost of the contract services becomes a major economic factor with an increase in uniformed guards, additional personnel to be cleared, and more incidents of theft, fire, accident, etc., to be investigated.
2. With the increase in contract security personnel, management finds it more difficult to maintain the supervision necessary to ensure their performance at a level satisfactory to the company.

The very nature of contract security services, as discussed earlier, forces them to hire a majority of employees who may be substandard according to the client company's criteria (substandard in the context that wages are sufficiently low to create frequent turnover and a lower caliber of trained personnel). Also, the loyalty of the contract personnel is divided, in most circumstances favoring the service that hired them. They do not have the same interest in the company as would a staff employee.

There are other factors as well, such as the company's inability to manage and control the contract employees directly without having to go through the contract service's management, the inability to hire and fire according to the client company's standards, and the inability to give incentive salary increases or promotions. Morale, particularly within the security operation, should be maintained at a high level; otherwise the whole system may break down, affecting the entire company's operation.

Adequate, competent, and instantaneous control of a security program is vital. When the company has "control" and can develop a security program according to its own standards and criteria, it will then have the ability to:

- issue or change instructions at any given moment depending on circumstances, which always leave room for exceptions;
- handle emergencies as they occur, with the knowledge that the security officers on duty and their supervisors are well trained, intelligent, and will respond in a calm, professional manner.

ADDED SECURITY NEEDS OF A LARGER COMPANY

Let us assume that our small widget-manufacturing company has now grown to a few hundred employees working two or three shifts. The company now faces additional security problems inherent in an industrial facility of its size.

Security guard coverage must be extended, not only in the interior of the buildings, but also to patrol the grounds surrounding the complex. Parking areas must be covered and traffic controlled. Usually a stationary post is established at the entry gate, not only to direct traffic but also to act as a primary information source for visitors.

Personnel clearance procedures become more stringent. If a government contract is involved, personnel clearance must be very precise in its methods and requirements in order to comply with government security regulations.

Interior traffic and access control relating to personnel and visitors must also be considered, utilizing identification badges and possibly color coding or electronic systems designed to limit access to highly sensitive or confidential areas.

Increased fire controls and equipment must be installed at specific locations, depending on the nature of materials stored or used in the manufacture of the product. Training in fire prevention and control must be provided not only to all security personnel, but to other employees who may become involved as well.

First-aid equipment and facilities for persons who may become ill or injured should be planned carefully.

Planning for a major disaster such as fire, explosion, earthquake, flood, etc., now becomes a major problem due to the increase in personnel. Careful and precise plans must be made in advance, taking every conceivable possibility into consideration, so that, in the event a disaster of any major consequence does occur, it will be handled calmly and efficiently with as little threat to life and property as possible.

Communications must be improved on from that of the smaller company. Considerations include the use of two-way radios and public address systems, the establishment of telephone procedures, and the posting of signs and notices relative to simple traffic controls or emergency procedures.

Key control systems, computerized or electronic methods of access to the complex, must also be designed to be functional and effective.

The installation of electronic hardware is needed to extend surveillance capabilities. Alarm systems, closed-circuit television, and computer systems are among the complex equipment requiring consideration.

Reporting procedures, forms, and files must be designed. Care must be taken not to overburden security personnel with paperwork, while still maintaining accurate records that will satisfy the many contractual, legal, and insurance requirements of the company (not to mention the many studies and statistics that must also be derived from reports).

Investigative procedures become more important as more thefts and other criminal activities occur and as the company acquires more secrets to protect. More trained investigators are required.

It should be clear by now that the company has grown to the extent where a contract security service will no longer be capable of maintaining the total protection program. A proprietary system with manpower under the control—direct control—of company management is necessary. Under the circumstances, a proprietary system is more economically feasible, more effective, more efficient, and better designed to save the company from loss.

INITIATING THE PROGRAM

The Professional Security Survey

Once the company has decided to develop a proprietary security program and phase out the various contract security services, the most logical first step is to have a professional survey conducted by a competent consultant. This specialist, as described in the previous chapter, is experienced in all aspects of protection and loss prevention. He should have the ability to evaluate risks and to design a program, complete with the necessary hardware, to meet the company's specific protection needs.

A security survey may be defined as an in-depth, on-site study of a physical facility and its property, environment, activities, and procedures in order to identify vulnerabilities and to determine the procedures and/or hardware necessary to provide security against those vulnerabilities. Arthur A. Kingsbury, in his *Introduction to Security and*

Crime Prevention Surveys, breaks down the survey in a slightly different way into four components:[1]

1. The *anticipation* of a crime or loss risk.
2. The r*ecognition* of that risk.
3. The *appraisal* or analysis of that risk.
4. The initiation or *recommendation of action* to remove the risk.

Each of these components suggests the degree of expertise that a security consultant must have. He must be able to anticipate the possibility of attack or loss, based on local conditions, the company's experience, and his own knowledge. He must be able to recognize a risk, even where there has been no history of loss, in any area of the company, whether it be a weakness in a door hinge or a shipping invoice procedure. He must then be able to analyze the probability and cost of each vulnerability, to evaluate existing protection, and to make specific recommendations that the company can follow to eliminate or reduce the vulnerabilities discovered.

The security consultant begins with an exhaustive study of the premises and activities conducted therein, using his eyes and ears and the touchstones of his experience. From that physical study he proceeds to try to identify any and all areas of risk in every part of the facility and in every operation. To do that he asks questions (of himself and of others in the company). Many security survey checklists, in fact, consist essentially of a series of questions grouped under appropriate headings.

The effectiveness of a security survey will ultimately depend on the comprehensiveness of the questions asked and the answers given. To cite only one example, consider the presence of a safe on the premises and the questions that might be asked about its security. Is the safe anchored? Is it in a highly visible location or in a secluded area? Is the area lighted? Is it checked by patrols? What kinds of locks are used? What is the safe's rating for resistance to attack or fire? If it has a combination lock, who has the combination? When was the combination last changed? Is an alarm system used to protect the safe? What kind of alarm? When was the alarm last tested? How often? How much cash and valuables are kept in the safe overnight?

While it is not possible to establish a universal checklist, with universally applicable sets of questions, there are general areas on which virtually all surveys will focus. Common elements of the survey of an industrial or business facility will include, at a minimum, all of the following:

A. General environment
    size and extent of facility, number of buildings, etc.
    neighborhood (high- or low-risk, urban or rural)
    access roads, parking
    adjacent structures
B. Perimeter barriers
    fencing
    lighting
    natural barriers (bluffs, bodies of water, etc.)

      landscaping (trees, brush, etc.)
      alarms
      guard patrols
C.   Exterior barriers
      doors and windows
      hardware
      walls (composition, openings, vents)
      roof (skylights, vents, ducts)
      outside storage areas
      parking areas
D.   Interior controls
      interior doors
      locks and keys
      alarms and surveillance systems
      container protection (files, safes, high-value storage)
      high-security areas
E.   Personnel and visitor controls
      personnel screening
      identification/pass systems
      package and property controls
      visitor access controls
      vehicle controls
F.   Fire and emergency planning
      extinguishing systems
      alarms
      flammable materials
      disaster and emergency planning
      first-aid and medical facilities
      safety procedures
G.   Procedural controls
      accounting
      materiel
      shipping and receiving
      sales
      purchasing
      cash and valuables.

In analyzing and evaluating each of these areas (and the list is *not*, it must be emphasized, all inclusive), the security consultant will look not only for security weaknesses but for the *best* solution for the particular facility. He will also look at each part in relation to the whole—barriers, lighting, locks, doors, grilles, alarms, guards, procedures, integrated into an overall balance of loss-preventive systems. And in each case the cost of security provided must be measured against the loss potential.

    The appendix provided at the end of this text suggests in greater detail most of the considerations that would apply to the industrial security survey, and the kinds of questions the consultant should ask—bearing in mind, again, that specific recommendations would be based on a company's individual circumstances and requirements.

Finally, after all of the above has been done and due to the threat of litigation, which has become all the more prevalent in recent years, the consultant must then obtain crime statistics from the local law enforcement agency. Those statistics, comprised of part I crimes for a period of 3 years prior to the evaluation, are studied and summarized, comparing the police reporting district, wherein the company being surveyed is located, with the surrounding reporting districts in order to determine the "foreseeability" of crime occurring in that immediate area of the company and the risk the company faces. The security design must ultimately meet that risk factor.

The job of the security consultant does not end with the initial survey. He should do more than analyze the company's needs and hand in a report. He should remain on the project, making necessary adjustments and supervising the installation of recommended protection, working closely not only with management but also with the chief of security.

The Security Director's Role in Planning

These introductory considerations have had as their focus the company in transition, which has not had its own in-house security department but has relied on, first, informal security and then on the use of contract services. In the latter stage the company may or may not have hired a chief of security to oversee the contract services program. If so, he will have gained valuable first-hand experience prior to the decision to develop a proprietary security department within the company.

If the company has relied entirely on outside services in the past, it is important that, as soon as the decision to go "in-house" has been made, the company should seek to recruit and retain the person who will be in charge of the security department. Ideally, the security director, or chief, should have the opportunity to work closely with the security consultant in analyzing the company's needs and developing a comprehensive program. He or she may have particular suggestions based on prior experience that will be helpful in the program's design. Moreover, since the security directory will have the responsibility for developing and managing the program, it is obvious that he or she should be involved in its planning at the earliest possible stage.

ESTABLISHING PRESENT AND FUTURE GOALS

Once the decision is made to develop a proprietary security system, the survey has been initiated, and the security director is on the payroll, management along with the security director and the consultant should confer at length and decide exactly what is to be expected from the program. From the consultant's analysis and the director's experience, management may learn for the first time the capabilities and wide range of services the security department can perform. But how are they to perform these services? To what extent should the department be utilized?

SECURITY'S EFFECT ON OTHER AREAS

The goals established for the security program have an effect on all areas of the company. A total program of security, including guard force, alarms, closed-circuit television, access and traffic controls, and rules and regulations, has a profound effect on everyone within its sphere of influence. The security personnel, management, employees, visitors, customers, and guests—all are affected by the program. If planning for security does not take into consideration all of its tangent effects, the program could spell disaster for the company as a whole.

Management will sometimes view security narrowly, simply as a means to stop thefts or other economic losses, without giving consideration to the psychological effects of a security program on other personnel, customer relations, labor relations, and general morale. Those psychological factors can have a far greater impact on the total production and economic outlook of a company than any series of burglaries, fires, or accidents.

"PERFECT" SECURITY

Carried to their extreme, security measures could make the normal operations of a company nearly impossible. Consider the familiar concept of the *absolutely safe* building, one that is impervious to burglary or theft, espionage or sabotage, fire or accident of any kind—in short, where there is absolutely no vulnerability to loss. Such a structure would have four impenetrable walls. It would be erected on a slab floor and would have an equally secure roof. There would be *no* windows and *no* doors. The building would be perfectly safe; it would also be completely nonfunctional.

The concept is not new. Thousands of years ago the Egyptians had the same idea when they built the pyramids; but even their solid masonry construction, using stones weighing as much as 30 tons each, could not stop penetration and the theft of valuable treasures. Today, we have steel.

The doorless, windowless structure would obviously be useless for the conduct of any activity inside. Let us compromise this "perfect" security system and see what happens. We will create a small opening leading into the interior, just large enough for a worker to enter. What additional security precautions must now be established to protect this access, permitting the accomplishment of work while retaining as much as possible of the absolute security we have compromised?

First, a door would be placed at the entrance. The door would be alarmed and watched by closed-circuit television, both on the exterior and interior of the building. A guard would be hired to monitor the cameras and to challenge the worker entering. If the building is to be accessible 24 hours a day, three guard shifts will be required, 7 days a week, plus relief security personnel.

Next arises the problem of proper identification of the worker attempting to gain access. As he approaches, the guard will scrutinize him and have him sign the register. The worker will then place in an electronic access computer slot a special electronic company pass bearing his photograph, signature, and thumbprints. The card is covered by a hardened vinyl plastic, rendering it unalterable. The computer will check the worker's file signature with the one he has just written on the sensitized writing surface, then compare his fingerprints on the card with the hand placed flat on the same sensitized surface. When the worker is satisfactorily identified, he will be permitted to enter the building.

There the worker will find himself in a small anteroom where he will undress, leaving his clothing and personal effects in a locker. He then steps into another room where he is fluoroscoped to make certain that he is not concealing any cameras, transmitting microphones, or other devices on his person. He then changes into special work clothing provided by the company.

Finally, the worker will enter a third room where he will undergo a polygraph examination to make certain that his attitudes and motives have not changed since his initial personnel clearance, and that he is not intending to commit any act of theft, sabotage, or espionage on this date.

The worker ultimately enters the plant just in time for the midmorning coffee break.

Bear in mind that the security required to admit this single worker involves not only the rotating staff of guards but also a fluoroscope operator, polygraph examiner, thousands of dollars worth of hardware, and the frustration of trying to determine how the fluoroscope operator and polygraph examiner should be admitted to administer the proper security clearance procedures to the worker. Obviously, too, these supplementary security personnel would have to be on a 24-hour schedule so that one crew would be on hand to admit the relieving crew. The process is almost endless.

"Perfect" security, then, is only a hypothetical concept—and near-perfect security is possible in theory but highly impractical. The task of professional security personnel is to compromise perfection, lowering the level of ultimate protection to create an environment that is safe but practical, where employees can work in comfort, moving freely enough to complete their tasks without too many barriers that would ultimately destroy morale and efficiency.

The human factor must also be considered. Security exists, after all, ultimately to protect the employees not only from fire, disaster, and accident, but also from the acts of other employees or outsiders, which could end in the company's demise and the loss of jobs. In addition, the security department needs the cooperation of the employees in order to function effectively.

MANAGEMENT POLICY

Management must consider all of the ramifications of security measures when the decision is made to commission a security director and develop the proprietary protective program. From the very beginning, rules and regulations must be established, along with the degree of enforcement and limits of exceptions. The authority and responsibility of security derive from management; security measures cut horizontally through all organizational departments and functions, and inevitably conflict arises between the goals of individual departments and the goals of security. The responsibilities of the security director must be explicitly set forth in written administrative policy, and the functions of the security department must be precisely defined, if the program is to receive the company-wide support it needs.

Although in practice the definition of the security department's function and activity will be a result of the security consultant's recommendations and the personal input of the security director, the decision to implement these recommendations ultimately belongs with top management. Simply put, the question is this: What does management require of security at present, and what will it require in the future, based on projected corporate growth? When the question is answered, the security director must be given the means and the authority to carry out the policy established.

BUDGET AND OPERATING COST FACTORS

Potential Loss Factors

What will the company spend on its security department? Sometimes there is not much of a choice when The Department of Defense and other local regulations enter the picture. These are discussed in other chapters dealing with specific topics; generally, however, the company must decide what its potential loss factor is, based on the value of various assets. What would the loss be, for example, if a fire destroyed the building or any portion thereof? What is the value of merchandise stored that is subject to theft? What effect would the loss of a million-dollar contract have, not only in income, but in cutting back production, layoffs, etc.?

Through accounting procedures and audits, a company can usually develop an educated guess as to its losses on an annual basis. It is the author's experience that anywhere from 8 to 20 percent of losses can be attributed to negligence and criminal activity when inadequate security programs are applied. In many companies, therefore, an arbitrary figure of 5 percent of gross income might be a reasonable amount to be budgeted for security. This figure, of course, must be flexible, and it is usually negotiable on an annual review basis.

Initial Cost Estimate

After a "ballpark" figure is arrived at, the security director must study the consultant's report and obtain bids from hardware and other supply companies, determining the selection of uniforms and equipment, alarm systems, CCTV, and miscellaneous supplies. He must develop the payroll factor for the personnel involved: security director and staff, guards, and support personnel. This budget must be based on a planned potential schedule of precise working hours plus an estimate of overtime and benefit costs.

If the initial cost estimate is not economically feasible, the consultant and security director must then begin the "compromising" procedure to bring the budget down to a practical level. Many times, for example, considerable cost can be saved by simply downgrading a closed-circuit television camera from a 1000-line resolution camera costing $1500 to a 350-line resolution unit costing only a few hundred dollars. The installation can be upgraded at a later date if necessary, but at least the basic coverage will be provided. There are innumerable ways to bring costs down, many of which are discussed in subsequent chapters.

Long-range planning may also provide for the gradual implementation of security measures over a period of time—even over a number of years. The most fundamental programs will be installed initially, and each year (or sooner, where feasible) additional components will be added until the comprehensive program is finally in place.

Flexibility

Above all, the security director should be allowed considerable latitude in determining how the funds budgeted for her department should be used. Limits must be placed on the amount of funds available and certain priorities will be established by various governmental regulations, but some degree of flexibility must exist. It is also important to maintain a "floating" fund to cover emergencies such as heavy overtime schedules, additional supplies, and other unexpected contingencies that inevitably arise from time to time.

REVIEW QUESTIONS

1. What is the primary determining factor in the decision to develop a proprietary security program?
2. Describe several potential problems in the use of contract security services.
3. Explain what is involved in a security survey.
4. Why should the security director work closely with the security consultant in developing the security program?
5. Discuss the statement, "'Perfect' security is only a hypothetical concept—and near-perfect security is possible in theory but highly impractical."
6. Describe the steps the security director goes through to develop a budget for the security program.

NOTES

1. Kingsbury, Arthur A., *Introduction to Security and Crime Prevention Surveys* (Springfield, Illinois: Charles C. Thomas, 1973), pp. 6–7.

Part II

ORGANIZING FOR SECURITY

Chapter 3

Security Organization and Staffing

The initial staffing of the security department is a critical step toward the ultimate development of an effective protective section. That first staff hired will receive collective training and for the first time actually place into operation those procedures which, up to this time, have been projected in theory only. Future personnel joining the staff will be entering into an already established program and will have to undergo training on an individual basis, or at least in smaller groups.

Bearing in mind that a security force is, by the very nature of its responsibility, a quasi-military organization, chain of command and strict organizational procedures should be established from the beginning. Independent initiative should be encouraged, but only within the scope of individual responsibility and within specific guidelines established by written policy.

Discipline is important, but discipline is effective only when it is based on respect for authority. For that reason, security personnel should be chosen very carefully and trained precisely in their professional conduct while on the job, exposed to other employees. It is that respect and discipline which will result in leadership in emergency or disciplinary situations.

THE SECURITY DIRECTOR

The selection of the best qualified executive to head the security department is crucial to the success of the proprietary security program. The qualifications—and remuneration—of the director should be established at a level that would interest a professional in seeking the position.

In the past, many companies felt that the ideal applicant for a security director's position was a retired law enforcement officer, preferably from the federal ranks. But former law enforcement officers often found it difficult to make the adjustment from civil service, with its inherent authority, to private industry and its civilian capacity. There is also a fundamental difference between the traditional law enforcement emphasis on *apprehension* of a criminal after the crime has been committed, and security's emphasis on *prevention* of crime or loss before it occurs. Former law enforcement officers who

27

take the time to learn and understand this difference along with acquiring the knowledge specific to security functions, such as applications of CCTV, locking hardware, access control (computerized and otherwise), and civil law restrictions on private persons, have the added advantage of their background, experience, and training.

It has been the author's experience while evaluating security departments with former police officers at their head that if the appropriate transition has not occurred, not only is the security head awkward and unhappy in his job, but the whole department has been mistrained; not necessarily poorly trained, but certainly inappropriately trained for the private environments in which they are employed. Many times, also, their morale is low and turnover is excessive or they have become too militaristic in their approach to their job and, in particular, in their relationships with other employees of the company.

Today, with the rapid development of security as a profession in its own right, many professionals are available from the ranks of industry, and many have the proper academic credentials in the security field.

Title for the Department Head

Although it may seem an inconsequential matter, some thought should be given to the title of the security department head. Of the titles most commonly used—director, chief, and manager—the main difference appears to be the degree of autonomy and responsibility delegated to the position. The title "security chief" or "chief of security" suggests the head of a department, which is more localized, of small to medium size. The chief's primary function is the direction of manpower, although his responsibility is often extended to include more technical areas such as the selection of hardware. A chief of security is usually (but not always) given directions by a company or corporate officer, commonly someone in middle management, who is not a professional security officer.

The "security manager" has even more limited autonomy and may, in fact, have to look to his superior for any significant decisions in the daily operation of the department. His superior is usually a company officer of lessor rank than would direct the activities of a "chief of security."

The title of security director implies a greater degree of autonomy and a level of responsibility that covers a wide spectrum of performance and policy making. Usually the director is at the corporate or middle management level of the company, answerable directly to someone in top management.

Qualifications of the Director

When applicants for the position of security director are being considered, several factors should bear equal importance in the final selection.

Educational qualifications would ideally be a 4-year degree in security. Because such courses are still limited, however, degrees in criminal justice, police science, or criminology are equally acceptable. If the applicant's other qualifications are extraordinary, a 2-year degree in these subjects may also be sufficient, depending on the judgment of the company officer doing the hiring.

The applicant should have a minimum of 10 years of full-time experience in security or law enforcement, with no less than 4 years in a management or full-charge supervisory capacity. Preferably, the past experience should be in an industry related, in terms of size and environment, to the hiring company. An industrial plant, for example, should seek a security director knowledgeable in the many requirements unique to a manufacturing environment and, possibly, Department of Defense security regulations should the company engage in production for the government or government-related projects. The applicant's technical expertise should be reviewed carefully with regard to his or her knowledge of the legal aspects of security, available hardware, and its applications. Also of great importance is that the candidates should be evaluated for their ability to manage and gain the respect of employees under their direction as well as other employees of the company with whom they will have constant contact.

When it comes to the final selection, one last question should be asked: Considering the enormous responsibility of property and lives at stake, is this the person who can meet, accept, and handle the challenge?

Source of New Directors

One major concern for many companies is figuring out where to look for candidates for the director of security position, especially at the corporate level. Should they go outside for their talent or promote from within the existing department?

Consider first promoting from within. Certainly, those officers currently on staff who have been with the company for an extended period of time, who have performed in an exemplary manner, who are mature enough to assume the responsibility of the job, who have attained the rank of assistant director or captain, and who have gained the respect of their fellow employees deserve the opportunity to advance to the leadership position of the department.

Certainly, too, promotion from within, all the way to the top, increases morale in the entire security staff. It suggests to employees that the company shares their feelings of loyalty with their fellow workers.

Upper level management may have some misgivings and concerns. Do the officers who are qualified for consideration as director of security have agendas based on their relationships with other employees in the department? Will the candidate be able to shift his or her concept of leadership from being "one of the gang" to that of a strict representative of the corporate structure where priorities often clash with Security Department objectives? Can the candidate assume the unique posture of authority necessary when dealing with corporate politics? In other words, will the new director's former position as a subordinate to the "new" peer group diminish his or her stature in their eyes, compromising the ability to negotiate on behalf of the Security Department? (Note that the author is not necessarily agreeing with all of the above concerns, nor is he commenting on their validity, only reporting what does exist at some upper levels of management.)

On the other side of the coin, let us examine some of the issues of consideration when seeking a director of security from outside the company and the existing Security Department. Many corporations that abide by the concerns noted in the preceding paragraph, seek a director of security from two major sources: from other similar industries or businesses and from the ranks of currently employed or former law enforcement officers. These searches are conducted either by the company's own Personnel Department or an executive search concern. Usually, the "word" is out that the company is seeking a qualified, experienced, professional and that "word" is directed to similar environments hoping to entice an experienced, working director who is seeking a liberal profit structure and benefit package.

Many companies feel that seeking out high-ranking law enforcement officers, such as a chief, will give them a political advantage within not only their geographical area, but within all other locations with a law enforcement agency, which, of course, includes all locations! The companies also believe that the training of a police official is far superior to that of any non-police-oriented security person; and, not being fully knowledgeable of the difference between "enforcement" and "prevention" techniques, they generally select the former peace officer. It is then up to the former peace officer to make the required adjustment on his own—and many of them do.

When the federal ranks are selected it is usually due to the stature of the background along with the belief that former FBI, Secret Service, or other federal officers' training and experience equates to their higher level of qualifications for the position of director of security.

It is the policy of many businesses to retain their directors of security, particularly at the corporate level, from the outside. They believe that a "stranger" at the top, particularly if their background is impressive and professional, will have a stronger impact on the department. Employees are less apt to test the new director's resolve as opposed to that of one of their own. The new director doesn't have any personal relationships within the department that might effect decisions regarding work assignments, terminations, or promotions.

Here again, the author is not suggesting which technique of hiring is more appropriate. They are both used religiously by companies with different goals, beliefs, and philosophies. It is suggested, however, that a new security officer, if he is planning on a future with that company and if he is hoping to attain a directorship some day, be aware of his company's policy and conduct himself accordingly.

The Director's Salary

Salary is an important consideration. Obviously, the more a company is able to pay, the more qualified an individual it will be able to recruit. Professional security directors in business and industry today earn anywhere from $50,000 per year and up depending on the size of the company and the amount its management is willing to budget in this area. Security directors at a corporate level, directing operations and establishing policy for a "chain" operation or a business with other facilities in different geographical locations, could earn considerably more.

Loss prevention, deterrence, and security in general are usually looked on only as expense items in the company budget rather than as contributors to profit. Mathematically it is impossible to compute a specific amount of money the security program is able to save. It is impossible to say that a theft, accident, or fire would have occurred if security had not been on the job, thus fixing an amount saved by prevention of the incident. Given the rapid increase of business crime and loss, in recent years, however, there is little doubt that the salary of an effective security director—and the cost of a comprehensive security program—will be more than covered by the actual savings realized under the program. Consider this rule of thumb: The more professional the security program and its leadership, the greater the savings to the company through fewer incidents of crime, negligence, and accident.

The Director's Role

The security director's task is basically administrative: establishing policy, planning operations based on statistical analysis of incidents, directing training, establishing liaisons, planning budgets for the security department, and generally overseeing the operation of his staff. His role conforms to the classic managerial concept of getting things done through others.

OTHER POSITIONS IN THE SECURITY DEPARTMENT

The type and variety of other positions that must be filled will naturally vary with the size and duties of the security department. Sample tables of organization for small (10 to 25 persons), medium (25 to 50 persons), and large (50 or more persons) departments are presented later in this chapter. Because even the small department may grow, however, it is useful to discuss the full range of possible assignments.

Assistant Security Director

The assistant security director shares responsibility for daily tasks, primarily to be prepared to assume the security director's position in case of an emergency and when the director is not available due to illness, vacation, or some other reason. The assistant security director also functions as the personnel officer of the department, interviewing potential security employees. Finally, the assistant security director should be a skilled investigator and conduct initial interviews and interrogations involving criminal activity within the business. He is the one who should review the reports of the other investigators and undercover personnel prior to their submission to the director for final review and determination. The assistant is in charge of plainclothes and investigative personnel.

Guard Captain and Lieutenants

The guard captain is in charge of all uniformed personnel on all shifts. This position is primarily administrative: hiring guards, evaluating procedures, maintaining logs and manuals, and continuing the updating process of training. Reviews and procedures should be discussed at a weekly meeting of the captain, assistant director, and director.

Lieutenant

Three lieutenants should be employed, one for each shift as "watch commander." The guard lieutenant's function is line and field administration as opposed to the staff duties of the captain. The lieutenant is directly responsible for the performance, conduct, and reports of the officers on the assigned shift. The lieutenant should possess strong leadership qualities as well as a working knowledge of security in general and the specific problems of the company. If possible, this position should be filled through promotional opportunities from within the department.

Sergeant

A sergeant should be appointed for every 10 to 15 security guards. His function is primarily field supervision and support. He is the officer who will give the people under his supervision the necessary basic on-the-job training. The sergeant will also review reports prior to their submission to the lieutenant. Once a month, the sergeant should prepare for the lieutenant performance ratings on each of his officers. He should also check supplies such as log forms, batteries, uniforms, equipment, etc., making certain each officer has what he or she needs to perform their assigned tasks.

Security Guard

The security guard's function is patrol and fixed post positions. Duties remain much the same regardless of the size of the facility, number of employees, or location, although the emphasis on specific responsibilities will be adapted to local conditions. The chief responsibilities concern access control and the protection of persons and property. Assignments include the following:

- Patrolling buildings, grounds and perimeters.
- Manning permanent posts, usually for controlling access of persons and vehicles.
- Guarding restricted areas.
- Controlling locks and keys.
- Enforcing employee and visitor ID systems.
- Enforcing company rules and regulations.
- Preventing damage to company assets.
- Observing and reporting fire and safety violations.
- Detecting and apprehending anyone violating criminal laws and reporting all violators of internal company rules and regulations.
- Carrying out special assignments during emergencies.

Note that an initial promotional level would be from "security officer" to "senior security officer," designated by a single corporal's stripe on the uniform sleeve. This elevation in rank implies an officer who, by virtue of length of service and successful completion of all training, has reached a level of performance in which he or she can act as a field training officer for new hires, along with being capable of filling in for the sergeant when necessary. It is also a recognition of excellent service and comes with increasing responsibility and the possibility of a salary increase, adding to the officers' morale and loyalty to the company.

Investigators

Nonuniformed personnel trained in investigative procedures, investigators follow up on all crime and incident reports involving fires, accidents, negligence, and employee dissension. There are also undercover investigative employees, usually recruited from an outside contract agency. These undercover operatives are specially trained investigators who work at normal skilled or unskilled jobs within the plant, posing as regular employees. Their investigative position with the security department is known only to a limited few within top management—usually an executive vice president of the company, the security director, and the assistant security director.

Clerical

Secretaries and other clerical employees are required to maintain normal office traffic in the security department. These individuals should be selected very carefully and should have extremely high security clearance ratings because of their exposure to highly sensitive material. Ideally, they should also have some background in and understanding of security procedures.

TYPICAL ORGANIZATIONAL CHARTS

The following organizational charts are merely suggestions of how small, medium-sized, and large security forces can be structured. An imaginative security director can establish variations for each size force.

Small Force

In the organization of the small force (Figure 3.1), two factors stand out. First, the security director here should probably be titled "chief of security," because the functions are primarily line and field duties, with responsibilities in the areas of investigations and other direct supervision along with administrative tasks. Second, the lieutenant is the

SMALL FORCE — 10-25 SECURITY PERSONNEL

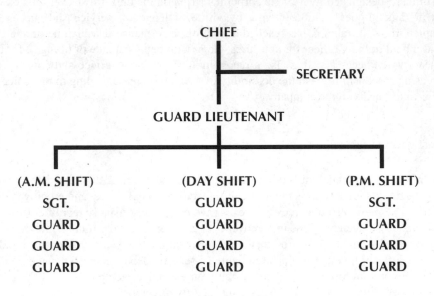

(A.M. SHIFT)	(DAY SHIFT)	(P.M. SHIFT)
SGT.	GUARD	SGT.
GUARD	GUARD	GUARD
GUARD	GUARD	GUARD
GUARD	GUARD	GUARD

Figure 3.1   Example of an organization table for a small security force.

overall guard supervisor, handling scheduling along with supporting the director, but note that the lieutenant is the primary supervisor of the day shift and no sergeant is necessary at that time.

It might also be a good idea to stagger the hours of the lieutenant so that he or she can have some time with the evening shift. For example, if the normal shift hours are 8:00 A.M. to 4:00 P.M., 4:00 P.M. to 12:00 midnight, and 12:00 midnight to 8:00 A.M., the lieutenant might be scheduled from 7:00 A.M. to 3:00 P.M. and the director from 10:00 A.M. to 6:00 P.M., or vice versa. In that way all shifts would have some degree of upper level supervision.

Medium-Sized Force

The medium-sized security force (Figure 3.2) requires some degree of administrative function during all three shifts; therefore, a lieutenant is scheduled along with a sergeant to assist. Because the captain is on duty during the day, only a sergeant is required on this shift—only 10 security guards are on duty and primary administration can be maintained by the director and assistant. The captain's main functions here are scheduling and field supervision. He should budget his time such that he is present physically at some time during all three shifts at various hours during the normal working week.

MEDIUM-SIZED FORCE — 25-50 SECURITY PERSONNEL

	DIRECTOR	
INVESTIGATOR	ASSISTANT DIRECTOR	CLERICAL
UNDERCOVER		
UNDERCOVER	GUARD CAPTAIN	
(A.M. SHIFT)	(DAY SHIFT)	(P.M. SHIFT)
LIEUTENANT	SERGEANT	LIEUTENANT
SERGEANT	GUARD	SERGEANT
GUARD	GUARD	GUARD
GUARD	GUARD	GUARD
GUARD	GUARD	GUARD
GUARD	GUARD	GUARD
GUARD	GUARD	GUARD
GUARD	GUARD	GUARD
GUARD	GUARD	GUARD
GUARD	GUARD	GUARD
GUARD	GUARD	GUARD

Figure 3.2   Example of an organization table for a medium-sized security force.

Large Force

As the guard force and nonuniformed personnel functions grow (Figure 3.3), many other branches can be devised, depending on the circumstances and needs of the department.

It should be emphasized, once again, that the illustrations given here are basic and have many variations; they are presented here only as examples of typical security departments.

LARGE FORCE — 50+ SECURITY PERSONNEL

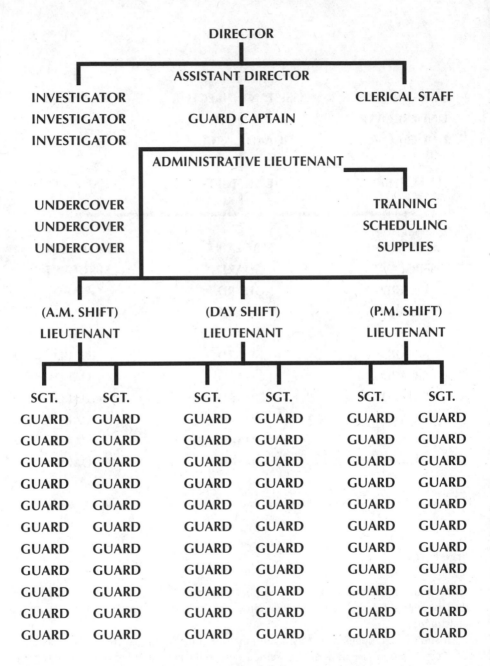

Figure 3.3   Example of an organization table for a large security force.

Chain of Command

The chain of command established by the various departmental structures should be strictly adhered to in an effort to eliminate confusion and create an environment of order and discipline. The smaller the force, the more informal the system may be, but it should be maintained.

UNIFORMS AND EQUIPMENT

During recent years a controversy has arisen regarding the normal police- or military-type uniform as opposed to the blazer. The proponents of the regular uniform say that the uniform itself acts as a deterrent; it maintains the atmosphere of a quasi-police or military organization, and it unquestionably identifies the individual as a security officer.

Those opposed to the regular uniform argue that the uniform has lost respect and is inflammatory, particularly to minority groups and immigrants from totalitarian countries where the uniform is feared. The blazer, on the other hand, still identifies the wearer as a security officer but is low-keyed and more dignified.

The author's experience suggests that both uniforms and blazer outfits have their place in industry, depending on the circumstances and environment. It is really a judgment to be made in individual situations, and there are many considerations. For example, a night patrolman walking the exterior of a complex should certainly wear a uniform that is easily identifiable from a distance, so that he will not be mistaken for a prowler by a passing police unit.

Another consideration is the degree of "formality" the company wishes to maintain. A blazer is obviously more informal than the uniform. Is that informality more relevant to the relations the security officer is attempting to establish with other employees or the public? These are questions that should be asked of each post and every position on the security staff and answered on an individual basis.

Where regular uniforms are worn, care should be taken to make the color combination distinctive and different from those utilized by local law enforcement agencies. In cases of emergencies when law enforcement officers are on the premises, there should be no confusion among nonsecurity personnel as to the degree of authority present and responsible. Also, it may be offensive to some peace officers if the impression is given that the security force is attempting to emulate policemen.

The uniform should be worn properly and be neatly pressed. It does represent authority and it creates the first impression that the wearer is competent, trained, and efficient.

Other Equipment

It seems almost ludicrous to have to mention the necessity for every security officer to carry a pen and note pad, but they are two of the most important items he can carry on his person. If the officer is to work night hours or be exposed to areas of the plant that are dark or where a power failure may occur, a good, strong sealed beam flashlight should be carried at all times. The flashlight should be at least a three cell, with a halogen or similar high-intensity bulb. The flashlight should *never* be used as or considered to be a weapon, due to recent civil court decisions in several states that gave large awards to plaintiffs claiming that being struck by a three- to six-cell flashlight constituted excessive force being used by the officer.

A pair of handcuffs is also standard equipment for both the uniformed and nonuniformed security officer. The set should be a standard U.S.-manufactured item with standard key, so that when prisoners are turned over to another officer or to the local law enforcement agency, cuffs can be exchanged between officers—eliminating the necessity of temporarily freeing the prisoner and placing a new pair of handcuffs on him.

Weapons

If the officer is to carry a firearm, the holster must be a type that is safe, with no chance that the gun can fall out, discharging when it hits the floor, or be grabbed by a suspect during a struggle. The so-called "clamshell," "snap-open," or other "fast draw" types are not suitable for security purposes.

A .38 caliber or 9mm weapon is recommended. Smaller firearms are less effective and, in a confined situation, larger caliber bullets could miss a target, travel through interior walls and kill or injure innocent persons. With any weapon there is always that possibility, but at least the potential can be minimized.

Tear gas canisters and/or stun gun units can also be carried on the person in a uniform container and are very effective defensive weapons.

MALE AND FEMALE SECURITY OFFICERS

In referring to persons throughout this text, we switch back and forth between referring to men or women. All references to security officers in any capacity are intended to imply either men or women, or both. It is the considered opinion of the writer that women function as efficiently as men, and in some instances where "detail" is necessary, more so; however, in other circumstances men are more suitable. It is up to the security director to schedule his officers on an equal basis except in those circumstances where a male or female is specifically called for due to unique situations such as checking men's or women's rest rooms.

Women are especially suited to conditions in which a female suspect must be interrogated or searched, or where children are involved. Women also seem to have a greater aptitude for detail work and function extremely well in supervisory positions.

Uniforms for female officers should be of the same color combination as those for the men. The selection of slacks or skirts depends, again, on the degree of formality desired.

REVIEW QUESTIONS

1. Discuss the different statuses suggested by the titles "chief of security" and "security director."
2. Describe the educational and experience qualifications for the position of security director.
3. Describe briefly the duties of the following: assistant security director, guard captain, guard lieutenant, investigator.
4. Discuss the arguments for and against the police- or military-type uniform for security officers versus the blazer.

Chapter 4

Duties and Responsibilities

MANUAL OF PROCEDURES

Rules, regulations, procedures, and all established, permanent directives must be set forth in a printed manual of procedures. The purpose of the manual is primarily to provide security personnel with a reference for those many details which, although assimilated through careful research, study, and trial and error, may be forgotten when little used over a period of time. The manual also serves as a training supplement for new personnel. It represents an accumulated wealth of knowledge and experience, not only of general procedures but also of specific routines established at the facility.

As time passes, many changes will occur in personnel, and it is virtually impossible to pass on all of the information by word of mouth, or to remember all of the many details necessary in the daily functioning of a department. Therefore the reference manual is vital. In addition, procedures change for many reasons: New buildings are constructed, new alarms installed, additional personnel hired, security clearance procedures upgraded or downgraded. These changes are added to the manual as it is continually updated and made available for daily reference.

The manual should contain detailed sections on the following subjects:

SECTION 1. Security Personnel Rules and Regulations
- A. Dress code and uniform requirements.
- B. Conduct on the job.
- C. Whatever rules the company establishes as justification for disciplinary action or dismissal.

Chain of Command
- A. List of the duties of each member of the security staff, from director to security guard.
- B. List of responsibilities of each officer relative to the men under his or her supervision.

Company Policy

A.　Information regarding benefits, such as insurance available to employees, overtime restrictions, etc.

B.　Policy on liaison with law enforcement, other employees, etc.

SECTION 2.　Specific Functions

A.　List of each post and patrol and outline of the duties of each position.

B.　Key and access control system.

C.　Alarm locations list.

D.　Instructions on special equipment (i.e., CCTV, communications).

E.　Maps and diagrams of plant areas.

F.　Fire equipment locations.

G.　Samples of logs and report forms.

SECTION 3.　Local Statutes or Other Government Regulations Affecting the Facility's Operation and the Performance of the Security Department

SECTION 4.　First Aid

A.　Equipment available.

B.　Policy of limited involvement.

C.　Hospital locations, phone numbers, and bed count.

D.　Insurance requirements regarding care and forms to be filed in case of accident or illness.

E.　Basic first-aid procedures.

SECTION 5.　Master Disaster Plan

A.　Emergency phone numbers.

B.　Evacuation procedures.

C.　Location of special equipment and instructions for its use.

It should be emphasized that all of the information incorporated in the manual should be contained in the training program provided to all new personnel. The manual is for reference, review, and updating only. In the case of an emergency, obviously, the officer should know what to do. He should never be in the position of having to take the time to read the instructions for the first time.

Ideally, each security officer should be issued a manual and provided with updated information and new pages for inclusion. If this is not practical, however, a copy should be located at every fixed post, with other copies placed at convenient locations within the security office, locker room, etc.

POST ORDERS

Very often, especially in larger organizations, the security manual is too extensive to be contained at every post at the facility, thus *post orders* would be more appropriate. Post orders are nothing more than the specific instructions to be followed by each security officer at each stationary post or patrol area. Those orders are located at the post or point where the patrol begins. Normally, the post orders are simply copied from the specific instructions contained in the Security Manual.

LOGS

The paperwork involved in maintaining an efficient security force is voluminous but extremely important for a number of reasons:

1. It is used for legal purposes in case an incident (criminal activity, civil negligence, or accident) must be resolved in court. Precise records and evidence must be maintained for presentation and/or reference by security personnel handling the matter, because most court calendars are months and sometimes years behind.
2. It is also used for statistical analysis in a continuing effort to upgrade the security program through a study of past performance.
3. Analysis of incident reports many times can reveal a pattern of activity, such as in a series of thefts, where methods of operation can be determined and proper countermeasures taken to apprehend the thief.
4. A study of patrol logs, relative to incident reports, can show where more efficient scheduling and timing of patrols would be a more effective deterrent. Logs are maintained by handwritten entry, mechanical generation, or computerization.
5. Logs are also a means of communication between security personnel working different shifts and assignments. Each officer coming on duty should read the log of the preceding shift in order to become familiar with the problems existing at that time and to prepare herself for situations that might arise.

Although many different types of logs can be maintained, three are basic:

1. *Telephone and complaint log.* A log should be maintained at the main security office listing all incoming telephone calls and nature of the complaint, calling party, call-back number, and disposition. Calls may also be recorded.
2. *Activity log.* At each fixed post location an activity log should be maintained, including shift changes, incidents reported by patrolling officers, times at which patrols are dispatched from that location, and brief notations of any unusual occurrences, referring the reader to the proper extended report form filed on that incident.
3. *Visitors log.* A visitors log should be maintained at each entrance and exit controlled by a security post. All persons passing through that location must sign in on the visitors log, noting their full name and address (confirmed by ID), time of entry, person visited, reason for visit, company represented, and time of leaving the premises.

Logs should be reviewed each shift by the shift supervisor, then passed on to the main office where they are reviewed by the captain. The logs should be maintained, in sequence, in the main assembly room for security personnel, where they can be reviewed by each relieving shift. Logs are usually kept available for about a month, then placed in a secure file where they can be retained for as long as 3 years for referral purposes. If space permits, logs may be retained indefinitely. Usually, however, they are destroyed after 3 years, with the exception of any material that may still be pending for court hearings, ongoing investigations, etc. The 3-year determination is based on the various state statute of limitation periods and may be adjusted according to local regulations. It is important to maintain all logs and reports for at least that period of time in anticipation of possible litigation defense.

FORMS

A form should be designed to cover every conceivable situation where reports or written communications are used frequently and are intended for filing and maintenance. The utilization of forms makes the preparation of written material convenient and uniform; above all, the form serves as a reminder to the person providing the information of all the facts required in each specific situation.

Take, for example, a "theft report form." In reviewing the theft reports, an investigator notes several thefts in the accounting office over a period of a month. He further reviews all reports, drawing from them all thefts in that area, compares the information, and learns that all items taken were petty cash and rolls of postage stamps. In addition, all thefts were discovered and reported on Thursday mornings; and in no instance was a forced entry of any kind noted.

In the circumstances just outlined, certain facts suggest that the thefts were perpetrated by an employee who probably has the opportunity to steal only on Wednesday nights. This further suggests someone on the night shift, or a maintenance employee if the regular night shift does not have access to that area. It is a simple task now for the investigative unit to plant, on a Wednesday, some cash or stamps dusted with theft detection powder, or a concealed CCTV camera and VCR, in order to try to apprehend the thief. It is also simple to check time records to see who works Wednesday nights.

The preceding example is intended to illustrate the value of a comprehensively designed report form. The same could apply to any type of incident, such as fire, accident, equipment malfunction, etc. In each case, reports can be reviewed and remedial steps taken to minimize future occurrence.

Finally, should the incident result in any arrest, court action, or insurance recovery, precise and detailed facts are a matter of record.

Sample report forms utilized in security reporting and documentation of events and occurrences, indicating the basic information required to make each report complete, are presented at the end of this chapter. The security director may amplify each form to suit her particular needs, including all information considered pertinent to special situations or important to the accumulation of specific research statistics. Reports, of course, can be handwritten or computerized.

Report Writing

Although forms are a convenient way of recording incidents in a uniform manner, containing all of the necessary elements for review and statistical purposes, narrative report writing is an important skill that must be learned by the security officer.

The narrative form allows the writer the latitude to present in detail the precise elements that constitute an explanation of the event. Narrative reports serve as a memory bank for cases that eventually terminate in the criminal or civil courts, many times months or even years later. Narration, when sufficiently detailed, contains intelligence that would not be included in most forms and that can be referred to in the future. Pertinent information may be included that is relevant to other incidents as well. Narration tells a story. It even permits the writer, in the proper context, to amplify and speculate on circumstances, drawing from the experience that has made him a professional. It allows him to utilize the skills for which he was trained.

The narrative report in itself is a skill. It requires the writer to have command not only of the language, but of the particular form of language peculiar to the profession. The report is a quasi-legal document, which, when properly formulated, lends credence to the writer as a professional security officer or investigator. It generates respect on the part of the reader for the writer, his abilities, knowledge, and, ultimately, the authenticity of the report and its contents.

The form of the narrative report is fairly standardized throughout both law enforcement and the security industry. First, it should be written in the third-person past tense. The past tense is used because the events related in the report did happen at a time in the past. "Third person" relates to the technique of the officer never referring to himself as "I"; such as "I then went to the car and drove to the office." The report should read: "The writer" or "This officer then went to the car and drove to the office."

In addition, the wording of the report should be somewhat formalized. Thus, the preceding sentence could read: "The writer then proceeded to his vehicle and returned to the office."

The report should contain the classic elements of a news story: who, what, when, where, why, and how. The events described should be related in a logical sequence.

The report should be completed as soon as possible after the incident. Like any good investigator, the security officer should strive for complete objectivity in his report, eliminating any personal bias. The body of the report should contain the *exact* observations of the officer, the *exact* statements of witnesses or suspects, and *exact* descriptions of physical evidence, locations, times, etc. Should the writer wish to speculate or offer opinions, they should appear only at the end of the report, on a separate page, and be clearly indicated as the writer's opinions. The opinions and speculations should be accompanied by sufficient justification for the conclusions. It is also important for the officer to develop a clear, neat manner of printing. Many people have difficulty deciphering handwriting, regardless of how neat or formalized it might be, and printing is the accepted norm in the profession.

ORDERS AND DIRECTIVES

Instructions issued to subordinates are always best given in writing; however, this may not always be possible or practical when emergencies arise. Therefore, any instructions given that effect a change in routine or an important notification of any kind should be followed up with a written order or memo at the earliest possible convenience. The written instruction not only serves as a clear reminder but also provides a record should any question regarding that instruction arise in the future.

There are three basic types of written instructions:

1. *General orders.* General orders are instructions that effect a permanent change or addition to normal operational procedures.
2. *Special orders.* Special orders effect a temporary change in operational proce-dure, usually indicated by a given time limit on the instruction.
3. *Memos.* A memo is a reminder of some specific special event, and a method of communication between shifts or specific personnel.

If forms are used in the preparation of written directives, color-coding usually increases their effectiveness, for example, green for general orders, red for special orders, and buff for memos. Unless they are directed to a particular individual, all orders should be posted in the security office and assembly location for security person-nel. They should never be placed in a position where persons other than security per-sonnel can observe and read them. Additionally, copies should be included in all log books at each post location in a section of the log book designed to contain such direc-tives. Each relieving shift should review that section of the log book daily.

A file should be established in the security office to maintain all written directives for a period of 2 to 3 years. The time element here is based on the possibility of the dis-covery of certain crimes committed in the past. Any orders or memos relating to inci-dents involved in those crimes could provide important evidence or information.

TRAINING PROGRAMS

In-house training programs should be established, at least in theory, before the first security officer is hired. The level of responsibility and the professional attitude expected of security officers are guides to the extent of the training program to be established. The method of training is also extremely important, and several possibili-ties exist in this area.

Books, pamphlets, logs, and other written materials, although required in the aca-demic process, are not a completely satisfactory method for a total training program. Many small security forces, however, do rely solely on written materials.

The classroom environment, with collective participation in a training program, is the only tried-and-true method of instruction where the student not only has the opportunity to learn but also develops pride in herself and respect for her fellow students who have been exposed to the same program.

The problem with the classroom technique is that normal turnover in a security department is small; newly hired officers come to work on an individual basis, or possibly two or three at a time—certainly not enough to form a class.

There is a partial solution to this problem, however. First, a progressive security director should schedule lectures or classes quarterly—or monthly if the budget allows—to present updated information and new techniques. In addition, groups of off-duty officers may be sent to the many seminars now available in the industry. This will enable the new officer to join the established group in the academic environment.

Secondly, the initial instruction should be provided by a training officer on a face-to-face basis, using as many audiovisual materials as possible. There are many excellent films and videos designed, written, and produced expressly for the security and law enforcement industry.

If the company can afford the investment, consideration might also be given to the purchase of a videotape unit. With this equipment the lectures and demonstrations given during the original classes can be recorded for use over and over again as new personnel are hired. New officers can also be trained in specific procedures by having them view a videotape of an actual patrol or a post where they are to be assigned, showing the route, procedures, emergency switches, etc. The new officer can view the tape and ask questions of the training officer present at the session.

It is important that the new officer be given a written test at the conclusion of each subject covered in training—not only to assess his ability to learn the material, but also to give him the sense of accomplishment that is so important in developing confidence and loyalty.

Training Subjects

A security officer should study a number of subjects in order to develop expertise and to meet his responsibility as a professional. Ideally, the officer should have acquired many of the basic skills prior to being hired by the company; the basic training which a prospective security officer has had provides an excellent means of judging his qualifications for employment. As a practical matter, however, in many situations an adequate pool of job applicants with prior security training is not available. In these circumstances the company's training program must provide for the following:

1. Minimum basic training for new security personnel
2. Training for experienced personnel to upgrade the officer's professionalism and expertise to a level desired by the company
3. Training specific to the position the officer is being hired for
4. Ongoing training for all personnel

All officers should have or acquire through training a working knowledge of the following subjects:

1. Duties and responsibilities of a security officer
2. Rules, laws, and regulations governing the authority of the security officer
3. General knowledge of local laws
4. Proficiency in the use of weapons (where applicable), including sidearms, shotguns, and chemical agents
5. Self-defense
6. First aid
7. Fire-fighting techniques
8. Public relations
9. Patrol procedures
10. Report writing

Periodic review and updating of these subjects should be part of the ongoing training provided by the company security department.

In addition, the new employee should receive specific training in the duties and responsibilities of her assignment. Training, in other words, should prepare the new officer for the specific functions of the job to be performed. In this respect, clear and well-defined job descriptions provide an essential foundation for the training programs. As the Task Force on Private Security observes:[1]

> Because private security personnel perform extremely varied services, clear job descriptions are invaluable tools for selecting and assigning personnel and for developing training programs related to the specific functions of each type of security position. Once the activities and responsibilities of a job are identified, the objectives and content of training programs fall readily into place.

Whenever the security officer is armed while on the job, there should be available, either on the premises, at a private, commercial gun club, or by agreement with the local law enforcement agency, a firing range where security personnel should be required to fire on a regularly scheduled basis, under proper supervision. Before being assigned a weapon, and periodically thereafter, each officer should be required to demonstrate an acceptable degree of competency and proficiency in the use of the weapon.

If the company is large enough to have a full-time training officer, he should be a qualified first-aid instructor. If not, the American Red Cross provides this service for free or at very little cost. Local fire departments will provide trained personnel to give courses in both basic and specialized fire-fighting techniques. Usually there is no charge for this service. Fire departments and other agencies will also provide instruction in disaster problems, evacuation, and other emergency procedures.

The company security department should also provide training sessions in the use of equipment utilized by the department, such as computerized access control systems, closed-circuit televisions, and communication devices. There should be lectures and classes on specific procedures to be followed in cases of major disaster and on the physical and psychological problems that are also involved in disaster planning. Obviously, there are countless possibilities of subjects to be taught, and the security training program should be continuous, not only for line officers but also for supervisory personnel. Training keeps the security officers alert, interested, involved, and prepared to perform their duties. It is also a major factor in maintaining high morale, pride, and loyalty toward the department and the company.

SUPERVISION

A person who has attained a supervisory position has, by virtue of experience and training, demonstrated a level of competence and expertise in the field sufficient to justify that promotion. The individual should also have exhibited an ability to direct the activities of their fellow employees and to assume the responsibility of sound, independent judgment in the decision-making process. The supervisor is an individual who has gained the respect of peers for that knowledge and judgment.

It is the supervisor's function not only to direct the activities of subordinates and to check their work to ensure its completion in a manner acceptable to management, but to support the people under their command through continued advice and instruction. The supervisor will also be actively involved in that part of the new employee's training program which includes on-the-job learning.

It is a good general rule to provide a supervisor for every 10 to 15 people in the field; this would be one sergeant for every 10 to 15 security officers, unless the lowest promotional rank is that of senior security officer. In that event, supervision could be extended to 20 or 25. The sergeant's time should be budgeted to provide him the freedom of movement to check posts and patrols in an unscheduled manner. He should also be scheduled to provide relief for personnel who must leave their post for one reason or another. Finally, the sergeant should make certain that all written or oral communications are distributed and understood by the officers under his supervision.

The watch commander or lieutenant of each shift usually divides their time between office administrative duties and additional field supervision, supporting the sergeants. At each higher supervisory level, there is a decrease in direct supervision and a corresponding increase in the delegation of responsibility to subordinates.

One final word on supervision (bearing in mind that this chapter is in brief only and there have been many lengthy books written on the subject): Companies are created to last far longer than any single working career. A good supervisor, from the director down to the sergeant, should have confidence in himself, in his ability to perform his job skillfully, and in his general professional knowledge. He should not have to play the game of "politics" or guard his position jealously. Good supervisors will make certain that all of the employees under their command are capable, ready, and prepared to assume the supervisor's position in an emergency when he is not present or if he is compelled to leave the position for any reason. Preparing those under his or her command to assume added responsibility is the mark of a good supervisor.

PROMOTIONS

Promotional opportunities must be provided to security personnel, even if they have to be created. The opportunity to advance provides the employee with some goal to be attained and helps to establish pride and loyalty.

Without question, the lower supervisory levels, such as senior officer, sergeant, lieutenant, and, in most instances, captain, should be drawn from the ranks of regular employees. The promotional process, and the opportunities it affords to the employees, creates the excellent morale and the positive environment that are vital to a properly functioning team operation. It is also the primary method by which the professionalism of the individual security officer is enhanced. As these officers develop expertise through experience, and exhibit academic progress through self-generated interest, they will become the supervisors, chiefs, and security directors of the future.

Moving up the ladder of promotional opportunities, the main criterion in the selection of officers for advancement should be knowledge of the job and ability to exercise mature judgment. The officer should also *want* to advance. The lieutenant's position, for example, when such an opening occurs through advancement or other change in the organization, is normally filled by one of the sergeants within the command, one who has demonstrated not only the ability but the desire to progress in a chosen field.

The selection process should be on a competitive basis, where the applicant for promotion must demonstrate the knowledge, skill, and potential for leadership through written and/or oral examinations. Mere seniority is not adequate justification for promotion, although length of service can be counted along with other determining factors.

REVIEW QUESTIONS

1. What is the twofold purpose of the manual of procedures?
2. Give four reasons why it is important for the Security Department to maintain precise records and reports.
3. Describe the three basic types of logs maintained by the Security Department.
4. What are some of the advantages of making a narrative report rather than filling out a report form?
5. What is the difference between *general orders* and *special orders*?
6. How can videotape be used advantageously for in-house security training?
7. What should be the main criterion in the selection of security officers for promotion?

NOTES

1. *Private Security: Report of the Task Force on Private Security.* National Advisory Committee on Criminal Justice Standards and Goals (Washington, DC, 1976), pp. 87–88.

(NAME OF COMPANY)
SECURITY DEPARTMENT
THEFT/BURGLARY REPORT

- -

DATE OF REPORT _____ TIME REPORTED _____

THEFT   ☐ VICTIM _____

BURGLARY ☐ SECTION EMPLOYED _____

UNKNOWN
MISSING   ☐ TELEPHONE NUMBER _____ EXT. _____

MISSING ITEMS AND VALUE _____

_____

_____

LOCATION OF MISSING ITEMS   _____

WHEN OCCURRENCE DISCOVERED _____

WHEN ITEMS LAST SEEN   _____

PERSON DISCOVERING ITEMS MISSING _____

METHOD OF ENTRY _____

FORCE USED _____

WERE THE ITEMS TAKEN

           COMPANY PROPERTY   ☐ INSURED ☐ YES   ☐ NO

           PERSONAL PROPERTY   ☐ INS. CO. _____

REMARKS _____

_____

_____

_____

_____   _____
OFFICER TAKING REPORT   REPORTING PARTY

_____   _____
SHIFT AND ASSIGNMENT   ADDRESS

(NAME OF COMPANY)
SECURITY DEPARTMENT
ACCIDENT/INJURY REPORT

- -

DATE OF OCCURRENCE _____ TIME _____

VICTIM _____ AGE _____

RESIDENCE ADDRESS _____ PHONE_____

WAS VICTIM: ☐ EMPLOYEE   ☐ VISITOR   ☐ VENDOR

BUSINESS ADDRESS _____

_____

EXACT LOCATION OF OCCURRENCE _____

MACHINERY OR EQUIPMENT BEING USED _____

WAS EMERGENCY FIRST AID RENDERED AND BY WHOM_____

_____

NATURE OF TREATMENT _____

AMBULANCE OR PHYSICIAN CALLED _____

TIME CALLED _____ TIME OF ARRIVAL _____

WHERE WAS VICTIM TAKEN _____

HOW DID ACCIDENT OR INJURY OCCUR (include names of witnesses) ___

_____

_____

_____

_____

_____   _____
REPORTING OFFICER   VICTIM

_____
SHIFT AND ASSIGNMENT

(NAME OF COMPANY)
SECURITY DEPARTMENT
REPORT OF FIRE/EXPLOSION/ELECTRICAL MALFUNCTION

- -

DATE OF OCCURRENCE _____ TIME _____

PERSON REPORTING OCCURRENCE _____

DEPARTMENT OR ADDRESS _____ PHONE _____

LOCATION OF OCCURRENCE _____

NATURE OF OCCURRENCE _____

EQUIPMENT INVOLVED _____

EMERGENCY MEASURES TAKEN AND BY WHOM _____

_____

_____

WHAT PUBLIC EMERGENCY SERVICE NOTIFIED _____

TIME NOTIFIED _____ TIME OF ARRIVAL _____

WHO NOTIFIED EMERGENCY SERVICE _____

DISPOSITION AND REMARKS _____

_____

_____

NOTE IDENTIFICATION OF
FIRE EXTINGUISHER USED   _____
AND IN NEED OF RECHARGE   OFFICER TAKING REPORT
AND REPLACEMENT ......
                               _____
_____   SHIFT & ASSIGNMENT

_____

(NAME OF COMPANY)
SECURITY DEPARTMENT
PROPERTY DAMAGE REPORT

- -

DATE OF REPORT _____TIME _____

VICTIM _____

PHONE/EXT _____

DEPARTMENT OR ADDRESS _____

PROPERTY DAMAGED (description & location) _____

_____

WHEN OCCURRENCE DISCOVERED _____ BY WHOM _____

HOW WAS PROPERTY DAMAGED _____

_____

IF VEHICLE WAS INVOLVED—LICENSE NUMBER _____

REGISTERED OWNER _____ DRIVER _____

IS PROPERTY INSURED _____ INS. CO. _____

IS DAMAGED PROPERTY COMPANY OR PERSONAL _____

WITNESSES _____

_____

PERSONS NOTIFIED AND DISPOSITION _____

_____

_____

REMARKS _____

_____   _____
OFFICER TAKING REPORT   REPORTING PARTY OR
                                                                  PROPERTY OWNER

_____
SHIFT & ASSIGNMENT

(NAME OF COMPANY)
SECURITY DEPARTMENT
LOST AND FOUND REPORT

- -

LOST PROPERTY ☐

FOUND PROPERTY ☐   DATE OF REPORT _____   TIME_____

PERSON MAKING REPORT _____

DEPARTMENT OR ADDRESS _____ PHONE/EXT _____

LOCATION OF PROPERTY WHEN LOST OR FOUND _____

DESCRIPTION OF PROPERTY _____

IDENTIFICATION OF DISTINCTIVE MARKS ON PROPERTY _____

_____

DISPOSITION OF PROPERTY _____

REMARKS _____

_____

- -

PERSON CLAIMING PROPERTY _____

DEPARTMENT OR ADDRESS _____

PHONE/EXT _____   IDENTIFICATION _____

OFFICER RELEASING PROPERTY _____

DATE OF RELEASE _____TIME _____

_____   _____
OFFICER TAKING REPORT   REPORTING PARTY

_____   _____
SHIFT & ASSIGNMENT   PROPERTY OWNER
                                                (signature when property
                                                released)

(NAME OF COMPANY)
SECURITY DEPARTMENT
MISCELLANEOUS INCIDENT REPORTFORM

- -

DATE OF INCIDENT_____ TIME _____

NATURE OF INCIDENT _____

REPORTING PARTY _____

DEPARTMENT/ADDRESS _____ PHONE/EXT _____

AUTHORITIES NOTIFIED _____

EXPLAIN INCIDENT IN DETAIL _____

_____

_____

_____

_____

_____

_____

_____

_____

_____

_____

_____

_____

DISPOSITION _____

_____   _____
OFFICER TAKING REPORT   REPORTING PARTY

(NAME OF COMPANY)
SECURITY DEPARTMENT
SECURITY OFFICERS DAILY LOG

- -

POST _____ DATE _____

TIME	OFFICER	ACTIVITY

(NAME OF COMPANY)
SECURITY DEPARTMENT
STATEMENT FORM

PAGE NO. _____

_____

_____
_____
_____
_____
_____
_____
_____
_____
_____
_____
_____
_____
_____
_____
_____
_____

_____

I declare under the penalty of perjury that the statements on this page are true and correct to the best of my knowledge and belief. I have read the statement and corrected all additions, errors and changes, initialing said changes in the margin. The statement was given voluntarily and freely and without threat or promise of reward.

_____

Chapter 5

Security Uses of Photography

In private security, the means for obtaining and analyzing evidence is limited to those areas that do not require the expertise of highly skilled scientists and technicians for admission in the courts. One of the most practical and certainly one of the best accepted types of evidence in both the criminal and civil courts is a photograph. The old adage "A picture is worth a thousand words" is certainly true in this instance. A photograph carefully preserves the condition of a crime scene or accident scene if the evidence is to be used for insurance settlements or civil litigation, and it eliminates the necessity of long descriptive reports that may be subject to interpretation and dispute. (This does not mean that written reports do not have to accompany the photograph, however, as we shall see later.) Photography also helps avoid errors of memory; a camera does not forget the image it has seen.

All security departments, regardless of size, should have at least one camera available, and all individuals assigned to security forces should have a minimal basic knowledge of the camera's use and methods for taking evidentiary photographs. As the security department becomes more complex, additional equipment can be added to the basic stock, which is usually an instant camera or two. Larger departments should also have one or more officers specially trained in photography.

PHOTOGRAPHIC EQUIPMENT

Instant Cameras

The Polaroid instant film development camera is the best and simplest method of taking a picture without the necessity of extensive training in photography. The instant camera's primary value is, of course, the fact that the operator sees the photograph within moments and can retake the picture if the first one is not reproduced properly due to poor exposure, unsatisfactory angle, or any other problem.

Although the instant camera does not furnish a negative, it is possible to have copies made at any photo supply store. Also, some of the later-model photocopying machines will reproduce a black-and-white Polaroid print well enough for use in additional copies of accompanying reports. The original photograph should always be retained in the original file copy report and preserved in case it should be required for evidence at a later date.

Standard Negative Film Cameras

A good-quality 35mm camera is also useful to have on hand due to its versatility. Numerous types of films unavailable for instant cameras can be obtained for 35mm cameras, along with a variety of lenses. The choice of films and lenses depends on the types of photographs to be taken, the conditions under which they will be taken, and the purpose they will serve. Lenses and films will be discussed at greater length later in this chapter.

Most models of 35mm cameras also have through-the-lens focusing, which allows the photographer to see exactly what is being photographed. The lenses available for 35mm cameras are also capable of wider adjustments for obtaining photographs under almost any conditions and for recording precise detail, where necessary, through focusing. Better cameras have interchangeable lenses. The 35mm camera is also capable of taking photographic slides for projection onto a screen for larger presentations such as in training classes.

Most importantly, 35mm camera film provides a negative from which any number of prints of equal quality can be made. These prints can be blown up to a much larger size than the original photograph, and specific portions of the original image can be isolated and printed independently. A classic example, from the author's own experience, is one where a defendant was cleared of a murder charge with the help of an enlargement of a photograph of him, taken by his wife. The enlargement of a portion of a store window behind the defendant showed a clock in the window, indicating the time the photograph was taken . . . approximately the same time as the crime occurred a hundred miles away. The photo, coupled with testimony establishing the date it was taken, helped exonerate the defendant. The precise detail, clarity, and resolution required for the enlargement would not have been possible with an instant camera.

Film negative cameras come in different negative sizes, such as 2-1/4 inches × 3-1/4 inches up to the standard 4-inches × 5-inches press camera. The latter are excellent cameras and, because of the larger negative size, produce extremely sharp, detailed prints. They are not necessary, however, for the normal security operation and are not recommended because of the level of expertise necessary to operate them and the higher cost of film and processing. The cameras are also larger and bulkier to handle.

Motion Picture Cameras

Motion picture cameras come in three basic sizes: 8mm, 16mm, and 35mm. There are, of course, other films used by the motion picture industry in the production of entertainment movies, but those are not practical for security or investigative purposes. The 16mm size film motion picture camera is the one most commonly used for investigative photography and the preparation of training films. The 8mm camera is primarily used for home movies and the 35mm for professional, theatrical films. The motion picture camera, whether silent or sound, is limited in its use and is usually considered a luxury that is affordable only for a security department of large size. Its use is usually limited to special needs such as obtaining a photographic record of strike violence that could result in property damage or bodily harm, or obtaining evidence of strike activities that violate court injunctions.

Motion picture records should, if possible, be taken of major fires or other disasters of serious proportion. Motion pictures are also extremely effective in preparing training films utilizing on-site locations.

Video

Videotaping equipment has in most instances replaced the 16mm camera, especially for training films and to obtain a record from closed-circuit TV surveillance cameras. Closed-circuit television cameras, used in conjunction with video recorders, are undoubtedly the most useful tool when conducting surveillance procedures; they are also utilized in traffic control, observing employees performance on assembly lines, critical machinery operation, etc.

Video cameras, formerly large and awkward, are currently very small, fitting into the palm of the hand. Thus, the name "palmcorder" has been designated for those units. They are very simple to use and require very little light. This subject will be covered in a later chapter devoted to closed-circuit television.

Digital Cameras

The technological advances in photography in recent years have paralleled the "computer age" and we now have the digital camera. This is a unit that, instead of using film, creates the image on a computer chip, which is then downloaded to a personal computer. As of the writing of this book the digital camera is still in a very early stage of development and, in the author's opinion, is not yet fully developed as a tool for security or investigative use. The quality of the final product is quite good. However, it lacks the versatility necessary for many applications required in the preservation of evidence or selection of lenses and films to photograph subjects where distance, close-ups, or other special framing or lighting elements are vital to the precise re-creation of the scene being photographed.

The current professional digital cameras that have the versatility necessary for security and investigative photography are expensive, costing upwards of $1000, plus all of the other paraphernalia necessary for the required compatibility with the computer for reproduction. Other digital cameras for general use currently come in two levels: the basic 640 × 480 resolution unit costing approximately $299 and the 1024 × 768 resolution camera at approximately $499. There is no doubt that the digital camera will continue to develop and, ultimately, will provide the user with the special lenses and other criteria for security and investigative use, along with lower, more cost-effective pricing.

When that time does arrive, along with the additional computer technology available to the camera, it will certainly be worthy of further consideration.

Types of Film

Various films are on the market for all types of cameras, with a variety of color combinations and speeds for use in almost any type of special conditions. For example, when photographs are to be taken under poor lighting conditions, a film of a higher speed rating should be purchased. These ratings are called "ASA" ratings; the lower the rating, the more light is required. For example, a film rated ASA 100 would be a good film for normal use such as in broad daylight or indoors with a flash unit. A film with an ASA rating of 400 would be used in situations where the light level is low.

When special conditions are to be photographed, a reliable film or camera store should be consulted for guidance in the selection of the type of film. One important factor to remember is that films of higher speeds tend to reproduce grainy prints, especially when blown up to sizes larger than the negative. The usual size of prints presented as evidence in courts is 8 inches × 10 inches.

Color films, too, utilize the ASA rating system; however, the grain factor in color prints is negligible. Color photography has another option in that films can be purchased to produce either normal prints or slides for use in a projection machine. Prints can be made from the slides as well. This is an expensive process, however, because it requires three separate development processes. First the film must be developed, then the resulting transparency (slide) must be mounted and prepared for projection, and finally a print made from the finished transparency. Slide projections do make excellent presentations, both in court and as illustrations during training lectures.

There are also very specialized films on the market. Infrared films can be used with special lighting, which is not visible to the naked eye; thus photographs can be taken in total darkness. Infrared flash bulbs, and other light sources, are used in conjunction with the film, and although a suspect creeping around a dark warehouse will hear the click of the camera, he will not see the flash and probably will not realize his activities have been photographed.

Ultraviolet films are also available for taking photographs of paintings, currency, serial numbers stamped in metal, or any other object where an alteration in the original is suspected. The ultraviolet photography will many times show the alteration as a "double image" on the film.

Lenses

The 35mm film camera is especially adaptable to various kinds of lenses, which can be changed at any time. These lenses range from wide-angle views to the standard 50mm lens, to a variety of highly powerful telephoto lenses for taking pictures at great distances. The author has found that the most generally satisfactory telephoto lens for most investigative photography during surveillance is 350mm. With a telephoto lens of this power, photographs can be taken of suspects about a block away. With some enlargement during the printing of the film, a photograph results that appears as if it were taken from only 3 or 4 feet from the suspects, with all the clarity necessary for competent evidence in a court of law. The suspects are not aware that they are being photographed.

A good 35mm camera, therefore, should be purchased in a case which includes three lenses: the standard lens that comes with the camera (usually around 50mm), a wide angle lens, and a telephoto lens. Prior to purchasing the equipment, the needs of the camera should be determined, based on the geography of the area where it is to be used. The proper lenses can then be chosen with the aid and advice of the camera sales-man who best knows the equipment and the lenses' capabilities.

USES OF PHOTOGRAPHY

Incident Scenes

Photographs are usually taken after an incident has occurred in an effort to preserve the image as evidence. For example, photographs should always be taken at the scene of an accident where bodily injury or property damage has occurred. Photographs should also be taken at the scene of any crime where observable evidence might be valuable in later prosecution in court, such as physical evidence left at the scene of a burglary: pry marks on a door, broken windows, footprints in the soft ground outside a window, etc. If a company vehicle is involved in an accident, photographs should be taken at the scene of the accident. If it is not possible to take pictures at the scene, the vehicles involved should be photographed before being repaired to show the damage.

When photographing crime scenes or scenes of accidents, it is important that the photographer take a picture both from a distance, showing the location and overall cir-cumstances, and a close-up shot of the damage or other special details which are of pri-mary importance to the investigation. Various views should be taken from different angles and distances.

Training Manuals

Photographs of the instant Polaroid type have been extremely valuable in preparing security officers' manuals where the use of emergency equipment and shut-off valves is carefully outlined. Where the manual describes the location of the equipment, switches, or valves, along with their proper use in an emergency, it is a simple matter to mount a photograph as an illustration so that the unit will be instantly recognizable to the officer. It is also extremely beneficial to mount a photocopy of the page describing some given emergency equipment (including the photograph) at the location of the emergency equipment; after reading the manual and proceeding to the area of the equipment, the officer sees the mounted reproduction and not only knows he is in the right location but also has a visual reminder of the proper procedures to follow.

Labeling the Print for Identification

When the finished print is available, either an instant Polaroid picture or processed film print, the print should be labeled on the back with the date and time the picture was taken, the name of the person taking the picture, the type of film used (including the ASA rating), the type of camera used and the camera setting at which the photograph was taken. Finally, a brief description of what the picture is supposed to depict and the title and number of the case should be recorded. A stamp can be made for stamping the backs of photographs that has the basic information on it and merely requires that the situation-specific information be filled in.

Some cameras also have a built-in date-time feature, which imprints the date and time on the photograph.

REPORTS

Whenever an incident occurs, a report is made out on a proper report form (see Chapter 4). It is important to include the fact that photographs were taken and to describe briefly the circumstances of the photographs, so that the pictures can be matched up with the information in the report for admission as evidence at a later time.

PRESERVATION OF PHOTOGRAPHS

Original instant camera shots (if copies were made) and/or the negatives from which prints were made must be preserved as the original evidence in the file copy maintained in the Security Department files. Camera stores sell inexpensive transparency containers especially for use in filing photographs and negatives. A supply of those transparency containers should be maintained as normal stock, along with some negative film can containers for film rolls.

REVIEW QUESTIONS

1. Why would an instant camera be the basic choice for a small security operation?
2. Name three advantages of the 35mm camera over the instant camera.
3. Name three security uses for motion picture cameras.
4. Describe three security-related situations in which still photographs should be taken and preserved as evidence.
5. Discuss the value of photographs in a security officer's training manual.
6. What data should be recorded on the back of each photograph?

Chapter 6

Security Office and Facilities

A security office or complex that is visibly clean, well organized, and well equipped not only functions more efficiently but also conveys an impression of professionalism. This is not only a matter of the space, furnishings, and equipment made available, although these offer an indication of the importance attached to security by the company. It is also important, for example, for the front counter not to become a repository for half-empty coffee cups and tired feet.

There has been much controversy regarding the proper location of the security office and facilities. Some management people feel that security should be "out of sight"; that it represents too much "police" authority. This view also holds that the strength (or weakness) of the department should be semi-secret, keeping the criminal element guessing—uneasily convinced that a guard will jump out at them should they try to steal anything.

The other side of the coin is the belief that security should be visible, displaying the fact that it is functional, operational, modern, and professional, thus adding to its efficiency the element of deterrence. That is not to say that security's presence should be flaunted through an overly prominent display—but security should at least be visible and available. The fact that security is not buried in the basement but is located in an active area of the facility also indicates management's support of the program and that security is considered an integral function of the company.

Examples of how various types of businesses contain their security facilities are as follows: Retail establishments, historically, maintain their security office in an area out of the view of customers, along with concealed observation stations designed to detect shoplifting activity. Commercial office buildings, in recent years, display their CCTV, computer, access control, alarm and communications systems at consoles located in the lobbies where they have become an effective deterrent to criminal activity.

In other structures where a high level of security coverage is maintained, such as in manufacturing plants or banking main vault and computer service centers, it is not unusual to maintain the security communications center, with visible computerized systems, and CCTV units in an area, possibly windowed, adjacent to the entry lobby. Hotels, like retail establishments, also maintain their security facilities outside the view of the public; the only exceptions being possibly a security desk or podium in the elevator lobby where room keys are requested prior to admitting persons to the guest room areas. Casinos also have security podiums in plain view.

As discussed later in this chapter, the equipment housed in the control center (CCTV, computerized access control systems, communications, alarms, etc.) should be visible both to employees and visitors if it is determined that the security facilities will, in fact, be visible. In addition, electrical and wiring problems must be considered and the control center should be centrally located within the premises—usually in or off a main hallway within the core of the main building. It would be more practical to have the rest of the security facilities also in the same immediate vicinity—adjoining if possible. The main office of the Security Department should have direct access to the other necessary areas such as the file room, assembly and training room, first-aid station, and locker facilities. Because the security office is often the focal point of activity, especially during an emergency or disaster, it should be easily accessible to all areas of the company.

The physical construction of the security area should be highly fire resistant, particularly in the vault and file room and in the control area, which houses the alarms, CCTVs, and communications equipment. It is also important that each section such as locker room, first-aid room, assembly and training area, and the individual offices be soundproof. Finally, it is extremely important that the security command area be equipped with an emergency power source so it can continue to function during natural disasters when municipal power is disrupted.

FILING SYSTEMS AND RECORDS

The importance of maintaining a comprehensive system of files and records within a security operation lies in the necessity of frequent and sometimes rapid referral to those records. It is also important that those records be maintained in a *secure* and *controlled* manner leading to absolute confidentiality. The same would apply to both manual and computerized filing. The person in charge of the records must be able to attest to the fact that the records have not been changed or altered in any way. The latter need stems from the probability of those records being used as material or evidence in the prosecution of a criminal matter or civil litigation in a court of law.

The first consideration is the manner in which the records are to be contained. They should be housed in a file cabinet of high-grade, fire-resistant steel, fitted with a plunger-type lock that secures all drawers. Additionally, the cabinet should be equipped with an exterior steel locking bar welded to the cabinet and a heavy-duty "changeable" combination lock. The lock combination can be changed on a regular monthly basis or whenever key personnel who had access to the combination leave the company's employ or are transferred out of the department. Although it is a cumbersome procedure, highly sensitive or confidential files should be locked and secured *at all times,* the cabinets being unlocked and relocked each time a file is removed or returned.

The process of removing or returning files should be accomplished by only one person in the office assigned to that task. The person requesting the file should sign his name on the file folder, along with the date and time of removal and reentry. Additionally, an "out" card should be placed in the file cabinet in the exact location of the removed file, indicating the name of the person who accessed the file, and the date and time of removal. In that manner the location of the file is known at all times.

Records and file cabinets should be maintained in a separate inside room, closet, or vault that can also be locked and secured each night when the office closes for regular business. If the night shift requires a record, only the lieutenant should have access to the file room. The room itself should be placed on the alarm list. Once the room is secured, a motion detection device should be activated on the interior. The file room should also be placed on the patrol schedule and checked during the patrolman's normal rounds. In areas where files contain extremely sensitive records or in a highly classified environment, the "double custody" system of removal should be considered. This simply means that when the authorized person obtains a file, a second security officer, who also signs the removal slip and witnesses the activity of the first officer, accompanies him.

If a computer system is utilized, the same caution should apply regarding the confidentiality of files. Additionally, it is most important, on a daily basis if possible, for files to be downloaded to a floppy disk or tape, depending on your system, to ensure the preservation of the information should the computer go down, losing its programming and/or memory. The downloaded disk should be secured in a fireproof vault, preferably at a different location from the facility.

Files can be retained for many years, depending on various factors. Space is the biggest problem, for manual records; however, inactive files can be stored away in a warehouse area or microfilmed, or scanned if they are to be upgraded to a computer system, if it is decided they should be retained indefinitely. Two points are important, however: (1) files should always be retained for a minimum period determined by the statute of limitations if they pertain to criminal or civil court related matters; and (2) if destruction is to be effected, it should be *total* destruction by shredding, pulping, or burning, conducted under the supervision of an executive officer. File index cards relating to that particular matter should be retained and the destruction method and date indicated thereon.

When the clerical staff is preparing files considered confidential, care should be taken that carbon papers and sections of carbon typewriter ribbons used during the preparation of the file are destroyed at the end of the day, and that any notes pertaining to the file are either inserted in the file folder or destroyed. A favorite source of information for industrial espionage agents when manual systems are utilized are just those items in an office: trash, carbon papers, and carbon typewriter ribbons.

Finally, care should be taken that the original notes, usually handwritten by the officer filing the report, are retained in the file. Many times, in court, an investigating officer may testify only from her original notes, and they should be retained for use at that time.

The types of data that should be filed are strictly up to the individual security department. Obviously certain materials should be retained, such as investigative files, crime and incident reports, logs, and correspondence. Files may also be established on many other pertinent subjects, such as available security hardware, academic and training material, new techniques, statistical analysis charts, personnel progress reports, and legal decisions affecting the Security Department.

A comprehensive "intelligence" file might also be maintained, with bits and pieces of information, which to law enforcement or security-oriented thinking, might prove valuable at some future date relative to a criminal investigation. Professionals in police or security work develop an instinct, over a period of time, for recognizing unusual events that are criminally oriented.

LOCKER ROOM

The company usually provides security personnel, in particular the uniformed guard force, with space and facilities for a locker room. Uniforms, which are normally furnished by the company, should remain on the premises and, unless special circumstances arise, should not be worn home by the officers.

Each officer should be provided with a standard clothes locker fitted with a lock to safeguard both the uniform when the officer is off-duty and his personal clothing and belongings when he is working.

There should also be an exposed rack where soiled uniforms are placed for regular cleaning service. Finally, the locker room should contain a full-length mirror and leather and shoe shining supplies. Some companies also provide a cot or two, with blankets, so that officers working overtime or double and split shifts in an emergency will have a place for a few hours' rest. The locker room should also have an adjacent rest room.

When female officers are employed, they should have similar, separate facilities. In smaller companies, or where adequate space is not available, it is acceptable for the officers to wear their uniforms to and from work.

TRAINING AND ASSEMBLY AREAS

Within the complex of offices housing the security department, there should be space allotted to serve as a combination training and assembly room. It may also be utilized as a lounge when not otherwise in use. This room should be furnished with school-type chair–desk combinations in sufficient numbers for the entire staff; a small 10-inch riser in the front of the room with lectern; and a large blackboard, projection screen, and television monitor with VCR. The room should also contain all of the training materials utilized in the academic program, including videotapes and shelves for books and magazines.

The training/assembly area should also contain bulletin boards where all updating information, notices, written communications; and previous log entries can be posted.

The training/assembly area is important to the operation of the department. It serves as the training room for new employees and as the location for updating lectures or class instruction provided to the department. It should also be the area where each new shift assembles for briefing by the shift lieutenant or sergeant regarding the day's activities and special events. Breaks and lunch periods can also be spent in the training/ assembly room. Security personnel are usually a close-knit group who like to mingle and exchange professional experiences. They also like to read industry periodicals and magazines. In effect, the assembly/lounge area is not only functional but is an important morale element as well.

FIRST-AID SUPPLIES

Large companies should have on the premises a fully equipped first-aid room, usually staffed by a nurse. Smaller concerns, however, may only have first-aid supplies available in case of emergency. In either case, the responsibility for first aid should be under the jurisdiction of the security department.

Each individual employee may secure basic first-aid materials such as bandages or aspirin. Any items or care beyond that, however, should be handled by someone with adequate first-aid training.

The American Red Cross offers classes in basic and advanced emergency first aid and *cardiopulmonary resuscitation (CPR)*. The only cost is a small sum for the first-aid book with which each student is supplied. It is strongly recommended that every employee of the security department be required to take this course as part of basic training. Small portable *defibrillators*, used to resuscitate heart attack victims, are now on the market and currently being used by security officers with special training in their use.

In larger companies where a training officer is maintained by the Security Department, he usually holds an instructor's card from the American Red Cross and can give the course on the premises to all security personnel and any other interested employees in the company. It is amazing how popular this course is to regular company personnel when it is conveniently offered.

First-aid supplies should be maintained in a central location, but smaller kits should be scattered around the plant where minor injuries might occur. Most pharmaceutical companies sell first-aid supplies in kit form. Large industrial first-aid supply kits can be purchased, which are already stocked with all necessary items, including specialized supplies depending on the nature of the product manufactured by the company. For example, if the company manufactures chemical supplies, a first-aid kit can be ordered that contains certain special items to render emergency aid for acid or chemical burns.

There should also be made available, somewhere in the plant, a room with a cot for employees who become ill.

Wherever first-aid supplies are available, there should also be a stock of accident/injury report forms, which should be filled out by security personnel or by the injured employee's foreman or supervisor, who in turn passes it on to the security department.

At the location where emergency first aid is controlled, there should be an up-to-date list of available public emergency services and phone numbers, the number and location of the company doctor, and a list of hospitals and their bed counts in case of major disaster with numerous injuries.

THE CONTROL CENTER

Some medium-sized and most larger companies will be equipped with computers, proprietary alarms, communications, and closed-circuit television systems which require a central control location and equipment console. The design of the console and the various electronic components house there will be discussed at length in a later chapter; here we discuss simply the facilities for its location.

The central control station is the nerve center of the entire security system. It should be manned continuously, 24 hours a day, by a competent officer who is well trained not only in the mechanical functions of the system, but also in the procedures for handling and processing routine and emergency situations as they occur. It is important to note here that the officers who monitor the system should be rotated, allowing as many qualified members of the department as possible to be given the opportunity to work with and learn the equipment and procedures. All too many times, the Security Department relies on just one or two officers to man the equipment, then suffer serious problems when those limited, trained officers, become unavailable due to vacations, days off, or illness.

The control center itself should be housed in an area that is secured at all times and highly fire resistant. It should also be soundproofed against external noises, because there will be times when the operator requires an environment conducive to extreme concentration. For that reason also, unnecessary traffic through the area should be discouraged. The door to the room should remain locked at all times. Access to the room should be through an automatic, remotely operated door lock, which is released by the console operator after he has identified the individual attempting to gain access.

There has always been a controversy regarding whether or not the control center and console should be visible as a deterrent. It is the author's opinion that it should. Although the contrary view holds that it is impossible to protect the area adequately if it is exposed to view, the possibility of placing the console in a room with a window exposed to an area of visitor and employee traffic should be considered. In highly sensitive security situations, bulletproof glass could be installed. The point is that, when a highly sophisticated and functioning system is observed, a potential intruder or individual with criminal intent may be deterred, particularly if they do not know the full extent of the system. Obviously, the TV monitors should not be facing the window, where they and the areas they cover could be observed by passers-by.

The control center is where emergency phone calls are received, alarms are activated, visual observations by CCTV indicate areas of trouble, and where patrolling officers can be dispatched to those areas by radio communication. As the most secure area of the company's premises, the control center should also be the location of key control cabinets and files of a highly sensitive nature.

REVIEW QUESTIONS

1. Discuss the considerations of visibility and accessibility in choosing the location of the security office.
2. What physical and procedural protection measures are recommended for security files and records?
3. Typically, what facilities should be provided in the locker room? In the training/assembly room?
4. What is the purpose of having the security control center exposed to the view of visitors and employees?

Chapter 7

Security Relationships

Unlike such defined and to some extent self-contained functions as production, shipping, and receiving, some organizational activities by their very nature affect *all* company operations. Finance and personnel are two examples; security is another.

Security controls may intrude into any department. If access controls are instituted, such as a gate with a guard, computerized access control, or employee identification pass system, all employees are affected. Theft is not restricted to shipping areas or the production line; it may occur anywhere in the company where temptation exists along with opportunity. For this reason theft controls must take into account possible vulnerabilities in any area of the company.

In this as in other respects, security cuts across organizational lines. The implementation and execution of the security program will be most effective when the security director reports directly to someone in top management—in smaller companies, often the president. The security director in most organizational structures serves in a staff relationship to the executive one level above and derives functional authority from that executive. The lower the management level from which security receives this authority and support, the less general acceptance for the security program there will tend to be throughout the company.

RELATIONS WITH MANAGEMENT

If the security program is to be successful, the authority and responsibility of the security director and the Security Department must be clearly defined in administration policy, preferably written policy. Where such policies are vague, or where the security program lacks management support, it cannot succeed.

Relations between the Security Department, and in particular the director, and company management are not always smooth sailing. The specific responsibilities of both will often come into conflict. Facing problems such as fiscal and budgetary deficiencies and increased production costs, management may feel compelled to cut back on security personnel, while continuing to expect the protection program to operate at a level consistent with its past performance; or they may suddenly decide to change rules and regulations for one reason or another, although the security director knows the change will compromise the established security program. Also, a very few management personnel—and although they are exceptions they are always a thorn in the side of the security director—will demand special treatment and expect to be the "exception" to established rules.

In special situations, internal company politics will place the Security Department in an awkward position. Requests will be made to bend or violate certain rules, sometimes for the benefit of one or another executive in an internal power struggle. In any such situation, the security director's position should be clear. He must assume the role of the professional, with loyalty directed toward that profession and to the company itself. Once sides are chosen, the director's long term ultimate survival is virtually impossible, regardless of which faction wins. As soon as the security director allows personal feelings or outside pressure to intrude on job performance, from that point on trust and confidence in him as an individual will be in question.

Industry is not an "easy" environment. In contrast with public law enforcement, internal company regulations can be and many times are changed, for no other reason than convenience to individuals in positions of authority. The security director lacks the job protections of civil service enjoyed by his counterpart in the public sector. Exceptions to established practices will inevitably have to be made because exceptions do occur. The director must remain flexible and understanding, and should have sufficient alternatives at his disposal to enable him to cover those exceptions without fatally compromising his position or his program.

GENERAL RELATIONS WITH PERSONNEL

The relationships between security personnel and regular employees of the company are unique. The normal "coworker" feeling does not exist. Even though the security officer is present to protect the company employees and the property that enables them to have employment, in the eyes of most employees security still represents *authority,* in almost the same image as that represented by a policeman. The terms "company cop" and "company spy" are used only too often in reference to security personnel, particularly by the rank-and-file laboring force and unskilled workers who comprise the majority of employees. Unfortunately, many labor unions also accept that image and will support their members in the contention that security oversteps its bounds and that many normal security procedures constitute an invasion of privacy.

It is difficult to get across to employees the fact that internal theft, embezzlement, and similar activities constitute crimes which, if not controlled, could have disastrous effects on the economic stability of the business. Few employees can recognize the real dangers of industrial espionage, for example, and the concomitant need for techniques and procedures designed to detect the presence of intelligence-gathering personnel and mechanisms for competitive organizations, especially where such activities include limited surveillance of employees and procedures to limit the movements and conduct of regular company employees.

Security should be aware of the potential for resentment toward security personnel and the authority they represent, and conscious efforts should be made to modify that

authoritarian image and to create an environment more conducive to mutual cooperation and respect.

It is very important, for example, that the security officer's attitude and conduct do
not impart a feeling of mistrust or suspicion. Employees' counsel and assistance should
be encouraged at every opportunity, including wherever possible the cooperation of
labor unions. Special effort should be made to demonstrate to employees that security
exists to protect and not to harass them.

Above all, beneficial relationships between employees and security will be fos-
tered when all security personnel act with a friendly, cooperative attitude, tempered
with fairness and equality. If it becomes necessary to interview or interrogate a suspect
or witness regarding a crime or other incident, the employee should be told of the circumstances necessitating the interview and be treated courteously and respectfully.
This does not mean that normal procedures of investigative firmness and a businesslike
attitude should be abandoned; but when employees have respect for the security officer
because they in turn are shown respect, information can be obtained most successfully.
Moreover, when the principle that all persons must be treated with equal dignity is
applied even toward persons arrested during the commission of a crime or after investigation strongly indicates guilt, the image of security will be enhanced, and many
uncomfortable or combative situations may be avoided.

It should be pointed out that security personnel often contribute to tension between
themselves and other employees by their attempt to remain "aloof." That is an unrealistic and misguided posture. A certain amount of paranoia—the belief that all persons are
guilty of something—is a miraculous armor that keeps policemen alive; but security
people are not policemen. They must combine their "police instincts" with the knowledge that their fellow employees are equally responsible to the same employer, and that
security's task is to permit them to function productively. "Command Presence," as it is
taught in the police academy, must be *modified* where *authority* is limited.

SELLING SECURITY

If security and safety programs are to have the support that is essential to make them
work, personnel at every level of the company must be "sold" on the importance and
necessity of loss prevention and safety measures. Top management support, as indicated, is fundamental; without it security will lack any "clout" at all, especially with
middle management and supervisors in other departments. Support of rank-and-file
employees must be won through educational programs as well as the attitude and conduct of security employees. Finally, supervisors must be convinced of the need for
security measures affecting their own departments; without their cooperation the program can quickly become undermined.

Selling security across departmental lines and throughout the company can be
done through both formal and informal programs. These would certainly include a
strong safety program obviously designed for the protection of employees; a good medical and first-aid program with accessible supplies; and frequent instruction as well as
visible signs of help available in case of emergency. Other programs might include a

security presentation during new employee induction sessions, ongoing audiovisual presentations, security tours, security bulletins, participation in department managers' meetings, security and safety posters, safety contests, and other activities.

The point is that recognition and acceptance of the role of security do not "just happen." There must be a visible and well-planned effort to get the message across that security is vital to the company's well-being—and to the well-being of all employees.

THE UNION FACTOR

In some situations the activities of security inevitably come into conflict with organized labor unions acting on behalf of employees. Unions have generally opposed the use of the polygraph, for instance, and have frequently sought to prevent the dismissal of employees caught in serious security violations. With regard to internal theft, it was not too many years ago that some unions considered the taking of company merchandise a "side benefit" of the job, insisting that the company had no right to restrict the activity. While this attitude has been modified in recent years, it has not entirely disappeared, as the following case history illustrates.

A major Los Angeles manufacturing firm had suffered an unexplained inventory loss amounting to more than $70,000 during a single year. A contract security firm was retained to investigate the loss. Undercover employees, four in number, were assigned to the manufacturing, stockroom, and shipping areas. Over a period of six months the investigation developed evidence of a ring of 15 employees within the company responsible for the thefts.

The operation was extremely sophisticated. Orders would be placed for merchandise from an outside source, or fence, for specific items in quantity. An accomplice working in the order department of the company prepared actual manufacturing orders, which in turn were processed normally through the production line. Following manufacture of the items, the special order was marked by other members of the ring in the stockroom area and placed in a special area of the loading dock, where two more members of the ring loaded it onto a truck. The truck was driven by yet another ring member, who would make a special drop of the stolen merchandise during one of his regular deliveries. The paperwork was then destroyed by all of the employees handling the order. It was a near-perfect operation, and the only possible method of discovery was infiltration of the ring by undercover agents over a period of time.

The investigation was successful. After all the necessary evidence was gathered, in an effort to make an "air-tight" case the local authorities were called in. With their assistance, arrests were made during one of the actual operations, which was placed under surveillance by the police. All 15 members of the ring, operating inside and outside the plant, were arrested. Twelve inside company employees all pleaded guilty to misdemeanor charges and were convicted in a court of law, resulting in their termination by the company.

Then the union stepped in. A demand was made for special union-company hearings for each employee. Following the hearings, the union decided that the employees should not have been fired, arguing that they had been punished sufficiently by the court and that, after all, stealing from one's employer was not unique. The company disagreed. The union threatened to strike unless (1) the employees were reinstated and (2) the company ceased all undercover operations, which constituted invasion of privacy of the employees. After due consideration, the company decided that the potential strike could prove disastrous—and capitulated.

While the attitude exemplified in this case is not as prevalent as it once was—enlightened union leaders have become more aware of the potentially crippling effects of internal crime, and labor arbitrators have tended to uphold the dismissal of employees for theft—nevertheless it remains true that employees caught in security violations invariably appeal to their unions for help, and few unions are reluctant to intervene on their behalf. A Supreme Court decision (*N.L.R.B. vs. J. Weingarten, Inc.,* 95 S. Ct. 972, 1975) has upheld the right of an employee to union representation during an investigatory interview, a condition that many investigators regard as crippling to any interrogation.

In these, as in many other circumstances, the security officer is caught in the middle. It can be a difficult position, and this is one reason why the morale of the security staff must be high. The attitude of the security officer should be even-handed and objective; he should not adopt an adversary attitude toward employees or their union representatives. He must be loyal to the company and his security director, but above all he must be loyal to his profession and to himself. The professional conduct of the security officer not only minimizes the potential for conflict, but in the long run contributes to improved relations with both employees and the unions representing them.

LIAISON WITH OUTSIDE AGENCIES

Establishing relationships with local authorities and, in particular, public emergency services is the responsibility of the security director, but which should also, in larger departments, be accomplished by each shift supervisor.

Relations with Local Police

It is an unfortunate fact that, historically, law enforcement people have not thought highly of security personnel. The "old man with a rusty gun" image of security is still all too prevalent. It has only been with the advent of higher level academic and other training programs in recent years that acknowledgment of the security officer as a professional, and as a valuable aid to law enforcement, is slowly surfacing.

A report prepared by the Private Security Advisory Council for the U.S. Law Enforcement Assistance Administration (LEAA) found that "In general, available literature and survey research indicate that a positive relationship exists between law enforcement and private security personnel and that they respect their complementary roles."[1] However, the Private Security Task Force also found that "only 25 percent of the law enforcement agencies had some policies or procedures for defining working roles with private security, and fewer than 20 percent had some procedures for cooperative actions with private security."[2]

What this research suggests is an increasing awareness in both the public and private sectors of the necessary role of private security in protecting private property and thus increasing the effectiveness of public law enforcement. But it also makes clear that the progressive security director should actively seek cooperative relations with public law enforcement officials.

An established mutual respect can be extremely beneficial to both parties. Any assistance sought by law enforcement personnel should always be furnished by the company Security Department. Since that cooperation must have the approval of company management, the policy should be established from the beginning of the director's tenure so that permission does not have to be secured on each occasion. While company management is generally favorably responsive to this type of cooperation, some companies will set limitations on the type of information that can be made available without prior approval. In those cases the company's requirements must be strictly observed.

Relations with Local Fire Department

The local fire department should also be contacted on the same basis as the police. Local fire officials are usually more "anxious" to establish relations with company security departments and will often, in fact, initiate the approach. Not only must the fire department inspect the premises by law, but it will normally be sincerely desirous of observing the precautions taken to guard against fire. It will want to learn what assistance can be expected if the fire department is called to an emergency, where to obtain quick access, and whether a competent security officer will be waiting to provide that access and information as to the location of the fire and the type of fire or emergency the responding firemen will face. Fire officials know only too well that their most formidable enemy is time, and that the quicker the response, the more apt they are to avoid a major disaster involving the loss of lives and property.

The fire department will also furnish free instruction in fire prevention and control to security personnel, and it is strongly suggested that those facilities be utilized to the fullest extent. Such training not only has the potential for saving great loss and destruction, but it also demonstrates to the fire department the company security department's desire to cooperate.

Emergency Care Facilities

Local first-aid and hospital facilities should be personally visited by the security director, who should learn what emergency care is available in case of accident, illness, or injury of any kind requiring outside assistance. Many hospitals have special treatment facilities that should be noted.

The security director should also request information regarding how many beds are normally available in a multiple-injury situation and how many emergency patients can be processed at a single time. With that information, should a major disaster occur involving multiple injuries, the Security Department is better equipped to direct ambulances to available facilities where injured persons can receive faster attention without overburdening the hospital staff.

Lists of all emergency phone numbers and persons to be contacted should, of course, be immediately available in the Security Department.

OTHER RELATIONSHIPS

There are other areas where the security director should seek and establish good relationships, such as with the security directors of other local companies where proprietary systems are maintained. An exchange of security information among companies in proximity is always valuable. Moreover, widespread disasters may strike many companies in the same area, and disaster planning should take into account this possibility.

The security director who establishes close contacts with his counterparts in other companies can often learn a great deal regarding new or different security procedures and equipment, and how those systems might be applicable to his own security program. In some situations, also, a lot of red tape can be eliminated by mutually cooperative security directors whose companies encounter common problems, such as a series of burglaries in the area affecting all manufacturing facilities, or the common circumstance of employees moving from one company to another and requiring security clearances.

If time and company policy permit, the director should also consider joining the local businesspersons' association or chamber of commerce—and he should actively participate and attend the functions of such groups. This can not only be beneficial to the Security Department in establishing local sources of information, but it is also good practice for the company to establish good community relations.

REVIEW QUESTIONS

1. Ideally, to whom should the security director report?
2. What are some potential problems in the Security Department's relationship with company management?
3. Discuss the relationship between security personnel and regular company employees. What can the security department do to foster an environment of mutual cooperation and respect?
4. Why is the local fire department usually eager to establish relationships with company security departments?
5. Discuss several possible advantages of the security director's establishing close contacts with his counterparts in other companies.

NOTES

1. "Law Enforcement and Private Security: Sources and Areas of Conflict," Private Security Advisory Council to the U.S. Department of Justice, Law Enforcement Assistance Administration, August 1976.
2. "Survey of Law Enforcement Relationships with the Private Security Industry," Private Security Task Force to the National Advisory Committee on Criminal Justice Standards and Goals, October 1975.

Part III

INTERNAL CONTROLS

Chapter 8

Access Control

LOCKS AND KEYS

Present technology within the general area of "access control" has, for the most part, substantially reduced the use of standard keys. Combination locks, card readers, remotely controlled entry and computerized systems, among other techniques, are advancing so rapidly, all of the above may very well become obsolete by the time you read about them in this book.

The primary reason for discussing key control techniques, based on the "hard key" method, is simply to emphasize the theory of controlled access. Also, keys are in fact still in use and will continue to be used well into the future, regardless of the extent of progress in that area. Many companies and small independent businesses simply cannot afford some of the more advanced systems available today.

Much of the theory of access control applies to any hardware or electronic application, thus, when reading the following, *card reader, sensitized ID badge,* or any other devise can be substituted for the word *key.* When the issues of key security and key control cabinets are being discussed, computerized systems should consider the programming and other entry code procedures designed to "protect" the method of access to the system by unauthorized persons.

KEY CONTROL SYSTEMS

There are some basic elements of key control that must be considered prior to a discussion of the types of keys to be utilized at a facility. Careful preparation for the maintenance and care of the system must be planned in advance of its installation.

Keys not in use must be housed in a tamperproof, locked control cabinet designed specifically for that purpose and located in some central area that is continually manned by security personnel. This area might be the control center, secured record and file room, or main security office, all of which were discussed in Chapter 6. If any of these areas contains a vault, that area would provide additional protection.

Keys should carry the highest level of protection required of all the elements under the jurisdiction of the Security Department; a loss, theft, or error in the key control system could compromise the entire security program and prove extremely costly.

Each key should be stamped with a *coded* number indicating the location of the lock it fits. Although it would be more convenient to stamp the location on the key ("Room 314," in a hotel/motel environment, for example), this should be avoided for obvious reasons.

Every key, whether issued or not, should have a corresponding hook or peg in the key control cabinet that is similarly numbered. A list of the code numbers and their exact locations may also be contained within the key control cabinet for easy reference. Most important, an inventory of keys remaining in the cabinet should be taken on a weekly basis and set up as a matter of routine.

As each key is issued, a file card should be made out containing the name and identification of the person to whom it is issued, along with a statement that he will not have that key duplicated. He accepts responsibility for that key by signing the card. The signed statement is an important psychological factor in impressing on the user the importance of the key and his responsibility for its care. In addition, a small tag bearing the name of the person to whom the key was issued should be placed on the peg from which the key was removed.

Upon termination of an employee, the return of company keys should be a requirement prior to the issuance of a final paycheck. The date of return should be noted on the key control file card, indicating that the key has been returned to the cabinet and the former user's tag removed from the peg.

Employees should be advised that the loss of a key must be reported immediately. To avoid the possibility that an employee would be fearful of reporting a loss, it should be made clear that there will be no recriminations regarding that loss. When a key is reported lost, stolen, or missing for any reason, the key locking cylinder should be changed as quickly as possible.

TYPES OF LOCKS

Various types of locks and keys are available that have been designed for high-security areas and are manufactured by all major lock companies. Some companies specialize in high-security locking devices. The keys and cylinders are designed so that—theoretically, at least—the key cannot be duplicated or the cylinder manipulated or picked. There is no system known to the author, however, which cannot be compromised. At best, locking devices only extend the *time* necessary to penetrate the system in some manner. The presence of a "good, strong security lock" should not create a complacent attitude as to the protection it affords. It should be supplemented with alarms, patrols, or other procedures, depending on the level of security required in that area.

The installation of the lock is also important, and the functioning of the lock should be inspected not only during installation but on regularly scheduled occasions throughout the year. The door itself should fit tightly against a good, strong frame, preferably of metal construction. The space between the door and the jamb should be small enough that a plastic card or other object designed to force the bolt into its receptacle will not fit. If there is too much space, the door should be adjusted or a device installed along the door jamb to secure the gap. Special "strippings" designed for just that purpose are sold by almost every locksmith. The technique of using a plastic credit card, or other flexible sheet, forced between the door and the frame is called *shimming,* thus the strippings referred to above are called, simply, *shim protectors.*

In addition, every good spring lock bolt has a safety feature, as shown in Figure 8.1. It works this way: When the door is closed, the bolt slides into the recessed metal receptacle in the door jamb. The safety bar, being wider than the bolt, rests against the metal plate and remains back as the bolt slides forward into the receptacle. When the safety bar is in this position, it locks the bolt forward where it cannot be retracted into the door by direct pressure alone (such as a plastic card). This feature should be checked by a security officer frequently; with use, the device sometimes loosens up and does not function efficiently. The checking method is simple: With the door open, press the safety bar back and hold in that position. Then press against the bolt to see if it holds firm. There should be no more than 1/16-inch play. If the tolerance is more than that, the lock must be serviced or repaired by the manufacturer or company locksmith.

Spring locks, such as those just described, are the least efficient but most convenient. Therefore, if an area is considered a high security risk, spring locks should be replaced or supplemented with deadbolt locks. The deadbolt lock must be turned with a key and cannot "slide" or "spring" into the closed position.

It is also important, regardless of whether a spring or deadbolt lock is installed, that the bolt itself be at least 3/4 inch in length. The length adds considerable strength to the device and minimizes the possibility of "forcing" the door.

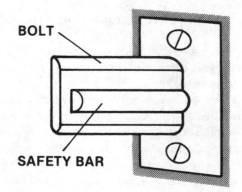

BOLT

SAFETY BAR

Figure 8.1

MASTER KEY SYSTEMS

Various methods are used to control multiple access to keyed doors. Obviously, each lock should have a separate key which fits only that lock, the key being issued to the person permitted access to that room. In most instances, certain levels of personnel require access to many different areas, and to carry 5, 10, or 20 keys becomes impractical.

For purposes of illustration, let us assume there are four buildings or areas in a complex: A, B, C, and D. Each area has 20 locked doors. Ten lead to manufacturing areas and 10 to other services such as sales, promotion, and maintenance. A supervisor requiring access to the 10 manufacturing area doors in Area A would carry a *submaster* key, cut and designed to open all 10. An individual requiring frequent access to the entire building of Area A would carry a *master* key fitting all doors. The same submaster and master system would be utilized in each of the other areas or buildings, B, C, and D.

Any individual cleared and permitted to have access to all doors in all areas would carry a *grand master* key. The only step above the grand master would be a rarely used *great grand master* key, utilized only when every lock, padlock, closet, file cabinet, desk, etc., is added to the system. The great grand master system is obsolete and should *never* be utilized in any company requiring even the most minimal security.

The danger in any master key system, of course, is that the loss or theft of any master key would require rekeying of all doors within its access area. Any loss of a master key should be investigated thoroughly.

Several other methods of access control can be considered, as discussed next.

COMBINATION LOCKS

There are doors and padlocks manufactured which utilize a combination lock mechanism as opposed to a key. It is recommended that a four-position combination be utilized. This not only provides more possible combinations to be used in larger facilities, but is also more difficult to open either by chance or by running through possible combinations carefully.

The value of the combination lock lies in the fact that there are no keys to be lost or stolen—and the cost of keys is eliminated. When an employee is terminated, it is a simple matter to change the combination.

Some manufacturers produce combination locks which also have a key cylinder to permit access by a mastering system for executive personnel, maintenance crews, and security officers. One point deserving emphasis is that security should maintain absolute control over any master key classification. *No submaster, master, grand master, or great grand master key should ever be permitted to leave the premises; they should be checked in and out each day with the Security Department.* Maximum security even requires any master key to be turned in whenever the carrier leaves the premises for short periods of time, such as for meals, outside business appointments, or any other reason.

CARD-KEY CONTROL

Where normal locks and padlocks are not used, specially sealed, proximity, sensitized, or magnetized identification cards can be utilized. These special cards respond to adjacent sensors or fit into slot receptacles next to the secured door and activate the locking mechanism.

Many of the computerized entry systems permit total access programming for the employee. Not only does it specify which areas and doors can be entered by the individual, but also the times of day and days of the week he or she has access. Additionally, based on the times the employee enters the business then leaves, either for lunch or at the end of the day, the computer also computes his salary based on an hourly wage. If the employee works over the time, programmed into the system, overtime too is computed.

IDENTIFICATION SYSTEMS

Many other types of access control systems are available that have highly sophisticated design; for example, a mechanism which activates when an entrant places her hand on a sensitized plate while a computer "reads" and compares her fingerprints with a set previously stored. Similar devices read the iris of the eye, which has patterns that are as unique as fingerprints. Such systems are designed primarily as identification systems in extremely high-risk areas.

Identification of the person attempting to gain access is a most important factor. It can be accomplished by sophisticated mechanisms such as those described in the preceding paragraph or by the physical presence of security personnel to check identification. Procedures for the logging of visitors were described in Chapter 4.

IDENTIFICATION CARDS

Employees of a company where internal security is controlled should carry identification cards sealed in hard vinyl, alter-proof plastic. The ID should show the employee's name and department, employee number, photograph, and thumbprint. It can also contain any other information the company considers necessary.

The identification card should be fitted with a small clip for attachment in plain view of the employee's clothing. It should be visible at all times. The card can also be color-coded, indicating the limits of the employee's access to the various areas of the facility. ID cards can, in fact, be the computerized key control card referred to in the preceding section.

Visitors to the company should be issued an identification card especially color-coded for limited access with an escort. In high-security facilities, no visitor should be permitted to wander freely through the premises. A visitor should be received at the front entrance and guided to his destination by the person he is visiting, by a member of that person's immediate staff (a secretary, for example), or by a security officer. The color-coded badges aid security personnel, or other regular employees, in observing an individual who is in an improper or restricted area, so that the individual can be challenged or assisted to his defined destination.

POSTED SIGNS

Signs are covered here under the general heading of "Access Control" because they are designed to direct or modify movement, not only leading into the interior of the premises, but also once an employee or visitor is inside.

The posting of signs serves a multitude of purposes and has great value if handled properly and discreetly. Many signs are required by statute or regulation, such as exit signs over emergency fire exits. All signs should be easily readable, brief and specific, and should be of a size consistent with their relative importance.

Directional Signs

Directional signs are designed to control traffic flow or are instructional in nature. They should be specific. Every fire extinguisher should have an accompanying sign indicating specifically the type of fire it *should* and *should not* be used on, and instructions on the use of the extinguisher. The same should apply to all pieces of emergency equipment available for general use by employees.

An example of a poorly designed sign accompanies one of the most important safety devices in almost every building with an elevator. It is one of the most critical life-saving devices used universally, yet very few people know what it does or how to use it properly, even though they see it almost every day of their lives. It is located on the floor-button panel in the elevator (usually at the top of the panel), usually colored red, with a notice, that reads "Use only in case of fire."

But what does this button do? Does it ring a bell? Activate an alarm? Call the fire department? Its function is simple. Most elevator doors are controlled by an electric eye; when a "body" breaks the beam by passing through it, either entering or leaving the elevator, the door will remain open. When no solid object passes through the beam for a few seconds, the doors close automatically and the elevator continues up or down to the next stop.

During a fire, enclosed hallways will fill with smoke. Thick black or grayish smoke filtering into the open elevator will act as a solid body, breaking the electric eye and causing the doors to remain open. The elevator will be immobilized and the occupants trapped. The emergency red button for "use only in case of fire" simply deactivates the electric eye function, permitting the elevator doors to close and the cab to leave the fire area.

The electric eye is inactive, however, only as long as the button is *held in*. As soon as the button is released, the electric eye is again activated and the doors will reopen. Many persons have merely pushed the button and released it, expecting it to accomplish its life-saving task in that brief moment. *It must be held in.* Many people have lost their lives simply because there was no proper explanation posted of that button's use.

Examples of other types of "directional" signs would be the identification of exits and routes to be used in case of emergency evacuation. In this context it might also be appropriate, under certain physical conditions, to paint color-coded stripes along the floor or walls for people to follow in case of fire. When smoke limits visibility, it is always safer to remain close to the ground (as heat rises), and the colored stripe can lead the individual to safety.

Warning Signs

Wherever a potentially dangerous condition exists as a necessary element of the environment, a large, clear warning sign should be posted indicating the nature of the danger—and, if possible, a remedy. An example would be: "WARNING—FALLING DEBRIS IN THIS AREA" (the nature of the danger), "WEAR HARDHATS" (the remedy). Other signs in this category do not require a remedy, such as "WARNING—HIGH VOLTAGE."

When the danger present is extreme, the "WARNING" indication can be used; if it is even more serious, "DANGER" may be more appropriate. If circumstances are such that the condition presents a hazard but no unusual remedy is called for and the employee's normal function must continue, "CAUTION" should be used, along with an explanation of the hazard. The sign is simply a reminder that special safety precautions should prevail.

Signs that notify employees of existing or potential hazards should also indicate the degree of hazard. If all signs read "DANGER" and some of the conditions are not in fact as serious as others, in time employees will tend to minimize the hazard and fail to recognize extremely dangerous conditions where they do arise and are posted.

Limitations

The third major category of signs are those that advise the reader of a rule, regulation, or law. They are notices that restrict or limit activity or state that some function must be performed. An example of the latter would be a fire regulation, "THIS DOOR MUST REMAIN UNLOCKED DURING BUSINESS HOURS." Limitation signs might include the following: "NO PARKING," "IDENTIFICATION BADGES MUST BE WORN AT ALL TIMES," "CAMERAS, FIREARMS, OR EXPLOSIVES NOT PERMITTED IN THIS AREA," and "NO SMOKING."

If the sign indicating a restriction in activity is based on a local ordinance, state or county statute, or government regulation, the citation should appear in small (but readable) print at the bottom of the sign.

Signs in General

The reader might assume from the preceding paragraphs that the author is suggesting that signs be posted for everything, resulting in wall-to-wall signs. This is not the case. Signs are extremely valuable as *reminders* of certain conditions or circumstances. If something is important enough to post, it is also important enough for instructions to be given verbally or by written notice on an individual basis. Even though the sign will not be read each time the individual passes by, it is observed and programmed into the employee's routine. It is also there for reference when he desires more precise information regarding its contents—but he has been conditioned to know that it is there.

The conditioning process can be carried one step further by color-coding the signs and not mixing the combinations. Signs in red usually indicate a warning of some kind. Green usually indicates a directional sign, and simple black-and-white an instructional sign. The heading of the sign should be in the appropriate color, with the added instructions in black and white or some other contrasting combination.

GUARD STATIONS

The location of posts manned continuously by security officers for access control purposes should be considered very carefully. It is possible to have too few, resulting in the potential of unauthorized entry into any given area, or too many, resulting in a waste of manpower and money. The latter also promotes poor relations with personnel, because it establishes a prison-like environment where the primary image is one of surveillance and mistrust. The resulting attitudes in this instance are not accurate or consistent with the company's intent; the fact remains, however, that the negative image does prevail and thus must be modified.

A female officer's presence can serve very well to soften security's normally authoritarian image. While they are trained security personnel, they also evoke the image of a regular receptionist, particularly if they are attired in blazers. The company must decide on the level of authority which they wish to be exhibited at each individual post.

Exterior posts, such as the main entrance to the parking area or any other exterior perimeter stationary positions, as well as exterior patrols, should be manned by a uniformed officer.

Officers assigned to stationary posts where ingress and egress are controlled should have specific procedures, materials, and communication sources to accomplish proper identification of persons entering and leaving the premises or controlled area.

1. Identification badges must be worn by employees passing through employee gates. The gates or doors should be narrowed to admit a limited number of persons at one time, enabling the security officer to observe badges and make proper

identification. While this is not a foolproof system, it does act as a deterrent to anyone hoping to "slip by" the officer.

2. The officer at the entrance gate should be provided daily with a list of terminations. If a terminated employee enters, the main gate post officer should notify the security officer at the employees' entrance. The former employee may possibly have some legitimate last-minute business to conclude at the company, such as picking up a final paycheck or claiming personal property. However, the terminated employee should not have free run of the facility and should instead be treated like any other visitor.

3. At main entrances where visitors enter, the officer must insist on proper identification by driver's license or other legally accepted documents. ID must have a photograph affixed.

4. The visitor should sign a visitor's log (legibly), indicating also his destination, the person he is visiting, the reason for the visit, company represented, date, and time of entry and departure.

5. When possible, the officer at the main gate post should be provided with a list of guests and visitors expected for that day. He should direct visitors to the proper entrance and parking location. Visitors whose names do not appear on the daily list should be cleared with the individual the visitor desires to see, or with the main company receptionist, prior to being admitted. The only exception to this procedure would be prospective employees applying for a position. They should be directed to the employees' entrance and handled by the officer at that station.

6. Visitors should be issued a visitor's badge. Once inside the building, they should be provided with an escort to their destination. Usually the person being visited will escort the visitor personally or send a member of her staff.

7. Deliveries should be routed to a specific location where incoming and outgoing materials are controlled separately. The loading and unloading of deliveries should be supervised by a security officer or other employee specifically assigned to that task.

8. Vehicles should be furnished with color-coded stickers, which are, in effect, parking passes indicating the section where parking is permissible.

In smaller companies, where manpower is not always available, closed-circuit television and intercoms have been effective in access control. The visitor can ring a bell and then be observed over CCTV as well as communicated with over the intercom. Once identification is satisfactorily accomplished, the door can be opened by remote control and the visitor admitted to an area where he will be met by an employee. In this manner, it is possible for one security officer to handle several entrances.

The process of limiting access to the premises is the company's first line of defense against penetration by many types of criminally motivated intruders. The degree of protection and the efficient, courteous manner in which it is handled will also leave the visitor with a favorable impression of the company in general.

REVIEW QUESTIONS

1. Describe the following protection measures for keys: control cabinet, coding, inventory, key control file cards.
2. What should be done when a key is reported lost, stolen, or missing?
3. Describe the various levels of a master key system: submaster, master, grand master, great grand master.
4. What are the three major categories of signs? Give an example of each type.
5. Describe the procedure to be followed by security officers at access control posts in admitting visitors.

Chapter 9

Personnel Clearance

The previous chapter explained how perimeter control is the first line of defense against intrusion by external forces. The verification and investigative procedures relating to the "clearing" of personnel hold comparable status by minimizing the risk of intrusion by criminal or disruptive elements from within. The importance of establishing proper procedures in this area, and the absolute necessity of following those procedures thoroughly and conscientiously, cannot be overemphasized.

In larger companies and major industrial complexes, the process of personnel clearance is contained within the Personnel, or Human Resources, Department. Security Department resources are utilized frequently, especially when high-level clearances are required either due to government contracts under Department of Defense requirements, or extremely sensitive, proprietary production or manufacturing processes. Smaller or mid-sized companies still may rely on the Security Department for their clearance procedures.

The controversy regarding the checking of an employee's background has become not only a legal but an emotional issue. On one hand, background checking is considered an invasion of the employee's privacy; on the other hand, it is the right of an employer to select employees in a manner that will provide some degree of protection against thievery and other intended criminal acts.

The relationship between an employer and employee should be one that is *mutually beneficial.* The employer desires an employee who is honest, loyal, conscientious, and efficient in the performance of his job. The employee desires comfortable working conditions, a good salary, adequate benefits such as retirement and insurance plans, recognition through promotions and wage increases, and, in general, a secure job and the ability to provide for his family's future.

Before accepting a position, the applicant will certainly seek information about the company in an effort to decide whether she wishes to work there or if she should look elsewhere for a position that would be more acceptable to her standards, desires, and qualifications. She is entitled to learn something about the company.

The employer, too, wants to know if the applicant is the right person for the job and is capable of performing assigned tasks. The employer also wants to know if the applicant is the kind of individual who will blend into the established environment and develop favorable relationships with coworkers and supervisors.

When employer and employee decide they are "right for each other," the result is a high level of morale, a safe, efficient operation leading to successful production, increased profits, higher salaries, better benefits, and a secure future for all.

EMPLOYMENT APPLICATION FORM

The first step in preparing for a complete pre-employment background investigation is to design an application form, one that not only tells company management the qualifications of the potential employee, but also provides sufficient detailed information to enable the investigator to verify the information provided by the applicant and to probe more deeply into areas the applicant has neglected to reveal which may be directly relevant to acceptance.

Areas may be "neglected" by the applicant by accident or by design. Possibly the applicant is concealing a prior criminal conviction that may directly affect his suitability for employment. A history of theft from previous employers should certainly preclude his being granted a position of trust with the company. Academic background and work experience should certainly be verified to ensure that the applicant's qualifications are accurately indicated in his resume or application.

The application form should be thorough and complete, with all specific information necessary to enable the contents to be verified and additional background developed. Figure 9.1 shows a sample application form that contains most of the information necessary.

Remember that there is currently considerable controversy surrounding the permissible information that an employer can request of a potential employee on the application form. The controversy will probably last for many years, and employers' practices will be revised many times and modified to meet the guidelines established by numerous court decisions now and in the future.

For example, the Supreme Court has made it clear that no employer may discriminate against a prospective employee because of the employee's age. Many employers, therefore, have eliminated the "Date of Birth" entry from the application form. Although there are no specific rulings on that particular item, it is the opinion of this author that the court did not intend to deny the employer, making a pre-employment investigation, the ability to distinguish between two individuals with the same name, when the date of birth is one important factor in determining the difference.

It is true that the Social Security number would make the same determination; however, there is also the theory that Social Security numbers should not be used for any reason other than filing Social Security benefits for the employee. (That is another study before the courts.) Also, it is the employer's right to search public criminal conviction records filed in the superior and municipal courts, and those records do not utilize Social Security numbers to identify convicted persons, but do use dates of birth to distinguish which one of thousands of John Smiths is the individual identified in the record.

For these reasons, this discussion will cover methods and techniques of pre-employment investigation including *all* of the information that is usable during the investigative process. It is left up to the individual company to utilize only that information which is legal at the time of the investigation.

(COMPANY NAME)

APPLICATION FOR EMPLOYMENT

- -

PLEASE PRINT

FULL NAME_____ MAIDEN OR AKA _____

ADDRESS _____CITY_____ PHONE: bus_____

res_____

SOCIAL SECURITY NUMBER_____ ARE YOU A U.S. CITIZEN ____

If non-citizen, are you able to provide proof of your right to be lawfully employed_____

DATE OF BIRTH _____ HEIGHT ____ WEIGHT ____ SEX____

HAIR_____ EYES ____ MARITAL STATUS/SPOUSE NAME _____

CHILDREN:

_____ ____ _____ ____

name   age   name   age

_____ ____ _____ ____

name   age   name   age

VEHICLE: 1) MAKE_____ YEAR ____LICENSE NO._____

2) MAKE_____ YEAR ____LICENSE NO._____

DRIVERS LICENSE NO. _____ STATE _____

AUTO INSURANCE CO. _____ HOW LONG _____

BANKING REFERENCE _____ CHECKING/SAVINGS _____

U.S. MILITARY RECORD (dates, assignment, type of discharge)

_____ CURRENT STATUS_____

SELECTIVE SERVICE NUMBER _____ STATUS_____

ARE YOU BONDABLE _____ Have you ever had a bond denied _____

PLEASE GIVE DETAILS ON A SEPARATE PAGE IF ANY ANSWER TO

FOLLOWING IS YES

Are there pending civil lawsuits or judgments against you   _____

Have you ever been convicted of a crime   _____

Have you ever been convicted of a crime under another name   _____

Have you any physical handicap, chronic disease or disability   _____

Have you ever had a nervous breakdown   _____

Do you have any outside business interest   _____

Do you require any special considerations or assistance

in performing your job   _____

Figure 9.1   Sample Application Form

TYPE OF EMPLOYMENT SEEKING _____   APPROX. SALARY _____

Will you take part-time employment _____   Hrs. Available _____

HOW WERE YOU REFERRED TO THIS COMPANY _____

Do you have any relatives or friends currently in our employ _____

ORGANIZATION, CLUB, OR UNION MEMBERSHIPS

_____

HOBBIES _____

ABILITIES:
DO YOU SPEAK A FOREIGN LANGUAGE _____TYPING SPEED _____

SHORTHAND SPEED _____   OTHER MACHINES OPERATED_____

SPECIAL SKILLS OR INTERESTS _____
EDUCATION:
COLLEGE _____   MAJOR _____

ADDRESS _____   GRADUATED _____   DEGREE _____

DATES OF ATTENDANCE _____

HIGH SCHOOL _____   GRADUATED _____

ADDRESS _____   DATES OF ATTENDANCE _____

OTHER SPECIAL SCHOOLING: (POSTGRADUATE, TRADE, TECHNICAL, ETC.)

_____

_____

HAVE YOU SERVED AN APPRENTICESHIP IN ANY TRADE OR PROFESSION

_____   DESCRIBE_____

EMPLOYMENT HISTORY (past five years, most current first)

COMPANY _____   SUPERVISOR _____

ADDRESS _____   PHONE _____

POSITION _____   DATES EMPLOYED _____

SALARY _____   REASON FOR TERMINATION _____

COMPANY _____   SUPERVISOR _____

ADDRESS _____   PHONE _____

POSITION _____   DATES EMPLOYED _____

SALARY _____   REASON FOR TERMINATION _____

Figure 9.1   Sample Application Form (*continued*)

RESIDENCE HISTORY (past five years, most current first)

ADDRESS _____ CITY _____ STATE _____

DATES OF RESIDENCE _____ RENT/OWN _____

ADDRESS _____ CITY _____ STATE _____

DATES OF RESIDENCE _____ RENT/OWN _____

ADDRESS _____ CITY _____ STATE _____

DATES OF RESIDENCE _____ RENT/OWN _____

IN CASE OF EMERGENCE, NOTIFY _____

ADDRESS _____ PHONE _____

RELATIONSHIP _____

PRIVATE PHYSICIAN_____PHONE _____

ADDRESS _____

PRIVATE MEDICAL INSURANCE COVERAGE _____

When was your last physical examination _____ Results _____

Are you willing to take a complete physical examination _____

Do you hold a security clearance _____ What Agency _____

When previously cleared _____ What company _____

I DO HEREBY STATE THAT ALL OF THE ANSWERS AND STATEMENTS IN THIS APPLICATION ARE TRUE AND CORRECT TO THE BEST OF MY KNOWLEDGE AND BELIEF AND UNDERSTAND THAT ANY FALSIFICATION HEREIN IS CAUSE FOR IMMEDIATE DISMISSAL OR DENIAL OF EMPLOYMENT. I DO HEREBY GRANT THAT (NAME OF COMPANY) HAS MY PERMISSION TO CONTACT AND INTERVIEW ALL PERSONS AND PLACES MENTIONED IN MY APPLICATION FOR EMPLOYMENT, AND TO CONDUCT A GENERAL INVESTIGATION INTO MY BACKGROUND HISTORY RELATIVE TO EMPLOYMENT

_____ _____
(DATE)   (APPLICANT'S SIGNATURE)

_____ _____
(DATE)   (INTERVIEWED BY)

Figure 9.1 Sample Application Form (*continued*)

Personnel departments and security officers responsible for personnel clearance investigations are cautioned to maintain a constant awareness of court decisions, legal opinions, and changes in the laws that affect their activities, and to adjust to changing circumstances.

PROTECTION OF APPLICANT'S RIGHTS

In considering the design of the application form, legal restrictions must be acknowledged carefully. The Civil Rights Act of 1964 and subsequent federal court decisions state that persons may not be denied employment based on racial, ethnic, religious, sex, or age discrimination. The application, therefore, cannot ask where an individual was born or what country he is from. It *can* ask if he is a U.S. citizen and what foreign languages he speaks. The application cannot ask the applicant's religion. It cannot ask whether the individual has ever been *arrested* or *dismissed* from another job for a crime; it can ask only if he has ever been *convicted* of a crime.

The Federal Consumer Credit Protection Act (Title VI, Public Law 91-508) also establishes criteria, not only for the methods and limitations of personnel clearance procedures, but also for the responsibilities incumbent on the employer to notify the employee regarding the intent to conduct the investigation, the areas the investigation will cover, and the results of the investigation.

The employee has the right to review her pre-employment investigation file *and* to dispute any findings by inserting, in writing, her version of any adverse information. This right of the employee is reasonable; there have been instances where an investigator has received inaccurate information through computer errors, mix-ups in individuals with similar names, or even from a former employment supervisor giving a poor recommendation because of nothing more than a personality conflict. Every person should have the right to correct errors such as these which might otherwise deny that person employment in a position for which he or she is qualified. Therefore, when a dispute to investigate information is filed, it is incumbent on the security officer to reinvestigate the matter and either confirm or deny the appeal.

The applicant's rights must be explained to him at the time he applies for the job. The safest manner of accomplishing this is to provide a written notice along with the application form. The notice should be signed by the applicant, indicating he has read it, and then filed in his personnel folder for later substantiation of notice if necessary. Figure 9.2 is an example of the type of notice the employee should receive attached to the application form.

Let us assume that at some point the applicant desires "additional information" as indicated in the preceding notice, and makes his request in writing. The next step would be to send him a letter or notice, with a copy retained in his file, as exemplified in Figure 9.3. If, in response to such a letter, the applicant requests to view his personnel file including the investigative report, he must be permitted to do so. His reading of the file should take place within the confines of the personnel or security office and under supervision, ensuring that the employee does not remove any materials from the file.

(COMPANY NAME)

PERSONNEL:
FOR THE PURPOSE OF COMPLYING WITH PUBLIC LAW 91-508, SECTION 606 (A) (1) ("FAIR CREDIT REPORTING ACT"), THIS IS TO INFORM YOU THAT AS PART OF THE PROCEDURE FOR PROCESSING YOUR APPLICATION FOR EMPLOYMENT, A PRE-EMPLOYMENT INVESTIGATION MAY BE CONDUCTED, DURING WHICH TIME INFORMATION WILL BE OBTAINED THROUGH PERSONAL INTERVIEWS WITH THIRD PARTIES SUCH AS MEMBERS OF YOUR FAMILY, BUSINESS ASSOCIATES, FINANCIAL SOURCES, NEIGHBORS OR OTHERS WHO HAVE PERSONAL KNOWLEDGE OF YOUR ACTIVITIES, LIVING AND WORKING HABITS. INFORMATION WILL ALSO BE SOUGHT REGARDING YOUR REPUTATION, CHARACTER AND BACKGROUND HISTORY. YOU HAVE THE RIGHT TO MAKE A REQUEST, IN WRITING, WITHIN A REASONABLE AMOUNT OF TIME FOR AN ACCURATE AND COMPLETE DISCLOSURE OF ADDITIONAL INFORMATION REGARDING THE NATURE AND SCOPE OF THIS INVESTIGATION.

_____   _____
Date   Applicant

Figure 9.2 Notice of Individual Rights in Background Investigations

(COMPANY LETTERHEAD)
THIS IS IN RESPONSE TO YOUR REQUEST FOR ADDITIONAL INFORMATION REGARDING THE INVESTIGATIVE REPORT WHICH MAY HAVE BEEN MADE IN CONNECTION WITH YOUR APPLICATION FOR EMPLOYMENT.

☐ NO INVESTIGATION WAS REQUESTED IN CONNECTION WITH YOUR APPLICATION

☐ AN INVESTIGATION WAS CONDUCTED. THE RESULTS ARE ROUTINE PROCEDURE IN THE EVALUATION OF YOUR APPLICATION AND COVERED AREAS OF RESIDENCE VERIFICATION, MARITAL STATUS AND NUMBER OF DEPENDENTS. AS APPLICABLE, OCCUPATION EMPLOYMENT HISTORY, GENERAL HEALTH, HABITS, REPUTATION, LIVING CONDITIONS AND CRIMINAL BACKGROUND WERE ALSO CHECKED THROUGH PUBLIC RECORDS AND INTERVIEWS WITH FRIENDS AND OTHER ACQUAINTANCES.

_____   _____
Date   Signature of Company Official

Figure 9.3 Notice of Investigation

INVESTIGATION PROCEDURES

Verifying Information on the Application

A great deal of information can be derived from the employment application. Ideally, *all* information furnished by *all* applicants should be verified carefully. However, few if any companies are willing to budget for a full field investigation of every applicant. Typically, this investigation is more intensive for top and middle management, and for technical or rank-and-file employees who are to be in sensitive positions or will have access to high-risk areas of the company.

The following procedures, then, represent the ideal.

1. *Current address* should be verified by conducting an interview with landlord or neighbors to ascertain actual residency, living conditions, ability to meet financial obligations regarding rent or payments, and general reputation. One or two former addresses should also be checked in this manner. This procedure may be conducted by telephone or in person.
2. *Former employment* should be checked through references obtained not only from the company personnel files but also from the applicant's former supervisor. Make certain that employment dates, salary, etc., agree with information provided by the applicant. This information should be obtained in person or by phone. It is possible to obtain information by mail, but this does not enable the investigator to ask questions or probe possible problem areas at the time of the investigation.
3. *Academic background* can be verified by mail. A photocopy of the applicant's authorization to obtain the information must be included with the inquiry.
4. *Personal references,* although not included in the sample application form, can be requested on the application and verified by the investigator. It should be expected, however, that the applicant would not list any sources who would be unfavorable to him. Investigation should also develop references not listed by the applicant. Favorable references are important and do add to the applicant's qualifications, particularly if the reference is knowledgeable about the applicant's ability to perform his profession or craft. The personnel investigator's task, however, is to develop any adverse information *if in fact it does exist.*
5. *Driver's license information* can be used to check with the state department of motor vehicles for any record of accidents or citations. The driving record may indicate a history of alcoholism or irresponsible tendencies, accident-proneness, etc. Not all states make DMV records available; however, it is the authors experience that the position of the state DMV departments changes from time to time.
6. *Military records* should be confirmed by having the applicant submit a copy of his or her service record (DD Form 214).
7. *Banking and financial history* should be checked through a telephone call or written correspondence to the bank listed on the application. Additionally, the company should subscribe to one of the major computer credit agencies and order a report from that source. Because credit agencies are sometimes inaccurate in their reports

because of computer error, mistaken identity or poor updating procedures, any information obtained from credit agencies must be reverified by contacting the credit references on the report.

Social Security Number

The Social Security number should be verified by observation of the applicant's Social Security card. This should be done in conjunction with seeing the applicant's birth certificate (or a certified copy if the original is not available). The birth certificate will show where the subject was born. The name should be the same as that on the Social Security card; if it is not, an explanation, with accompanying substantiation, is in order.

Social Security numbers are coded by the government. The first three digits indicate the state where the card was issued. In all probability, this will be the state where the applicant began her working career. The following is a list of Social Security numbers and the states they represent.

001-003	New Hampshire	449-467	Texas
004-007	Maine	468-477	Minnesota
008-009	Vermont	478-485	Iowa
010-034	Massachusetts	486-500	Missouri
035-039	Rhode Island	501-502	North Dakota
040-049	Connecticut	503-504	South Dakota
050-134	New York	505-508	Nebraska
135-158	New Jersey	509-515	Kansas
159-211	Pennsylvania	516-517	Montana
212-220	Maryland	518-519	Idaho
221-222	Delaware	520	Wyoming
223-231	Virginia	521-524	Colorado
232-236	West Virginia	525	New Mexico
237-246	North Carolina	526-527	Arizona
247-251	South Carolina	528-529	Utah
252-260	Georgia	530	Nevada
261-267	Florida	531-539	Washington
268-302	Ohio	540-544	Oregon
303-317	Indiana	545-573	California
318-361	Illinois	574	Alaska
362-386	Michigan	575-576	Hawaii
387-399	Wisconsin	577-579	District of Columbia
400-407	Kentucky	580	Virgin Islands
408-415	Tennessee	580-584	Puerto Rico
416-424	Alabama	586	Guam, Amer. Samoa,
425-428	Mississippi		Northern Mariana Islands,
429-432	Arkansas		Philippine Islands
433-439	Louisiana	700-728	Railroad Retirement Act
440-448	Oklahoma		

The first step in analyzing the application form should be to decode the Social Security number in order to learn where it was originally issued. The work history, education, and past residence sections of the application should then be reviewed to see whether they relate to the state where the card was issued. If they do not, the applicant should explain why. Possibly the applicant is attempting to conceal his history in one state due to a criminal conviction or other adverse background. Or perhaps the application form simply does not request information going back far enough in time to cover his history in that state. In either case the discrepancy should be probed, with the question asked directly in an interview with the applicant. At least at this point the applicant will realize the investigation is thorough. If his answers are not satisfactory, consideration must be given to denying him employment.

Personnel investigations sometimes reveal that an applicant has used two or more Social Security numbers on previous application forms with past employers—indicating an attempt to conceal true identity for one reason or another.

It is of interest to note here that very few job applicants are aware of the coding system for Social Security. As a matter of fact, surprisingly few personnel departments are aware of or use the number codes for verification.

Criminal Background

A check of the applicant's criminal background must also be made. In most states, criminal convictions are a matter of public record; felonies are filed in superior court and misdemeanors in municipal court. Some jurisdictions also have a gross misdemeanor category, normally also filed at the lower court level. It is therefore a simple matter to check those files physically. If the investigator is fortunate, the file may also contain a complete probation report, which can also be used to verify and complete information on the application form.

If the records are not publicly available, assistance may be sought from the local police department or other private sources. In this context, a complete set of fingerprints should be obtained from the applicant as part of the hiring procedure. If the company has a government contract that requires a level of security clearance, the government agency involved will assist in obtaining the criminal background information. Often, states that require security officers to complete firearms training will check the officer's criminal record with either state criminal files or the FBI, or both.

Public Records

Finally, a check of all available public records should be considered. A wealth of information is available to the investigator in public records. It is not possible to discuss these records in a specific way, because each state and county varies in its filing procedures and availability of records. Some states, for example, maintain record systems that are not available publicly, but are released only to "interested parties." In such cases, the release form at the bottom of the application, signed by the applicant, may suffice.

It took the author 3 years, during which time thousands of letters were written and the replies analyzed, to compile a comprehensive listing of records maintained in the 50 states and more than 3000 counties in the United States. Only a brief examination of the records can be presented here, based on the California system (a system that can be matched in most states with a little effort). Although it is not necessary for the investigator to check all of the following sources in all cases, it should be left up to the investigator and personnel department to determine which records are pertinent to a particular investigation.

Voter's Registration.   The applicant should be listed here if he has ever voted in the county. The record will show address, former address, occupation, brief physical description, and political affiliation.

Department of Motor Vehicles.
1. *Driver's license.* Furnishes a complete physical description, birth date, and, in some states, photograph, fingerprint, or both.
2. *Registered vehicles.* Shows license numbers, vehicle make and year, description, serial number, and both legal and registered owner.
3. *Accidents and violations.* Lists all auto accidents and violations, showing address at the time of the incident and disposition of the case.

Birth Records.   Includes place and date of birth and information on parents, such as mother's maiden name, address at time of birth, occupation of parents, etc.

Marriage Records.   Includes age, description, and address of both parties.

General Civil Records.   The civil indexes are usually divided into two sections: superior court and municipal court. The records will list all lawsuits, divorces, probate matters, etc., for the subject, either as plaintiff or defendant. Divorce records are especially valuable, as the interrogatories usually go into detail as to employment record, assets, where the marriage took place, date, and children's names, ages, and birthplaces.

Tax Records.   Divided into two groups: secured (real property) and unsecured (personal property such as furnishings, boats, airplanes, etc.). This file will list all property owned by the subject and its location and value, including the amount of taxes paid and whether or not the subject is or has ever been delinquent.

Grantee–Grantor Index (Superior Court).   This filing lists all financial transactions regarding real property, deeds, loans, homesteads, etc. Also included are judgments, mechanic's liens, and any other miscellaneous records an individual wishes to make a matter of record.

Criminal Records.   Not only does this source indicate the subject's convictions, but will also go into prior arrest and conviction history and possibly a very thorough background investigation conducted by the probation department, usually going back to the subject's early childhood and school record as well as employment history.

State Corporation Files.   Usually located in the corporation commissioner's office, these files will show any business that has incorporated and applied for a permit to issue stock. Information in this file will provide background information on all officers of the corporation, along with an indication of the financial structure of the business and individuals. The same information can be obtained from the county division of corporations, showing all fictitious names of companies, their owners, partners, business structure, etc.

The preceding list of public records is basic. There are many more public records available. There is a section in the National Archives in Washington, DC, for example, that maintains all passenger lists of ships coming to the United States as far back as the 1800s. Probate files, census reports, death records, and credit records (for a small fee) are available. A quick look at the telephone directory under city, county, state, or federal listings will provide the names of agencies maintaining public files available for the asking. The Mormon Church, in Salt Lake City, maintains probably the largest library of genealogical records in the country, if not the world. Those records too are available.

Also, for a small fee, credit reporting agencies are available; however, any information obtained from those sources should be verified very carefully, because many times computer entries are not accurate due to errors in entering the data or confusion about individuals with similar names.

After all the existing files are searched, the analyst can, from the background report, produce a complete and accurate picture of the applicant under investigation, along with the other information provided through confidential sources and interviews with former neighbors, employers, etc.

Over and above the manual technique of record searching, the computer is the greatest source of background data available to the investigator. If the researcher does not have the computer skills necessary to access all the sources for investigative purposes, there are investigative agencies and computer operators who specialize in that area and are available to perform that function, usually for a fee.

UPDATING

One important factor should be considered. People do undergo physical and emotional change for many reasons, such as sudden financial stress (possibly due to serious illness), philosophical readjustments, alcoholism, addiction to dangerous drugs, morale problems, etc. Years may pass without incident; then, suddenly, for one reason or another, the employee becomes antagonistic over real or imaginary injustices. Financial stress may be the catalyst that precipitates a personal crisis resulting in the theft of company merchandise or the selling of trade secrets to a competitor. The situation of the distressed or disgruntled employee is not as rare as security people would hope. The potential must be recognized.

An effective way to minimize this danger to the company, or at least to provide a warning of potential problems, is to make periodic, brief reinvestigations of the employee's application and current living habits. The object of the updating process is to make certain that stresses which were absent during the initial pre-employment investigation have not been manifested suddenly. In a high security risk situation, this periodic updating is mandatory.

Should a problem appear during reinvestigation, the employee can be counseled regarding the condition. If possible, the company can offer help. Most of the time this practice is extremely beneficial. Appreciation of the company's concern for his welfare solidifies a feeling of loyalty on the part of the employee. If the counseling proves to be ineffective or is resisted by the employee, consideration should be given to transferring him to an area of less responsibility and lower risk to the company; or, as a final solution, terminating him.

POLYGRAPH EXAMINATION

The scientific instrument most widely used in determining an employee's honesty and fitness is the polygraph, which records physiological changes of a subject under questioning, measuring blood pressure, respiration, and the galvanic resistance of the skin. The test is designed to enable the examiner to detect deception.

There is some controversy over the use of the polygraph in employee honesty testing. Some union contracts rule out the polygraph; some states prohibit its use by law. Legislation in some states specifies that no applicant for a job may be denied that job based on a refusal to take a polygraph examination, nor can an employee be terminated for refusing the test.

In jurisdictions where the polygraph is permissible, however, it has proved to be an effective aid in employee investigations. The applicant can be tested for the truthfulness and completeness of information provided on the application form. By avoiding a major portion of the physical investigative techniques, which would otherwise be required, a considerable amount of time can be saved. In some companies there is a policy of offering the job applicant a choice: She can take the polygraph test, thus processing her application more quickly, or she can have the full physical investigation conducted, which might delay the start of her employment.

The value of the polygraph test lies both in its time saving and in the accuracy of the test in detecting deception by the applicant in statements made on the application form. The test does not replace the necessity to verify past employment and other statistical material regarding the applicant; an employee should never be approved or disapproved by virtue of the polygraph test alone. The test must be supplemented to some extent by the normal investigative process.

It should also be noted that all polygraph examiners are not equally qualified. Their performance and experience should be carefully checked. The safest selection process is to obtain a referral or reference from the local law enforcement agency.

THE PSE

Another instrument used for honesty testing is the Psychological Stress Evaluation (PSE) unit, which records voice patterns for analysis. There is no general agreement, however, on the level of accuracy of the PSE. Those examiners who utilize the PSE strongly defend its results; many others question its accuracy. A number of independent studies, including those conducted by the U.S. Department of Defense, suggest that the PSE is not only inaccurate but that it can be intentionally defeated.

The PSE does have its value; it does, in fact, register stress in the voice patterns. A major problem in its utilization in investigative procedures is that there is no way of determining with certainty the source of the stress. Stress in the voice patterns can be caused by factors other than attempted deception. The system can even be manipulated by an individual knowledgeable about how it functions. The author, for example, whose early education and work experience were in the field of radio broadcasting as an announcer, was able to defeat the PSE examination by employing voice techniques. The PSE unit was unable to detect the deception. The polygraph, on the other hand, even if unable to produce conclusive results, can at least enable the examiner to detect the use of intentional measures of deception on the part of the subject being examined.

A number of states have banned the use of the PSE, including the state of Virginia, where one of the units is manufactured.

LEVELS OF CLEARANCE

As previously indicated, not all employees have to be subjected to as thorough an investigation as that described in this chapter. The degree of investigative effort and depth of background history required depend entirely on the amount of responsibility to be held by the applicant and the extent to which he will be exposed to confidential material. This is a matter that must be decided by the company, and it should be examined very carefully.

Job level and exposure to sensitive material do not always correspond. For example, a janitor or maintenance man is not a skilled craftsman, but he may still be one of the few employees who has total access to all areas; thus he should be cleared at a high level. Each position must be judged by criteria that determine the vulnerability of the material to which access is gained and the clearance necessary for the individual granted that access.

In a situation where a government contract is involved, the government agency responsible for granting that contract will establish the levels of clearance for each area and employee having access to that area.

REVIEW QUESTIONS

1. What method is recommended for explaining to the job applicant his rights with regard to pre-employment investigation?
2. In a background investigation, what are some of the most important points to be verified in the following areas: current address, former employment, driver's license?
3. What do the first three digits of a Social Security number indicate?
4. List five types of public records and briefly discuss the kind of information found in each.
5. What is the reason for conducting periodic reinvestigations of employees?
6. How are the polygraph and the PSE, respectively, able to detect stress?

Chapter 10

Document Control

The preservation of company documents of any kind (reports, plans, blueprints, business records, correspondence, billing and order forms, etc.) should be accomplished in five basic ways:

1. The initial protection of the original paperwork by storage in a manner resisting damage from fire, water, theft, aging, and humidity
2. A supplementary backup system of microfilming and its storage methods
3. A system for controlled release of documents designed to maintain the confidence and security of the material contained in the documents
4. Computerized document storage accessed by special codes, depending on their level of confidentiality
5. Downloading documents, each day, to microtape or floppy disk, to preserve data in the event of a computer failure or breakdown. Disks should be stored in a secured manner, off the premises, and maintained for corporate or business reconstruction should a major catastrophic event strike the area (e.g., fire, flood, earthquake, terrorist attack).

FILE CABINETS AND SAFES

Average file cabinets, such as those purchased from a stationer, are safe neither from fire or water damage nor from theft, even though the cabinet may be fitted with a lock. Specially constructed file cabinets are required to provide adequate security for valuable company documents.

The safety factor in file cabinets and safes is usually measured in "resistance time"; special security cabinets and safes are constructed to withstand, for a specified period of time, high degrees of heat (paper will ignite at 292°) and penetration by drilling or other actions by a burglar. The cabinets should also be waterproof, sealed against flood or water damage resulting from a fire situation, and humidity controlled.

It is not necessary for every file cabinet in the company to be of a special security type. The type of cabinet required depends entirely on the level of protection necessary for the contents. The more confidential or secret the documents, the greater the protection required. In determining the value of various documents, the company should not over-look the importance of paperwork (billing, taxes, payroll, etc.) in its operation. These records have critical value to the company apart from secrecy considerations.

MICROFILMING AND DOWNLOADING

All important documents and records should have backup copies. Damage, destruction, or theft can occur under extraordinary circumstances regardless of the safety factor provided by file cabinets and safes. The technique of microfilming is also an enormous space-saving device, making room for new and current documents. Stored microfilm can be referred to when necessary, or hard copies can be made from microfilm for replacement purposes.

Microfilm copies should be stored in a location separate from the premises where the originals are maintained. They must be kept in security containers designed to afford the maximum degree of protection possible.

There have been numerous instances where a company has been physically destroyed (by fire, for example) and its continued existence depended entirely on its ability to recover the paperwork through a backup system of microfilm copies stored at another location.

The same holds true for computerized records. Microtapes and downloaded floppy disks should be maintained in the same manner. The downloading, however, should be accomplished on a daily basis and also stored off the premises.

DESTRUCTION

Whenever the decision is made to destroy records and other documents, whether they are originals, microfilm, or computer download copies, they should all be subjected to *total* destruction. Simply throwing an important document in the trash, even if it is first torn a couple of times, makes it an easy target for an outside element bent on intelligence gathering. As insignificant as that document may appear, it has some value to someone when pieced together with other apparently insignificant items.

The easiest and most convenient method of destroying documents is by using a shredding device. Larger companies have a shredder in every office where important records are kept, and employees in that area are instructed to run *everything* through the shredder. Smaller companies have a single shredder in a central location. Employees either take paper to that location or place paper to be destroyed in a pickup box where a security officer makes regular rounds, retrieves the items, and then destroys the items or supervises their destruction.

Documents and records can also be collected periodically and burned in a furnace designed for that purpose, or placed in another device known as a pulping machine, where the paper is subjected to high-temperature water and chemicals, then compressed. Some manufacturing firms use the by-product of the pulping process as packing material in the packaging and shipping departments.

Erasure of computer disks should be complete along with elimination of the hard drive data.

ACCESS LIMITATIONS

The company should maintain a document classification system that identifies records and documents according to their relative importance with regard to the degree of confidentiality of the contents. The system has two basic requirements. First, the documents should be stored in security cabinets and safes as described earlier in this chapter (the higher the level of classification, the more secure the cabinet). Second, access to the documents should be limited to persons cleared at a level commensurate with the importance of the information.

If the company has a government contract requiring the maintenance of classified documents or materials, the Department of Defense will establish the criteria for the classification process. Certain basic principles of document classification, however, should be considered in all industrial firms, regardless of whether or not government contracts are involved.

The three basic levels of classification designated by the U.S. government are (as an example), in order of descending sensitivity, TOP SECRET, SECRET, and CONFIDENTIAL. The government has requested that private businesses develop their own security clearance designations, restricting the use of the classifications listed to government agencies or to work being done under government contracts for such agencies. One major U.S. corporation uses the following model:

Government Classification	Corporate Classification
TOP SECRET	Special Controls (S)
SECRET	Company Confidential (C)
CONFIDENTIAL	Private Confidential (P)

Whatever the terminology adopted, these three levels of classification provide the basis for a functional system. At the lowest level of the restricted information ladder are those documents or records that are (adopting the corporate example above) "Private Confidential." They are "off limits" for any of a number of reasons. They are simply nobody's business. Revelation of this kind of information could create problems for the company. Release of partial information without full knowledge of a situation might start rumors through the plant, cause morale to drop, or reputations to be placed in question. Someone passing by a secretary's desk and observing a partially written letter or an open personnel file with one piece of negative information on top could, by passing along such information, create a personnel problem. Similarly, someone reading a letter from a customer questioning a price quote might wrongfully jump to the conclusion that a contract was being canceled and 200 jobs eliminated.

These examples are not as incredible as they seem. They are not even exaggerations—they have occurred. It is reasonable, therefore, to assume that any information not released officially for public or employee consumption should be considered Private

Confidential and maintained in a manner that would preclude anyone from "accidentally" acquiring the information.

The next step up in information restriction is the "Secret" or "Company Confidential" classification. This is information that is considered important enough in content that its release could pose a threat to profitable company operation. Examples might include manufacturing processes, customer lists and bidding schedules, blueprints, or any other information that would aid criminal activity, such as providing insight useful to dishonest employees intent on theft, extortion, blackmail, embezzlement, espionage, or sabotage.

The "Top Secret" or "Special Control" classification should be attached to that information which is considered the *most* important to the company's survival. An example would be a new process, design, or product that is being readied for the market, the loss of which to a competitor would result in the rival company's ability to produce the same product at a competitive advantage. Top Secret classification at the government level would be attached, for example, to new weapons, aircraft, parts, materials, or information that would affect the national security if shared with others.

Obviously, there are other intermediate classifications that could be utilized, should additional levels of control be required.

The more important the information, the more carefully the documentation should be stored and released to individuals. Those materials or papers considered Private Confidential, Company Confidential, or Special Control should be so marked or stamped for identification. Persons having access to the higher levels of classified materials should be processed and cleared more carefully by the pre-employment investigative process. The investigation should be intensified and brought up to date for employees being promoted to areas where the level of confidentiality increases. At the Special Control or Top Secret level, the honesty, integrity, and reliability of the employee must be assured to the highest degree possible.

Papers and information considered Company Confidential should be retained on the company's premises and used there only; they should be locked and secured whenever they are not in actual use. Persons seeking documents classified at this level should be held accountable, signing for such papers upon release and return.

Controls for Special Control or Top Secret material should be even more stringent. Such information should not be viewed or used by a single person alone; another employee or security officer similarly cleared for that level should be present.

Computerized documents and other data, depending on their level of clearance, should require an access code plus the name of the person viewing the material. Information relating to the access of information should be maintained within the computer record system, reporting on the employee accessing the data, the terminal used, date, and time. That information should be reviewed on a daily basis by a security officer assigned to that task.

One general rule is that papers, records, materials, and areas of the company should be accessible only on a "need to know" basis, and that any individual violating that premise should be investigated or questioned as to intent. It is the responsibility of the Security Department to ensure the integrity of the system.

REVIEW QUESTIONS

1. In regard to file cabinets and safes, what does "resistance time" mean?
2. Where should microfilm copies of documents be stored?
3. What are three methods of totally destroying documents?
4. What are the two basic requirements of a document classification system?
5. Describe the three basic levels of document classification, suggesting corporate terminology for equivalent government classifications.

Chapter 11

Fire Prevention and Control

Prior to discussing the specific remedies available in the control and prevention of fire, a basic understanding of what a fire is is necessary. For that purpose, let us examine a classic concept. In order for fire to occur, three environmental properties must be present: oxygen, heat, and fuel. These necessary elements of fire are often represented by a triangle.

A chain reaction occurs when the three properties are present in the proper proportions and under the proper conditions. This chemical reaction or rapid oxidation creates *fire*.

The only ingredient of fire missing from the triangle is ignition. Ignition can be caused by any number of forces, such as a match or lighted cigarette, spark, internal combustion, or heat from friction raising the temperature to a level that would ignite the fuel. Temperature for ignition varies, depending on the fuel present. Paper will ignite at 292°; some wood at between 500° and 800°, depending on the type of wood.

To extinguish a fire, one of the elements, or one side of the triangle, must be removed. To prevent fire, the elements (oxygen, heat, or fuel) must be eliminated or controlled.

TYPES OF FIRES

Let us take the theory of fire one step further and examine the manner in which fire is categorized into four classes. An understanding of the proper classification of fire is vitally important to the security officer, as it will aid him in knowing how to extinguish the fire. It is also of tremendous value, when reporting a fire to the fire department, to advise them of the nature of the fire so they can respond quickly with the proper equipment.

Class A. In a Class A fire, the fuel is comprised of normal combustible material such as paper, wood, trash, draperies, fibers.

Class B. In a Class B fire, the fuel is flammable liquid, such as gasoline, oil, grease, cleaning fluids, alcohol.

Class C. Class C fires occur in live electrical circuits where current is flowing. Computers, electric typewriters, motors, generators, light switches, and electrical outlets may be involved in Class C fires.

Class D. In a Class D fire, the fuel is a combustible metal such as magnesium. This is the rarest of the four types of fire.

In many instances fire may be of two simultaneous classes, and in rare cases, three. For example, if a Molotov cocktail, or gasoline fire bomb, is thrown through a window into an office, the result is a fire involving both the ignited gasoline *and* those normal combustible materials which are ignited as the result of the burning gasoline: furniture (wood and fiber), trash, drapes, paper, etc. Thus, we have both a Class A and B fire. The method of extinguishing such a fire is complex and could prove dangerous if only the method normally used to put out a Class A fire were applied.

COMBATIVE METHODS

Each type of fire requires a different fighting technique, and it is important that only that technique be applied.

Class A fires require saturation by *water* or *water fog*. The fuel that has been ignited and is burning should be cooled below the ignition temperature. Water will extinguish the flames and the cooling will prevent reignition. Caution should be taken *not* to use a carbon dioxide (CO_2) extinguisher because its cooling effect is only temporary; although the flames will be extinguished almost immediately, the heat will quickly rise back to the ignition point and the fire will be rekindled. The rekindling effect can be almost explosive in nature.

Class B fires require that the flammable liquids be smothered, depriving them of the oxygen necessary to create the fire situation. Thus, CO_2, special dry chemical extinguishers, or water fog should be used. Foam extinguishers can also be used, but they are less effective. Caution should be exercised here *not* to use a stream of water, because the flammable liquid will float on the water, still ignited, and spread the fire rapidly rather than containing it.

Once the flammable liquid has been extinguished, water should be used as a follow-up to extinguish the Class A fire created by the flaming liquid. CO_2 has only a temporary cooling effect and the dry chemical or foam does not have the penetration necessary to be effective on Class A fire fuel.

Class C electrical fires must be extinguished by a nonconducting agent such as CO_2 or dry chemical. Water conducts electricity; electrocution has resulted in situations where an unknowledgeable secretary, for example, has poured water from an extinguisher onto a sparking, smoking electric typewriter. This is a prime example of how employee education and *properly labeled* fire equipment are an absolute necessity.

Obviously, the power circuits should be shut off if electrical fire occurs, usually at the fuse box or circuit breaker if the overload has not already done so. For safety's sake this should be done first, but it may not always be possible due to the location of the fuse box or lack of knowledge of its whereabouts.

It should be noted that at one time Halon was considered an excellent fire fighting agent, especially where computers were involved; however, it was determined that the Halon had very destructive properties, affecting the ozone layer, thus its use and manufacture were discontinued.

Class D fires are rare, occurring only under certain manufacturing conditions. They are not found in average buildings or industrial facilities. The only effective way to extinguish this type of fire is with a special dry powder.

FIRE EXTINGUISHERS

Although there are many specialized extinguishing units on the market, only the basic types that should be used under normal conditions are discussed here. If any type of extinguisher not mentioned here is under consideration, the fire department should be consulted first to find out whether that type of extinguishing unit is effective or recommended under the conditions where it would be used. For example, although carbon tetrachloride extinguishers are still available, they are no longer recommended by the National Fire Protection Association and are illegal in some states because of the potential danger and side effects of the chemical.

Water Extinguishers

There are three basic types of water extinguishers.

Pump Action.   The pump handle must be plunged up and down with one hand while a stream of water is directed through a hose held in the other hand.

Soda Acid.   This unit appears to have a small wheel at the top. This wheel is actually intended to be the base when the unit is turned upside down. When the unit is turned upside down, an acid chemical comes in contact with baking soda, creating a gaseous pressure and forcing water to be expelled through the hose.

Although this unit is effective, the one problem lies in the fact that once the water begins to flow, there is no shut-off valve. The entire contents of the extinguisher will be emptied at a single use.

Pressurized.   The pressurized extinguisher is the most effective and easiest to use. The container is under constant pressure and the water is released by squeezing the handle. The water flow can thus be turned on and off as needed.

It is important prior to using this unit to look at the valve indicator to make sure there is sufficient pressure in the extinguisher to make it usable. As a matter of fact, most states require an annual inspection to ensure the pressure in this unit is maintained at a normal level. It is a good idea to have security officers check all pressurized units every other month by adding that function to a normal patrol route.

Water is also available through normal fire hose installations, possibly even from ordinary garden type hoses in the area. Water from these sources can be applied in two ways:

1. *Water stream.* A solid stream of water can be used on all Class A fires. The stream should be applied in a sweeping motion. The user must be cautious not to enter an involved area, thrusting forward with fire on all sides, and become trapped if fire rekindles behind the user.
2. *Water fog.* A special nozzle on the end of the hose allows water to be dispensed in a light but saturating "mist." The effect is to lower the temperature of the fuel without spreading the flames. The cooling effect is very quick and is most efficient on both Class A and B fires. This method will also reduce the smoke factor.

Dry Powder and Chemical

The primary ingredient in dry powder extinguishers is baking soda. It is effective on Class D fires because it is nonconductive and smothers (eliminates oxygen) and coats the fuel.

In addition to baking soda, dry chemical extinguishers add other chemicals which make them effective on Class B and C fires. The newest type of dry chemical extinguisher, actually called an ABC extinguisher, is effective on all three classes because it not only inhibits the flame but acts as a coolant and penetrates sufficiently to be effective on Class A fuel.

Note that the powder and chemical type extinguishers, although most effective, leave a residue that could do as much damage as the fire itself. If there is time to determine an alternative method of fighting the fire, this fact should be considered. Usually, however, the fire danger itself and the potential of spreading should be of primary importance.

Carbon Dioxide (CO_2)

Carbon dioxide extinguishers, also maintained under pressure, provide an immediate cooling effect. They are most effective on Class B and C fires—without leaving a residue as do dry powder and chemical units. The cooling is temporary and will extinguish the fire in electrical circuits and combustible liquids. It cannot be used on Class A fires, however, and water should be used as a follow-up if necessary. In the case of an electrical fire, once the extinguisher has eliminated the flames, the power should be shut off leading to the source of the short circuit and fire.

Seals

One final word of caution regarding fire extinguishers. Every extinguisher, regardless of type, bears a small lead seal. This seal is usually attached to the safety key, which must be removed prior to activating the extinguisher. The seal is placed there by the company that charges the extinguisher and certifies its preparedness for immediate use. This process is required by law. If the seal is not properly attached or appears to have been tampered with, *do not use the extinguisher.* A missing or tampered seal may indicate either that the extinguisher is not functioning properly, or—as has occurred in instances where emotional labor disputes are taking place or a terrorist or an emotionally disturbed employee is bent on destruction—that the extinguisher's normal contents have been replaced with gasoline or some other volatile fluid.

As mentioned earlier, it is an excellent idea to have a security patrol check the fire extinguishers every month or two, on a regular schedule, to check not only the pressure but also the seals on every unit on the premises. If a unit does not appear to be in order for any reason, the extinguisher should be replaced with a spare. The questionable unit should be examined and recharged by the fire extinguisher maintenance company.

FIRE EXTINGUISHER PLACEMENT

Extinguisher units should be placed liberally around the premises. The added cost of a few extra units is the best insurance a company can have. Immediate accessibility of an extinguisher has many times saved costly property damage and lives. The lack of proper equipment could result in total destruction of a sensitive area of the premises.

It is important that specific hazards be identified and the proper extinguisher placed in the immediate vicinity. In production areas, for example, where flammable liquids are utilized in the process (Class B fire potential), a dry chemical or CO_2 extinguisher should be mounted close to the danger area and carefully labeled with a sign over the unit stating how and under what circumstances it should be used. Care should be taken not to place the unit too close to the danger area; otherwise the location of the extinguisher may itself be involved in fire. The planning of its exact location depends on the circumstances.

Where electrical fires are possible and a CO_2 extinguisher is available, make certain the instructions over the unit also include the location of the main switch, circuit breaker, or fuse so that the current can be turned off.

In storage rooms where materials are placed awaiting transit or other use, an extinguisher should be placed immediately outside the door leading to the room, as well as one to the rear of the interior of the room in case an employee is trapped inside.

Wherever multiple hazards are present, an ABC extinguisher should be placed, alleviating the necessity of an employee having to decide which extinguisher to use. Indecision wastes time—and time is the biggest ally of fire.

SPRINKLER AND HOSE SYSTEMS

Sprinkler Systems

Sprinkler systems provide a vital means of combating fires. Actually they are nothing more than a piping system containing water under pressure, running along the ceiling structure, with valve heads placed in strategic areas over combustible matter. Each valve head is set to open, releasing a spray of water, when heat rises to a preestablished temperature (usually around 280°). In most instances, several valves will be activated in the vicinity of the one that is actually activated by the heat, thus wetting down the surrounding area and aiding in the control of fire spread.

A sprinkler system is the most effective method of controlling fires automatically. Although costly to install, it usually pays for itself in a few years due to reduced insurance premiums resulting from the system's installation.

Most sprinkler systems use water flow; however, under special circumstances, sprinkler systems may utilize dry powder or CO_2. The primary example would be over the cooking stove in a restaurant that maintains a sprinkler unit, containing powder.

There are several types of automatic sprinkler systems:

- In *wet pipe* systems, water is held in the pipes throughout the system. When heat ruptures the seal in a sprinkler head, water flows instantaneously.
- In *dry pipe* systems, air is kept in the pipes under pressure; valves (usually at the main riser) keep water out of the pipes. When a sprinkler head is ruptured, the pressurized air escapes and water rushes into the pipes. Dry pipe systems are especially used in areas where winter freezing of wet pipes may be a problem.
- The *deluge system* is also a dry pipe installation. Again, water is held at the risers by valves. The difference is that the sprinkler heads (or some of them) are open in a fixed position, designed to direct water flow in a chosen direction. The system may be activated manually or automatically.

Note that in many business, commercial, and industrial facilities a variety of components can be used in an integrated fire protection system, including both wet and dry pipe automatic sprinklers for some areas; foam, water, and soda-acid fire extinguishers in appropriate areas; different types of detectors and automatic or manual signaling systems. Automatic alarms may prevail in office and warehouse, manual fire alarm stations in the production areas. Expert advice should be sought in the design or reevaluation of any fire protection system, and the firm's insurance carrier as well as the local fire department should be consulted.

Hose Systems

The average business and office building as well as other facilities will be equipped with the standard 2-1/2-inch hose, folded or on rolls, in an enclosed cabinet that is predominantly red in color and is identified for emergency fire use only. The cabinet may also contain an extinguisher of an appropriate classification for the immediate environmental hazards. The hoses are equipped with nozzles that deliver either a solid stream of water or water fog, again depending on the nature of combustibles in the vicinity of the installation. It is recommended, however, that the nozzle have a self-contained adjustment feature to deliver *either* stream or water fog.

The above installation is usually a "standpipe" system, indicating that the main pipe and water supply is a vertical piping installation leading to similar outlets at the same location on each floor. The water supply in the standpipe system is separate from that which is supplied to the sprinkler system in the building, thus either or both can be used without drawing important and needed pressure from the other. In high-rise or multiple story structures, the standpipe is usually constructed within the enclosed fire stairs or fire wells to provide added protection for the installation.

It is also important that fire hose installations be located near an exit; thus if the individual using the equipment is unable to contain or extinguish the fire effectively, a safe retreat is immediately accessible.

Two persons are necessary to operate the hose system. The first stretches the hose to its full length while the second turns on the water flow, *after the hose has been stretched.* If water is turned on during the time the hose is still partially coiled, the extreme pressure will fling the hose about like a whip and possibly injure the individual handling the nozzle.

Once the fire has been extinguished initially, it is important that the individuals remain by their stations at the hose to protect against rekindling, at least until the official fire department arrives to check and clear the area.

Hose Houses

Industrial hose houses enclose outdoor hydrants and provide shelves or racks for hose and other equipment. When the house doors are open, all equipment should be readily accessible. The National Fire Protection Association has set minimum requirements for the contents of hose houses. They should include the following equipment as a minimum:

- at least 100 feet of hose coupled to the hydrant with a play-pipe attached,
- an additional 100 feet of hose on the shelf,
- a fire axe,
- a crowbar,
- an extra play-pipe,
- a play-pipe holder,
- a hydrant wrench, and
- two hose and ladder straps.

Periodic inspections (at least monthly) should be made to ensure that all equipment is in place and in good order. The hose house should be kept free of weeds, dust and dirt, snow, and other obstructions. Hose and standpipe connections should be checked to make sure the valve is not leaking.

FIRE DOORS

Placed at strategic locations throughout the building, fire doors are intended to isolate various sections of the facility, protecting one area should a fire break out in another section. They are placed at walls, which are of solid masonry construction as opposed to fiber dividers. Fire doors are usually designed to close automatically by the use of any one of several devices, such as electromagnetic releases activated with the regular fire alarm in the area, or a fusible link activated by a rise in temperature. In office and large apartment buildings, fire doors are most commonly found in garage areas.

The doors themselves are constructed of metal and should be inspected for breaks, rust, dry rot, or other damage. They should be kept clear of debris that might impede their closing function, and they should be operated manually during regularly scheduled inspections to ensure their proper operation.

When areas of the building are not in use, such as on Sundays or other nonworking shifts, the fire doors should be closed. This not only affords protection when personnel are not on the premises, but also ensures the proper function of fire doors through constant use.

FIRE ALARM SYSTEMS

Numerous systems are on the market today that have been designed specifically for early detection and warning of existent fires. The alarms should be studied carefully and selection based on the type that would be most efficient under the specific conditions of the individual company, its premises, and manufacturing processes.

Alarm systems involve both *detection* and *signaling* devices. The major types in use today are described next.

Detectors

Smoke detectors utilize photoelectric light beams which detect the presence of smoke from a smoldering object. This technique can give sufficient warning prior to the outbreak of flames. *Ionization detectors* are sensitive to "particles" created during the early stages of a fire. The method responds to infrared emissions also and is extremely effective in explosion situations, because the response is measured in microseconds.

Thermal detectors or heat detection units respond either when the temperature reaches a specific degree or when the temperature begins to rise too rapidly from its norm (called a rate-of-rise detector).

Sprinkler water-flow detectors are used, as the name suggests, in automatic sprinkler systems. They combine a seal that melts when heat rises to a designated temperature, causing water to flow, and pressure switches that are closed by the water flow and trigger an alarm.

Signaling Systems

Regardless of the type of alarm system installed, it should be coupled to additional local warning systems that sound bells, sirens, or lights to notify persons in the vicinity of the fire; and/or to monitoring stations. The latter may be proprietary if the facility operates its own fire-fighting department, or more commonly a central station that immediately notifies the fire department. In some areas direct lines to the fire department are used. The system should also be tied into the central control system maintained by the security department, pinpointing the exact location of the fire and activating evacuation and fire-fighting procedures.

Most alarms, whether local or remote, are coded, not only to indicate the location of the fire but also to distinguish between drills, trouble warnings, all-clear signals, or actual fire alarms.

Manual Fire Alarm Stations

Many structures use manual fire alarm stations, or boxes, either to supplement or in place of automatic systems. Most are the familiar wall-mounted box with a lever or trigger behind a breakable glass panel. The alarm must be activated by someone at the scene. The alarm may be *local* only (in which case the station will be identified with the word "local" printed on it), activating flashing lights or a bell, siren, or buzzer audible in the immediate area; or *remote*, which usually combines a local audible or visible alarm with the transmission of the alarm signal to a monitoring center.

Where manual fire alarm stations are part of the fire response system, they should be located close to hazardous areas and in sufficient number to provide adequate coverage for the entire facility. It is important also that responsibility for giving the alarm be given to specific individuals in each area (the foreman or supervisor, or a member of the fire brigade in that area). Otherwise it is all too easy, in the excitement and confusion attending a fire, for everyone to assume that "someone else" has pulled the alarm. This can mean a costly delay in alerting company or public fire units.

FIRE PREVENTION PLANNING

Employee Education and Training

One of the first and most important truths to be understood about fire prevention in the business environment is that it is everyone's job. All employees have a stake in fire planning, not only for their personal safety but also because of the disastrous economic effects of a major fire on any business. Moreover, the activities of many workers in industrial facilities are more directly related to the risk of fire than in other settings, and by the same token employees are often more involved in the response to a fire. In addition to security personnel, plant supervisors, foremen, and even individual workers may have specific assignments in the event of a fire. In office buildings, apartment houses, and small businesses, volunteers should be solicited throughout the premises and/or maintenance personnel trained to handle special functions.

Whole books, of course, have been written on fire training, as on every aspect of fire prevention. The *Fire Protection Handbook* produced by the National Fire Protection

Association and *Essentials of Fire Fighting*, published by Oklahoma State University and validated by the International Fire Service Training Association, belongs on every security director's shelf, as do other appropriate NFPA and other publications on fire prevention. It is possible here only to touch briefly on some of the essential aspects of the subject.

Training programs and demonstrations are generally available from the local fire department. Security personnel and members of the fire brigade (see below) should have extensive training in fire protection and prevention. The regular employees of the company can either attend these training programs or be given instruction by the security staff.

Fire *training programs and films* should be available to every employee of the company. They should be presented at least twice a year, ensuring that instruction will be provided to all new personnel. Constant reminders are also important, such as *pamphlets and signs* warning of specific fire hazards and frequent inspections by security personnel or the plant fire inspector.

All employees should be instructed on what to do in the event of a fire, including not only how to help in fighting a fire but also orderly evacuation procedures. *Fire drills* should be held periodically so that employees have an opportunity to walk through the evacuation procedure. During the stress and potential panic of an actual fire, that experience could save lives. All employees should be instructed carefully about conditions which create potential hazards, and those who might be involved in fire fighting should know how to use extinguishers and water hoses, as well as the location of such equipment and of manual fire alarm stations.

In companies that do not have their own fire brigades, thought should be given to appointing supervisors in each area (and on each shift) to act as *fire wardens,* whose responsibilities should include directing the evacuation of personnel. Under stress conditions it is important, especially in heavily populated areas, to have knowledgeable leadership in order to prevent panic. The supervisors assigned to fire warden duties should receive additional training in fire prevention and be totally familiar with the premises. They should also be selected for their leadership qualities and ability to perform calmly under stress. The importance of this function should not be minimized.

In most industrial facilities, and especially those in which the fire hazard is high because of the nature of the products or manufacturing processes, there should be a *fire marshal* or *fire inspector.* This person should receive special instruction in fire prevention and fire-fighting techniques and be thoroughly familiar with the building layout and any potentially hazardous locations or conditions. It is desirable in all but the smallest facilities for this to be a full-time assignment.

Private Fire Brigades

The use of fire brigades made up of company employees is widely prevalent in industrial facilities. In most situations their function is not to take the place of the public fire department but to provide the initial quick preventive action prior to the arrival of the public fire fighters. The latter may be delayed by traffic or weather conditions. The fire station may be some distance away from a suburban or rural plant site (in which case the private fire brigade becomes even more essential); or, in the case of natural disasters such as floods, hurricanes, and tornadoes, the fire department may be swamped with more calls than it can immediately handle.

An employee fire brigade has many things going for it. Its members are on the scene and can take immediate action, often allowing small fires to be put out before they become serious hazards. They are also more thoroughly familiar with the company facilities than any outside firemen can be.

It is impossible to generalize on the size of a private fire brigade, since the determining factors—public fire department response time, size of the facility, and specific fire hazards—vary for each business. However, it is important that the brigade, whether large or small, be organized in a command structure. There should be a brigade chief with overall responsibility, preferably a supervisory employee, and assistant chiefs for other shifts to take over when the chief is off duty. Each member should be trained in specific duties in the event of fire. Since training time is usually limited, any employees with previous experience (such as members of local volunteer fire departments) should be actively recruited for the brigade. In larger facilities, the brigade may include several fire companies, and each company may include several fire squads to provide complete coverage for the plant. It is important that there be at least one brigade member in every area of the plant during each shift.

Fire Emergency Plan

Whether there is a fire brigade to assume responsibility in the event of a fire, or whether this falls on the security officers, the specific duties of all personnel who might be involved in the response to an emergency should be put down in writing.

There are two primary objectives in the response to any emergency: first, to minimize danger to persons; and second, to minimize property damage as much as possible. Some of the specific duties to be assumed by security or fire brigade include the following:

- Provide immediate first aid for injured persons, and remove them to safety.
- Oversee evacuation of all personnel from the area.
- Control spectators and others not involved in fire fighting.
- Meet the fire department and direct them to the area of the fire, giving information as to location of the fire and the type of emergency.
- Shut off machinery, electrical power and gas lines, fans, blowers, etc., which might create new hazards.
- Ensure that the alarm is given as quickly as possible. (Responsibility should be assigned for each manual fire alarm station.)
- Man extinguishers, hoses, fire pumps, and other available equipment.

Again, it should never be assumed that "someone" will grab the proper fire extinguishers, give the alarm, or activate the fire pump. The major point is that these and all other responsibilities should *never* be left up to chance, but should be specifically designated in the fire emergency plan.

Fire Reports

Chapter 4 provides a sample report form to be used in the event of a fire. It is important that accurate reports of all fires, regardless of how small, be maintained not only for insurance purposes, but also for study of the circumstances in an effort to avoid a recurrence of the incident.

In compiling a fire report, *all* employees in the area of the fire should be interviewed and questioned about any unusual circumstances, conditions, or odors that may lead to determination of the cause of the fire.

The possibility of arson should also be considered in all cases. Should any circumstance give rise to suspicion of arson, the authorities should be notified immediately. The authorities will want to know if there have been any local disputes with employees or any other persons that might have prompted a serious retaliatory effort.

BUSINESS AND INDUSTRIAL FIRE HAZARDS

It is impossible in a general security text to do more than touch on the fire hazards that exist in business, commercial, industrial, and residential settings, since this is a complete subject in itself. Moreover, the particular hazards cover an enormous range for different environments. Even good housekeeping rules—one of the most essential aspects of fire prevention, and one in which security can play an active role—must be tailored to the specific situation.

The subject is so important, however, that some of the most fundamental considerations should be mentioned.

Awareness of Risk

Paradoxically, those businesses which daily confront a high fire hazard because of the nature of the product or manufacturing process tend to have the best fire safety records, while those business or residential complexes that would appear to be "safer" environments often have a greater incidence of fire loss.

The explanation is obvious enough. Where there is a strong awareness on the part of both management and employees of the need for fire safety, and where rules of fire prevention are assiduously practiced, the danger can be minimized. But where there is a casual attitude, carelessness, or neglect—generally accompanied by the feeling that "it can't happen here"—the real risk increases drastically.

The fact is that all business facilities operate with some degree of fire hazard. Hazards come not only from those substances whose dangers are immediately recognized, such as flammable liquids, but also from many other easily overlooked sources, such as dusts and trash. A review of the more common fire hazards would include the following:

1. *Light materials*, such as textiles (which produce fine lint), and materials that produce fine shavings. These materials are easily ignited and can cause a rapidly spreading fire.

2. *Dusts* of all kinds, whether from materials such as wood and starches, or as a by-product of machinery (grinders, conveyors, pulverizers, etc.). Accumulations of dust can explode with devastating force.
3. *Flammable oils and greases.*
4. *Flammable liquids* (vaporizing), such as gasoline, paint thinner, and naphtha.
5. *Flammable gases*, usually found in closed containers or piping systems. Any seepage or spill, or failure to close outlets, creates a serious fire hazard.
6. *Painting, welding, or cutting* operations.
7. *Heating processes*, such as furnaces, ovens, and forges.
8. *Electrical hazards* from frayed lines or cords, overloading, arcs, and sparks.
9. *Static electricity*, which can accumulate rapidly in a manufacturing facility.
10. *Spontaneous combustion* hazards, from grains or coal piles, stored plastics, oily waste materials and rags, etc.

The giant plastics industry, for one, has created a whole new range of fire hazards. As one authority has written, "The entire flaming family is around when plastic is born. Not only gases and liquids, but also solids. Solidified resin is often ground or pulverized into finely divided form before use. The fillers . . . include a number of combustible powders, and . . . many finished plastics are explosive when reduced to dust during processing or fabricating. Flammable liquids are used as solvents in making plastic paints, adhesives, or coatings. Lubricants that reduce stickiness in molding processes are often flammable, especially if the mold is still hot."[1]

Flammable Liquids

Many industries make common use of a wide range of highly hazardous flammable liquids—fuels, paints, thinners, cooling agents and oils, etc. Their presence is so familiar that the risks they create can all too easily be taken for granted.

It is the vapors produced by a flammable liquid that burn with great intensity—and can easily explode. The flash point of a liquid is the temperature at which a flammable liquid gives off enough ignitable vapors to become a serious hazard. Many flammable liquids have flash points below room temperature. A few examples[2] follow:

Acetone	0 degrees Fahrenheit
Alcohol (ethyl)	55 degrees
Gasoline	45 degrees
Lacquer thinner	30 degrees
Naphtha	52 degrees
Toluol	40 degrees

As pointed out before, fire prevention in the industrial environment is everyone's business. In the control of flammable liquids, however, that responsibility must be specifically defined at every stage. It falls primarily on management in planning, and on supervisors and those under them in the day-to-day operations which require the use of dangerous substances. Precautions must be exercised in shipping and receiving, storage and handling, dispensing and use, and disposal of wastes. Security's responsibility will include monitoring good housekeeping practices, noting fire hazards on patrols, inspecting fire equipment, enforcing such regulations as no-smoking rules, initiating the alarm when fire breaks out, and, in some circumstances, attempting to put out localized fires with the equipment available, until the arrival of fire-fighting personnel.

Industrial facilities are not the only types of businesses with high-risk factors. Commercial office buildings also have unique features, depending on the tenants occupying the structure. Residential complexes, supermarkets, shopping centers, restaurants, and stores each has its own special areas of consideration when it comes to fire prevention and control.

REVIEW QUESTIONS

1.   Describe the four classes of fire and the proper extinguishing technique for each.
2.   What type of water extinguisher is most effective and easiest to use?
3.   Why is it important to check the seal on a fire extinguisher before activating the extinguisher?
4.   Why is it important that fire hose installations be located near an exit?
5.   What is the purpose of fire doors?
6.   List five specific duties of the fire brigade (or security personnel in the absence of a fire brigade) in the event of fire.
7.   Why do industries with a high fire hazard tend to have better fire safety records than "safer" industries?
8.   What is meant by the *flash point* of a liquid?

NOTES

1.   James H. Meidl, *Flammable Hazardous Materials* (Beverly Hills: Glencoe Press), p. 235.
2.   The fire and explosion hazard factors for more than 700 flammable substances are described in Chapter 12 of the National Fire Protection Association's *Handbook of Fire Protection.*

Chapter 12

Emergency and Disaster Planning

Any commercial, retail, industrial, or residential complex, of any size or type, can be faced with an emergency, whether it involves a minor work accident or a major disaster such as fire, flood, building collapse, tornado, or other type of threat. No company can consider itself immune. By the same token, no management is free of the responsibility to prepare to meet any emergency that might reasonably strike.

Emergency and disaster plans are designed to fulfill that responsibility. Their purpose is to anticipate what can happen and to provide for prompt, effective action, should it happen. The goal of all emergency planning is threefold:

- The safety of people (employees, visitors, patrons, guests, etc.)
- The protection of property, with minimum loss or damage
- The restoration of normal operations with minimum delay.

Advance planning is essential to all of these goals. While it may be impossible to predict all possible emergencies or the particular circumstances that may be confronted, it is possible to anticipate most hazards and how to cope with them. Advance planning enables the company to call on the best thinking of key personnel in every area—production, safety, security, engineering, maintenance, finance, personnel, etc.—so that the planners can think through all eventualities and the best ways of meeting them. It makes possible the determination of what emergency equipment and facilities will be required so that they can be available when needed. It enables management to designate responsibility and delegate authority for emergency action, with a clear understanding of that authority and responsibility. It also makes possible the training of key personnel in essential emergency response.

One of the major problems in any emergency is confusion and the panic that can easily follow. Everyone in the company, from management down to the line employee, must know what to expect. Each person should know what he is to do, who is in charge, where he should go if an evacuation is ordered, and so on. If key personnel have been trained in their responsibilities—or key groups of people in a larger organization—they will provide the reassurance, the sense of order, the clear direction that will not only minimize losses but also reduce the threat of panic.

Another benefit of advance planning is mutual aid. This involves coordination and liaison with outside agencies, such as fire and police departments, local utility companies, hospitals, local government officials, and news media. It may also be possible for neighboring organizations—other companies, offices, stores, etc.—to plan for mutual assistance in an emergency, thus greatly expanding the resources available to each organization. In a general disaster, of course, *all* may be affected.

Also of great importance in a disaster or destructive incident of any dimension is the preparation of reports, photographs, and damage assessments to be presented to insurance carriers following restoration of normal business activities. The insurance companies should, of course, be notified as quickly as possible, because they will in all probability want to dispatch their own investigator and adjuster to survey the damage and determine the probable cause of the incident.

EMERGENCY PLANNING MANUALS

Whether in manual or other form, emergency plans should be put down in writing. Moreover, it is not enough to have generalized plans. Each aspect of the emergency response must be precise and specific. One of the points to be stressed is that a general "game plan" cannot be adopted for use in all emergencies. Some elements of the plan may be the same—including the makeup of the emergency team and the assignment of areas of responsibility. The specific details of planning will be different for a fire, for example, than for a flood, a leak of toxic chemicals, or an approaching hurricane. The equipment needed, the specialized skills to be called on, the urgency of response, these and many other factors will be different for each type of emergency.

Emergency planning, then, will include plans for each type of emergency or disaster, with priorities assigned for each potential risk and greater emphasis placed on the most probable hazards.

Among the items to be included in the written plans, or manual, will be the following:

1. Statement of policy
2. Description of potential hazards, with risk assessment
3. Description of the facility, including size, construction, location, access roads or other means of transportation, entry points, type of operations, hours open, number of personnel on hand at each shift or stage of operation, building plans, utilities lines, etc.
4. Emergency organization, showing the chain of command, responsibilities of each position, with a succession list
5. Emergency facilities, including the emergency command center, evacuation routes, assembly points, and communications and alarm systems and their locations
6. Emergency equipment and supplies, including medical and first aid, fire-fighting equipment, salvage equipment, food and water supplies, with their locations
7. List of mutual aid agreements
8. List of outside agencies, with emergency phone numbers

9. Shutdown procedures
10. Physical security procedures
11. Evacuation procedures
12. Other related items applicable to the specific organization.

Too many company manuals, of whatever kind, simply gather dust on a shelf or remain forgotten in a drawer. The emergency planning manual should escape this fate, by means of an ongoing program of training and testing. Key personnel, including supervisors and maintenance and engineering staff with emergency responsibilities, as well as specialized crews such as fire brigades, rescue teams, and first-aid trainees, should be involved in active training programs for emergencies. It is also necessary periodically to test both equipment and people to make sure that they function according to plan.

TYPES OF EMERGENCIES

Most companies are well aware of the hazard of fire, and few fail to take this threat into account through the installation of alarms, sprinkler systems, fire extinguishers, and other precautions. The impact of Occupational Safety and Health Administration regulations has made all companies exceedingly aware of the danger of accidents and environmental hazards, and the requirements for safety and health standards. But there are many other perils that can be equally if not more disastrous. Before any company can make effective emergency plans, it is necessary to begin—as in all security planning—with risk assessment. What emergencies are most likely to occur? At what times? What is the potential for injury or property loss? How often will a given emergency arise? A variety of industry, government, medical, and other agencies can provide needed input, which can be supplemented by local experience.

It is possible in this space only to comment briefly on some of the most common emergencies.

Fire and Explosion

Fire and, in some types of operation, explosion are the most serious hazards commonly threatening many types of businesses and industrial facilities. The best planning will involve prevention, as discussed at length in Chapter 11. But the details of response to the event of a fire or explosion should be spelled out in the emergency plan. Small fires can be contained by prompt, localized action, often the responsibility of operating personnel at the scene. Plans must also include fighting a major fire, specifying equipment available, types and locations; responsibilities of the fire brigade or other assigned fire-fighting forces; alarm and communications systems; availability of public fire response; shutdown, evacuation, and other procedures. Planning must also include the eventuality, in a major disaster, that the local fire department will not be able to respond, and that there will be interruptions in power and even water supplies.

Windstorm (Hurricane, Tornado)

The Atlantic and Gulf Coast states are particularly subject to hurricanes. The central and south-central states in the "Tornado Belt" experience this devastating threat more than other areas, but tornadoes also occur, if less frequently, in most parts of the United States. And even those areas not subject to these extremes may be visited by windstorms that can cause extensive damage to property and danger to personnel.

Building design offers the best protection. Although it is not economically feasible to design buildings capable of withstanding a direct hit by a tornado, it is possible to design hurricane-proof buildings where this risk is plausible. If windstorm risk is high, provision should also be made for emergency shelters for employees and the assignment of key personnel to control special hazards (such as broken power lines).

Earthquakes

Earthquake damage is most probable along the Pacific Coast of the United States, and in this region building design and construction should take this risk into account. Utility lines, water pipes, etc., can be constructed with flexible connections and be free of rigid structures. The greatest danger to personnel occurs from building collapse and falling debris, especially glass, but fire is another serious threat. Planning should include the possibility of providing emergency water sources for fire fighting.

Building Collapse

Again, good design and building maintenance offer the best protection. In older buildings, especially where heavy machinery is in use and/or where heavy stockpiling is carried out, special attention should be given to safety loading and potential structural damage.

Floods

Properties in low-lying areas contiguous to bodies of water (rivers, streams, lakes) are subject to the threat of flooding on at least an annual basis. Design and location, especially of vital facilities, should take this hazard into consideration. Provision for dikes, whether permanent or temporary, should also be made.

Work Accidents

While most work accidents are isolated and contained incidents, they are real emergencies for those involved and in the immediate vicinity. The emergency plan must define the response to any type of accident, particularly with reference to care of the injured, shutdown of equipment, etc. The reporting of accidents should be preplanned and very specific as to both emergency response for the victim, consideration for the tangent effects on witnesses and other persons in the area, and documentation of the incident in writing for future review and study. It important to review the record of the incident, in an effort to prevent future similar accidents. It is also important to maintain careful and precise documentation for insurance coverage and potential litigation.

Many accidents in the workplace will involve more than an isolated danger, especially where hazardous chemicals or toxic vapors are involved. Here the emergency situation will call for preplanned procedures for evacuation, medical care and treatment, oxygen supplies, shutdown of feed or utility lines, etc., depending on the particular hazard involved.

The risks involved in manufacturing processes that require the use of hazardous materials demand special care in the handling, distribution, storage, and labeling of such substances. Local and state codes and ordinances regulate the use, storage, and handling of hazardous materials, but planning should always cover the possible failure of such safeguards, through cracks in containers, leaks, spills, accidental ignition and explosion, etc. Prevention is the best protection—but emergency planners must always ask, what if procedures break down? What if something *does* happen?

Other Hazards

It is impossible in a general discussion to examine all of the potential emergencies that can confront a given facility. The community, the physical location, neighboring installations, the type of operations, size of the facility, history of weather extremes—these and many other factors affect the localized threat. In addition to the special perils briefly described, provision must be made for the possibility of sprinkler leakage and other water damage, leaking storage tanks, ice, snow and freezing weather, riot and civil disturbance, vandalism, sabotage, bomb threats, aircraft and vehicle accidents, and many other emergencies—even terrorist attack.

Emergency planning involves a realistic assessment of each potential special hazard, evaluating the cost of preparedness, and weighing that against the risk to people and property. When needs have thus been determined, they must be translated into a detailed plan of action for each possible emergency.

BASIC EMERGENCY PLANNING

A basic emergency plan should outline the steps involved in a swift, orderly transition from normal to emergency status. It should answer the familiar questions of who, what, when, where, and how. It should specifically designate the authority necessary to declare an emergency and to carry out the emergency plan. While specific plans will necessarily vary for each company and facility, a basic plan should include, at a minimum, the following:

1. An emergency command post or center
2. An emergency organization (chain of command)
3. An alarm or warning system
4. Communications, internal and external
5. Shutdown procedures
6. Evacuation procedures
7. Provisions for medical care and first aid.

The Command Center

The emergency response should be directed from a command control center. In small facilities, of course, it may not be possible to set up a separate emergency office. The control center may simply be the management or security office. In larger organizations a permanent emergency command center will be established. What is important in all situations is for everyone to know what will be the "nerve center" for emergency actions. In a company with widely dispersed facilities it may be necessary to have an emergency control center in each location, but there should still be one centralized overall command center to which the others report.

As with other aspects of emergency planning, there should also be a backup—an alternate location for the command center in the event that the primary center is itself involved in a disaster.

The command center should ideally be located in a protected area, but it must be readily accessible to key personnel. It should be well equipped, especially with communications facilities (telephones, including cellular telephones, two-way radios, public address system). Essential emergency records should be maintained at this location, as well as maps and building plans, location of utilities, lists of emergency equipment and supplies and their locations, organizational chart with names of key personnel and their phone numbers, a list of emergency phone numbers for all outside agencies, and any other records essential to the emergency response.

Chain of Command

The emergency plan should effectively establish an emergency and disaster organization within the company, with the authority and responsibility to act promptly in any crisis.

Director.   The director or administrator of the emergency plan should be a member of top management (the higher the better), since he must have authority to act and speak for the company. The director is responsible for emergency planning, liaison with outside agencies and other cooperating companies, and seeing that preparations are indeed made in keeping with adopted plans. He will have the authority to declare a state of emergency, causing the emergency plan to be activated.

A succession list should designate those members of management, in order, who will assume the authority and responsibility of the director in his absence.

Emergency Chief.   In some situations the emergency director will also assume active command of the emergency response. In many other cases, however, a manager directly involved with operations will function as emergency chief. In the industrial setting, the plant manager is commonly the person-in-charge when an emergency is declared. An alternate with closely related authority and qualifications should also be named. (Many emergency plans designate two alternates for each key member of the emergency organization.)

The emergency chief will be responsible for:

- Classifying the emergency and initiating action
- Activating emergency forces
- Ordering shutdown, partial or full, as necessary
- Ordering evacuation, partial or full, as necessary
- Reporting to the director (or management)
- Making emergency announcements
- Requesting mutual aid or other assistance as necessary
- Coordinating emergency actions.

Emergency Team.   Responsibilities should be clearly designated for each aspect of the emergency response. Normally the existing organizational chain of command will be reflected in the assignments of the emergency team. Those responsibilities may include fire fighting, rescue, first aid and medical care, transportation, communications, security, engineering, maintenance, finance, and public relations. Department managers and supervisors will have assigned responsibilities for their own areas and personnel that are integrated into the overall plan. Alternates should be named for each assignment, and plans should cover each shift as well as those times when the plant is not operational because it is shut down or manned only by a skeleton staff.

The point should be made that the same responsibilities in emergency situations exist for small or large operations. In the latter there may be trained units for each function—fire brigades, rescue squads, wardens to direct the movement of personnel, evacuation squads, the security force, and so on. In smaller facilities operations personnel may be required to perform each of these and other emergency functions. In either case the assignments should be spelled out and understood. No one should have to wonder what he or she is supposed to do in the turmoil and confusion of a disaster.

Alarm or Warning System

In almost all industrial plants a fire alarm system exists, incorporating both a local signal as a warning to personnel and, in most cases, some method of communication with local fire departments, whether by means of alarm boxes on or near the plant, direct connection to the fire station, or connection to a central station. (Types of fire alarm systems are discussed in Chapter 11.)

In addition to fire alarms, other emergency alarms will usually originate from the emergency command center, or will be touched off on authorization from the emergency chief. Existing public address systems may be used for emergency announcements and alerts. In some shops a manual alarm or bell is used for all warnings. Some means should be established to identify fire and other emergency situations by distinctive signals.

Communications Systems

Emergency planning should include means of internal and external communications. In addition to the alarm system, the command center should have, as already mentioned, telephones adequate to handle emergency communications coming in or going out. The center may also use messengers, two-way radios, or even bull horns, depending on the situation. Remember that both electric power and telephone service may be interrupted in a disaster. Provision should be made for emergency power and for battery-powered radio communications. It is also possible that cellular telephones may remain operable when telephone wires and cables are disrupted.

Plans should provide for rapid external communications with:

- Fire departments
- Police
- Hospitals
- Emergency/ambulance services
- Utility companies
- Civil defense agencies
- Management and key employees not present
- Adjacent plants, buildings, or firms affected
- Mutual aid sources.

Shutdown Procedures

Any major disaster, fire, explosion, or other serious emergency may require shutdown procedures, either for the affected area or the entire business operation, depending on the circumstances. Emergency plans should detail the orderly procedures for shutdown. These procedures should follow the pattern of scheduled normal shutdown of operations, adapted for the emergency timetable. Priorities must be set so that, if there is little time or inadequate warning, the most essential steps can be taken quickly. These may include the following:

- Shutting off power to machines and fans
- Shutting off feed lines, gas lines, etc.
- Closing windows (opening them in the case of bomb threats)
- Clearing aisles

- Closing valves
- Covering, anchoring, or otherwise protecting equipment
- Plugging vents and pipes
- Shuttering or otherwise protecting doors, windows, and vents.

Operating personnel may have specific assignments for shutdown, such as shutting down machinery and equipment they are working on, clearing aisles, taking precautions against fire where flammables are used, etc. Building maintenance and engineering personnel, because of their specialized knowledge, will be involved in the shutdown procedure. Security will also have special protective responsibilities during shutdown.

Evacuation

Evacuation procedures are one aspect of emergency planning that will be relatively uniform for almost all situations—that is, the same evacuation routes, exits, secondary routes, and assigned rendezvous or assembly points should be used wherever possible. Employees familiar with one evacuation procedure for fire should not be called on to follow a different route or procedure in another emergency, allowing, of course, for the possibility of routes being blocked, unsafe, or otherwise impassable.

Apartment complexes, hotels, and motels will require individual notification of residents and guests. Business environments normally will have some access to mass communication devises, such as intercoms and loud speakers. Audible warnings, such as bells or siren-type systems are also utilized in residential structures but, without some direction and guidance, panic may result. It is important that in apartment structures and hotels or motels, there be some employee personnel available to guide people to a prearranged assembly area, such as a parking lot or adjacent building where they can receive further directions and information. There should also be sufficient posted notification of how and where to proceed in the event the audible alarm system is activated. Hotels and motels should have this information posted inside the individual rooms, along with a simple map or sketch of the emergency route to be taken.

The emergency chief is responsible for ordering evacuation on notice of a situation dangerous to personnel. Advance training and instruction should enable all personnel to respond to an evacuation signal in an orderly manner, without panic. Exit routes and exits should be clearly marked. Larger companies may also have wardens whose job it is to direct and lead employees to safety. This responsibility is sometimes assigned to security personnel.

First Aid and Medical Care

The goals of emergency planning were described at the beginning of this chapter as (1) the safety of people, (2) minimizing loss or damage to company property and assets, and (3) recovery of operations as soon as possible. The first of these concerns, people, must be the primary objective of emergency action.

Larger organizations will have an organized medical and first-aid system in place, with a company doctor who should be in charge of both planning and action involving emergency medical care. Companies that do not have a full-time doctor should consider an arrangement with a local doctor who can be available for consultation and on call during an emergency.

There should be close coordination with local health and medical services during planning. The availability of hospitals or clinics in the nearby vicinity and the accessibility of ambulance service are primary considerations.

If a doctor or industrial nurse is not employed by the company, individual employees should be trained in first aid. The American Red Cross, National Safety Council, insurance carriers, and other agencies can provide assistance in training programs.

Emergency medical and first-aid planning must provide for the following:

- Emergency medical equipment and supplies
- Establishment of a first-aid station during an emergency
- Emergency procedure for handling injury accidents
- Removal of injured or otherwise affected persons from danger
- Emergency first-aid care at the scene when necessary
- Quick-drenching or flushing facilities where employees might be exposed to corrosive materials
- Transportation to health care facilities when necessary, either by ambulance or company vehicles
- Operating a casualty identification, tagging, and reporting system
- Interview and clearance of *all* personnel at the scene of a disaster.

EMERGENCY SECURITY RESPONSIBILITIES

The security director, like the safety professional, should always be involved in emergency planning; in most situations she will be part of the planning committee. As a practical reality, in many companies the emergency organization is built around the existing security force.

Whether this is the case or not, security will have specific responsibilities in any emergency situation. Acting in her normal protective role, the security officer should have some training in crowd control and maintaining order, essential duties during any serious emergency. While on patrol the security officer must observe potential hazards, violations of policy, signs of unauthorized intrusion, etc. This experience also comes into play both in the prevention of accidents and emergencies and in the emergency response.

While specific duties will depend on both the nature of a crisis and the local conditions, among the special responsibilities that generally fall on security in emergency and disaster situations may be the following (the list is by no means complete):

1. *Control of access.* This will include maintaining records of all persons entering or leaving a facility during the period of emergency.

2. *Traffic control* (vehicles), including providing for unimpeded access of outside emergency units. Security, for example, will meet responding fire department or bomb squad units, provide information as to the location and type of emergency, and in some circumstances provide escort service.
3. *Protection of property.* Physical security becomes even more essential when a facility is evacuated or in the confusion accompanying a major disaster.
4. *Prevention of theft,* looting, sabotage, or espionage.
5. *Direction and control of personnel.*
6. *Direction and control of evacuation procedures.*
7. *Assistance in first aid,* rescue, and other emergency needs.
8. *Protection of vital information,* documents, records, etc.
9. *Control of hazardous areas,* classified areas, and high-value areas or property.
10. *Establishing communications with outside agencies* such as local law enforcement, fire department, hospital and ambulance services, Red Cross, etc.

Additionally, security's general protective function in any emergency may include assisting injured employees, guiding employees and visitors to safety, crowd control, preventing panic, fire fighting, and other special duties governed by the local circumstances.

In this connection a word should be said about the conduct of the security officer during a crisis situation. The nature of his role requires the security officer to be able to handle himself and others under stress conditions. Historically, panic can be as dangerous to personnel as any of the physical factors involved in a disaster of major proportions. The security officer should be capable of providing a solidifying element in a crowd of disorganized, confused, and frightened individuals. Bearing in mind that almost all emergencies he will encounter will be temporary conditions, the security officer should conduct himself so as to inspire confidence. He should remain calm, even-tempered, and in control of himself. Such conduct can make as important a contribution to the minimizing of danger in a crisis as any other security responsibility.

In a major disaster, there are never enough trained personnel on hand to do everything that must be done. Security officers may be pressed into a variety of functions, and security personnel may also need to enlist the aid of other persons, selecting quickly from whatever personnel are available. In such circumstances it is essential to remain alert and sensitive to individual reactions. Following a serious explosion, a major accident, bombing, fire, or other emergency, many individuals will be dazed, shocked, and disoriented. When calling on someone to deliver a message if communications are not functioning, or to aid in an evacuation or rescue operation, the security officer (or anyone acting in a position of authority during the crisis) should first be certain that the individuals called on are rational and reliable. When time permits, shocked individuals may also be given innocuous tasks to give them a certain sense of responsibility that will aid in recovering their composure and avoiding panic, and yet not endanger others.

BOMB THREATS

Since the late 1960s terrorism has become a way of life, not only for politically motivated dissident groups but also for individuals who, for one reason or another, believe that the creation of fear or terror will achieve some goal, satisfy a desire for revenge, or simply "get attention." Bombings, real or threatened, appear to be the ultimate destructive weapon employed by these terrorist groups or individuals. One study group, the National Industrial Conference Board, released a report in 1971 which found that 90 percent of major firms in the United States have been threatened with bombings.[1]

Preventive Security

The primary preventive measure to minimize the threat of a bomb is constant vigilance. This applies to the normal security patrol routine, during which guards on patrol should observe all items that seem unusual or out of place. It also applies to regular employees, who, more than any other persons, are familiar with those areas of the plant in which they work. Through daily exposure they know the environment and its contents intimately, and they will more quickly spot something that does not belong there. These regular employees should be made constantly aware of the potential of bomb threats and of sabotage, and they should be encouraged to report any unusual items or conditions to the security department.

Additionally, all packages and other deliveries arriving at the plant should be routinely inspected. In high-security facilities these inspections should even include the lunch pails of employees if these are carried into sensitive areas. It is recommended that such personal containers as lunch pails be left in a locker room or special employee storage location, separated from the production area.

Bomb Threat Preplanning

As with all potential emergencies, the bomb threat can best be met without confusion and panic when the threat response has been carefully considered in advance. Preplanning should include the following:

- Identify help available from police or military bomb disposal squads or other agencies. The threatened organization should know the emergency phone numbers, procedures to follow in order to obtain aid, and what help is available. (For example, will the summoned agency conduct a bomb search or only disarm and remove a device that has been found?)
- Prepare target lists of (1) vulnerable and easily accessible areas where a bomb might be planted, such as rest rooms, stairwells, trash receptacles, and fixtures, which should receive special attention in a bomb search; and (2) high-value areas, such as record storage areas, flammable storage areas, and main switches and valves, where a bomb could cause substantial damage or loss of assets.
- Investigate the possibility and legality of recording bomb threat telephone calls.
- Provide training in the bomb threat response for key personnel, including security, search teams, evacuation procedures, and most particularly telephone switchboard operators or other employees most likely to receive a bomb threat call.

Telephone Bomb Threat Procedures

The majority of bomb threats come in the form of a telephone call warning of the danger. In most such instances the bomber is intent only on emphasizing a cause and not actually causing any injury or fatalities. Most calls are, in fact, hoaxes, either made as a "joke" or with malicious intent to cause disruption of operations and create an element of fear. When a bomb has been planted with the intention of triggering it, the bomber almost invariably provides a warning in time to provide for safe evacuation.

When a telephoned threat is received, the person taking the call (usually an operator) should remain calm and follow prescribed procedures:

1. Keep the caller on the line as long as possible by asking him to repeat the message. At the same time activate a recording device (if available) which should be maintained on the line for just that purpose. An alternative, wherever possible, is to signal another person to get on an extension line as a witness to the conversation and also to make observations that might be missed by the first operator.
2. Request the caller to give the *location* of the bomb and the *time* it is supposed to detonate. These are the two most vital pieces of information. The operator should emphasize the threat to the lives of innocent parties while attempting to obtain the information. Additional questions should seek to learn what kind of bomb it is, what it looks like, how it will be set off, how big it is, and—very importantly—why the bomb was planted.
3. Listen carefully to the caller's voice and note any special characteristics such as accent, dialect, and speech patterns. Also observe the "tone" of conversation and whether the caller appears calm, tense, nervous, drunk, etc.
4. Note any background noises or ambient sounds that may help in identifying the location from which the call is made. (Does the voice sound "hollow" as if the caller is in a phone booth? Are there background traffic sounds, such as trains, machinery, aircraft?)
5. Record the exact time the caller begins the conversation and terminates the call. Notify the security department and local police authorities. Normal routine would be to notify the security department, which will then follow up with calls to the appropriate authorities: law enforcement agencies, the fire department (placed on standby), and medical and ambulance services (placed on standby).

The Evacuation Decision

One of the most important considerations when a bomb threat is received is the decision to evacuate. This is a matter of judgment and depends entirely on the circumstances of the particular threat, and the decision should be made by a senior member of management. If a formal emergency organization is in place, the decision to evacuate a threatened area, building, or entire facility will be made by the emergency director or emergency chief to whom such authority has been delegated.

It might be assumed that, in the interest of safety for personnel and others on hand, evacuation should always be the preferred response. Such is not the case. Harassment and interruption of operations is, more often than not, the purpose of the bomb threat call. Achieving the desired result only encourages more such calls, approximately 98 percent of which *do not involve actual explosives.* (Of some 10,000 bomb threats reported to the New York Police Department in 1972, for example, approximately 9700—or 97 percent—involved malicious false alarms.[2])

Nor is evacuation always the safest procedure. It may delay or impair the search for a bomb, both by diverting the attention of security and by removing employees who might otherwise help in the search. Evacuation itself involves some risk to personnel, because fear and panic may accompany an urgent decision to evacuate. Finally, if the bomber's intention is to harm personnel, the bomb may well be planted along evacuation routes, in lobbies, hallways, or assembly areas.

Normally, then, the decision to evacuate will be made only when a suspect device has actually been found or when there is other compelling evidence that the threat of an explosion is real.

The Bomb Search

The intensive bomb search will usually be conducted by company personnel, either specially trained search teams, security personnel, or, in smaller organizations, key personnel for each department or area of the facility.

Employees can best search their own work areas quickly and safely, since they are most familiar with what should or should not be there. Security or assigned search teams should then search the target areas noted earlier where bombs are most likely to be placed. Special attention should be given to areas and objects readily accessible to outsiders, such as lobbies, elevators and stairways, restrooms, trash containers, and plant stands.

Upon entering an area to be searched, the searchers should first stop to listen for any unusual sounds, particularly ticking or hissing sounds. The most effective technique used by search specialists is to divide an area or room into three visual "layers" and to search from the bottom up, looking always for foreign objects, things out of place or disturbed, anything that looks strange.

If a bomb, a suspected device, or simply an unusual and unidentifiable object is found, *no one who is not specially trained in bomb disposal procedures should touch the item.* The search team's work ends when a suspicious object is found. At that point, local police or other designated bomb disposal specialists should be notified, the area should be evacuated for a minimum distance of 300 to 400 feet in all directions, and all emergency, fire, and rescue units should be called to the scene.

If, on the other hand, the search results in an area, building, or facility in question being declared "clean" and safe, an orderly procedure should exist for concluding the search, reporting the incident in detail, and, in the event that evacuation has occurred, reoccupying the site and resuming normal operations.

Bomb Blankets

A variety of "bomb blankets" are available that can be stored in the security office or emergency headquarters. If there is time in a particular bomb threat situation, and if it is safe to do so, the blanket can be placed over the suspect device until bomb disposal specialists arrive to help contain the potential explosion.

Bomb blankets are cumbersome and heavy. Usually two or three persons are required to carry and place the blanket properly. Training in this procedure is imperative; the bomb blanket should be used only by trained security personnel. And, as previously emphasized, *under no circumstances should the device itself be moved or touched.*

As an alternative to the bomb blanket, sandbags or mattresses may be placed around a suspected device. However, metal objects such as desks, chairs, etc., should never be used to form such a barrier.

STRIKES

Among other concerns that come under the heading of emergency or contingency planning is the labor strike. Although not always an emergency in the usual sense, a strike can cause a serious crisis, especially when so prolonged that disagreements and tensions turn into bitterness and anger. For this reason contingency planning for a strike should not wait for the time when a contract is about to run out and strike talk is heard. Plans should be made, and policies determined and made known, long before the strike threat becomes real.

Unions vary from company to company, in differing trades or professions, and among skilled and unskilled laboring forces. Their policies are affected by such factors as the geographical location of the facility, the strength of union membership, the loyalty of the members, and affiliations with other unions in sympathy with any given causes. The company's relationship with the union is unique in that they are bound together contractually and through the labor laws established by the U.S. government. Terms of particular union contracts with management vary, and, to add to the confusion, one company may conceivably have contracts with several unions, representing different segments of the labor force in the facility and establishing individual guidelines for different categories of personnel, whether they are engineers, maintenance employees, dock workers, or truck drivers.

Plans, then, will be based on local circumstances. They will also reflect past history of labor relations (for example, whether strikes have been short or long, peaceful or violent). And they will be affected by the attitude of local law enforcement. Police have been known to be reluctant to take notice of disruptive incidents on a picket line. Like security personnel, police may be caught in the middle between friends and neighbors on the picket line and others who are not striking. While the company should always insist on the rightful upholding of the law, at the same time emergency strike plans must be cognizant of all factors, including relationships with police and other local authorities.

The Decision to Shut Down

When a strike occurs, the first decision facing company management is whether or not to shut down or continue operations. This determination will be made, of course, long before the strike deadline arrives. Many advance preparations, such as the building up of inventories of raw materials and finished products, will depend on that decision.

The question of shutting down or remaining operational will turn on many considerations, including the type of business and its contractual obligations, the ability to continue operations with non-union or supervisory personnel, the nature of union picketing activities, the willingness of non-union employees to cross the picket line, the cooperation of law enforcement, and many other factors.

If the decision is made to shut down the plant, it will still be necessary to make plans for the strike period. Management must still have access to the facility. Some maintenance and supervisory staff may also be required to enter the plant, and provision must be made for this access. Finally, the security force will normally remain on duty to protect the facility against unauthorized access, vandalism, theft, and other potential losses.

Operations during a Strike

If the plant remains open and the attempt is made to continue operations after a strike begins, many complications must be anticipated in contingency planning.

During an actual strike, emotions often run high, and violent outbreaks are always a threat. The union and its striking members come under protections of federal law, and the company may not do anything to impede the right to demonstrate, nor can the company conduct so-called "strike breaking" activities. The company also has its legal rights. Through the courts it can appeal for injunctions limiting the strikers' activities, specifying the number of persons permitted on the demonstration line, limiting the locations of the demonstrations, guaranteeing the right of access to the facility, etc.

The National Labor Relations Board (NLRB) will also provide independent referees to observe the activities on both sides and note any violations of the orders and agreements. The NLRB representatives recognize the frustrations inherent in the emotionally charged strike situation and attempt to mediate disputes as they arise, but their role is essentially that of observers.

Among the specific considerations to include in emergency strike plans are the following:

1. Establish temporary headquarters for management away from the plant. Temporary warehouse facilities may also be required.
2. Arrange for checking of telephones for wiretaps; have conference rooms cleared of "bugs" or eavesdropping devices.
3. Prepare and maintain files on union leaders and officials.
4. Prepare and maintain complete lists of all employees, union and non-union, for emergency communications.
5. Have company counsel prepare to obtain necessary court injunctions against violence, mass picketing, denial of access, or other violations that may occur.

6. Provide for testing the picket line at facility entry points. (Cool heads should be chosen for this difficult assignment.)
7. Select observers for each entrance to make written reports of any incidents.
8. Designate photographers to record incidents on film and/or videotape. Logs should accompany such photographic records, identifying those involved, the time and place. (Note that it has been ruled an unfair labor practice to take photographs of lawful union activity such as peaceful picketing, distribution of handbills, etc. Pictures should be taken *only* of clearly unlawful activity.)
9. Make arrangements regarding deliveries, either by way of non-union trucks or by delivery to off-site locations.
10. Make preparations for possible blockading of personnel inside the plant. Food, water, blankets, beds or sleeping bags, etc., should be stocked in a secure location on the plant site.
11. Provide for communications with the media, the public, law enforcement, and civil authorities. Public relations should be the responsibility of a single spokesperson; during this difficult situation the company should speak with one voice.
12. Instruct all non-union and supervisory personnel in the avoidance of any direct conflict with strikers, including acrimonious verbal exchanges and the like.

Conduct of Security Personnel

In the strike situation the security officer's role is a very difficult one. They must remain on duty, alert to possible violations that could cause injury or damage to persons or property. Security represents company management in one sense, but they are also employees—and many of the strikers are well known to the officers. Some security forces are also unionized, a factor that further complicates the situation. Commonly, striking employees will appeal to the security officers as coworkers, demanding that they display a sympathetic posture and support the union by refusing to function as "tools of management." Ideally, if the security officers are to remain neutral during any labor negotiations or strike activities, they should be independent.

This problem underscores the desirability of security personnel remaining slightly aloof from other employees during the normal course of their activities on the job. The security officer should be courteous and friendly, but too much fraternization on a day-to-day basis should not be encouraged. Like the public police officer, the professional security officer must strike a middle-of-the-road posture, somewhere between being "one of the guys" or a "mechanical robot," between being a "buddy" or an unsympathetic disciplinarian. The security officer must at all times be viewed as a professional, one who is fair, just, efficient, responsible, and sincerely interested in the welfare and protection of *all* persons without prejudice. When the security force conducts itself in this manner during normal times, its protective role will be more readily accepted during a strike.

In a strike situation security personnel should remain extremely low key. They should not present an image of a company barrier, a wall of armed, stern, strike-breaking guards. This impression will only antagonize striking workers, precipitating confrontations, jeering, rock-throwing incidents, and the like. It will also adversely affect the security officer's position in the plant after the strike is over.

The security officer should become clearly "visible" only when extreme trouble threatens and violence or destructive activity is imminent. The officer's position should be one of understanding but firm dedication to the task of averting trouble. When trouble does threaten to escalate, the attempt to neutralize a potentially violent reaction should be conducted by a security executive, preferably on a one-to-one basis with the apparent leader of the crowd. The ranking security executive should attempt to appeal to the strike leader's better judgment, pointing out the ramifications of violence and how it can adversely affect the union's position. If this strategy does not appear to be fruitful, then—and only then—a show of force may be necessary. That display of force should be in the context of calling in the local police and their riot control task forces, who should replace the security officers immediately upon their arrival at the scene. Obviously, police should be notified of the troublesome situation at the earliest moment, and placed on alert.

Should the company decide that a show of strength at the outside perimeter is advisable on a continuing basis, utilizing uniformed security officers, this is an instance when it would be advisable to retain a contract guard service whose personnel are unknown to the striking employees. The guard service should, however, be under the supervision of in-house personnel, and they should be carefully restrained from any independent action not directly ordered by a staff security supervisor.

REVIEW QUESTIONS

1. What must be the *first* concern in all emergency planning?
2. A large chemical plant is located in Oklahoma City. Suggest a priority for four different major catastrophes for which emergency plans should be made.
3. What are the reasons for establishing an emergency command post?
4. Why would the plant manager in an industrial facility be a logical choice for the emergency chief?
5. Why might emergency shutdown procedures be especially important in an industrial facility?
6. Describe some of the specific responsibilities of the security department in an emergency.
7. Make up a "target list" for a bomb threat response plan, identifying areas that might be likely places to plant a bomb in an industrial facility.
8. Give two different reasons why evacuation might *not* be advisable in response to a bomb threat.
9. Discuss the merits of this statement: In a strike situation, security's role is that of a "protective wall" around the company.

NOTES

1. Release No. 2488, August 16, 1971, National Industrial Conference Board, 845 Third Avenue, New York, New York 10022.
2. Graham Knowles, *Bomb Security Guide* (Los Angeles: Security World Publishing Co., Inc., 1976), p. 2.

Chapter 13

Theft and Pilferage Controls

THEFT AND PILFERAGE

In industrial and commercial settings, unlike retail establishments where customers are also involved, theft and pilferage are normally conducted by employees of the company. The major problem usually lies in the area of tools and other company equipment, in a manufacturing plant, along with the products that are being manufactured. Hospitals, hotels, schools, general offices, etc., also have items that could be subject to theft. If the items are small enough they may be taken intact; if they are larger, more complex units, then individual parts may be stolen. Retail businesses will be covered in a separate chapter.

Pilferage of Small Items

Several years ago a contract company was providing security services at an industrial plant that manufactured large organs. The largest model was an enormous five-keyboard-level professional instrument designed for use in major theaters and churches. Obviously the unit was much too large to be taken out in an employee's lunch box—but it was. Over a period of 2 years a trusted stock clerk methodically removed every component of that organ piece by piece and reassembled it in his garage.

The truth of the matter is that neither the security personnel nor the company executives were aware of the theft. It was a complaint by the employee's neighbors to the local police department about the noise and music coming from the garage late at night that disclosed the theft. When the officers arrived, responding to the noise complaint, they were suspicious as to how a hundred-dollar-a-week stock clerk came into possession of a $40,000 organ, and their questioning of the suspect ended in a confession.

The preceding anecdote should emphasize the basic need for a deterrent in minimizing the potential of small items being removed from the premises. Security personnel must be stationed at the employees' exit, in industrial facilities, where all containers are subject to being examined prior to leaving the building. This is an extremely sensitive area of control, because most people are rightly offended by this lack of trust in their honesty.

I should point out also that the majority of employees are honest and would never consider stealing company property. It is those few who are dishonest, however, that make this technique necessary. To avoid creating ill will and morale problems, the employees should be made aware of the justification for this action. Spot-checking should suffice initially and be increased if heavy losses are being experienced. Spot-checking will also act as a deterrent.

Many companies require their employees to leave personal items in a central area or locker room prior to entering the plant and that secure area is under constant surveillance, either by establishing a guard post at that location or a closed-circuit television camera. In that manner, because the company knows that no materials have been placed in the containers brought in by the employees, the necessity of examining them upon leaving is eliminated. The CCTV surveillance of the area will also ensure the safety of the employee's belongings. Care should be taken *not* to place the camera inside the locker room as that would obviously be a violation of their privacy.

It is also possible that the employees may carry items out in their pockets or purses. This is a problem that can only be minimized through the alertness of security personnel on duty, at the exit at the end of each shift. For a number of reasons, a personal search of each individual would be totally impractical.

In an industrial and/or manufacturing environment, usually, if the smaller items and tools are distinctive by virtue of identification stamping and numbering, making them easily recognizable as company property, the theft of those items will be discouraged. It is also important that tools be maintained in a central, attended location. A record should be maintained of all tools checked out, and they should be checked back in carefully after use. All tools should be accounted for after each shift.

Parts used in manufacturing should be similarly controlled and accounted for, with "breakage" and defective units turned back in, reported, examined, and either returned for repair or destroyed in a proper manner. All too often a part will be reported as broken in order to justify the checking out of another similar unit, whereas in fact the first item was stolen, the breakage report merely a cover to explain the loss.

Removal of Stolen Items in Trash

Another favorite method of removing company property from the premises is through the trash. Small items are disposed of in a trash receptacle, then recovered later, after the trash has been placed outside the building, ready for pickup by the trash removal truck. In other instances employees will arrange with the trash pickup truck driver for him to search the trash after he has left the premises and keep the stolen items, to be delivered to the employees at a later time. Rings of thieves have been discovered comprised of a single trash truck driver working together with several employees at various facilities along his route. It is for that reason that the security department must carefully control the disposal of trash from within the company. Control should be in three stages: (1) Inspect the individual containers when they are emptied into the larger pickup containers; (2) maintain outside trash containers in a secure area; and (3) supervise the loading of trash into the pickup trucks if possible.

THEFT PREVENTION

The techniques just mentioned are only a few of the most popular techniques for stealing from an employer—the possibilities are so extensive, and the dishonest employee so ingenious, that entire books have been written on the subject of internal theft. The most logical methods of combating internal theft include the following:

1. Constant surveillance and vigilance by the security staff should be maintained, both visually and through closed-circuit TV and should cover assembly areas, loading docks, entrances and exits, trash disposal, locker rooms, employees' parking lots, stock rooms, tool rooms, parts department, accounting and billing procedures, and order desk operations.
2. Frequent inventories should be taken in stock and equipment rooms of supplies, parts, and raw materials utilized in production, and ratio factor studies should be compiled in an effort to ascertain whether those raw materials and parts can be accounted for in the finished product. Establish a reasonable percentage accountable for defective materials, breakage, etc. Then, if that percentage shows unaccountable increases at any given time, an investigation should be instigated to explain the losses. If they cannot be explained, a theft problem has been identified and isolated, depending on the materials unaccounted for.
3. Undercover investigators can be employed, either on a long-term basis or temporarily injected into the identified problem area in an attempt to infiltrate the theft ring or identify the suspects either through observation or the "grapevine." Employees at the working or laboring level usually know or suspect what activities are taking place and who is responsible. Most of the time they will keep it within their own peer group, rather than "inform" to management and become outcasts among their fellow employees. That is the primary value of having an undercover agent working within the group.
4. Each incident of theft should be investigated thoroughly, regardless of how minor the loss. (All unexplained losses should be considered suspected thefts until proven otherwise.) Reports should be taken and employees directly related to the area of loss interviewed. Not only will the interview technique produce surprising results in many cases, but also the fact that attention to the problem is rapid and thorough initiates a strong deterrent effect.
5. It is most important to maintain careful records of all incidents of suspected theft and to review the reports frequently in an attempt to develop a method of operation, specific area of loss, shift most frequently victimized, time elements, nature of items taken, etc. Once a method has been established, undercover or interview techniques should be instigated. Statistical reviews are particularly valuable and informative in office buildings, hotels, motels, and hospitals where contract maintenance crews are employed along with in-house people. In those areas, theft detection powders and other "plant" techniques are extremely effective.

THEFT DETECTION

Specific theft detection methods can be used for some problems. For example, in one case, a large law firm, located in a major high-rise office building, experienced a series of thefts where petty cash had been taken from desk drawers throughout various areas of the firm to which certain maintenance personnel had access. Secretaries who could state for certain that the cash was in place the night before always reported the thefts early in the morning. It was therefore clear that suspicion could be laid to a cleaning person, working nights between the hours of 5:00 P.M. and 8:30 A.M. There were several persons involved. Who was guilty?

One evening, several "plants" of marked, identified money, consisting of small bills in sealed envelopes, were placed in various secretaries' desk drawers. The serial numbers were listed and the bills dusted with invisible fluorescent powder. Approximately an hour before the cleaning people were scheduled to end their shift, a uniformed officer, patrolling the building, checked on the envelopes of cash. As soon as one was discovered missing, several officers awaited the cleaning people as they left the building through a controlled exit and subjected them to an ultraviolet light test of their hands. Faced with the sudden realization of the evidence, the one who "glowed" readily admitted the theft. If he had not, a search would have turned up the bills with the identifying serial numbers.

Note that when theft detection powders are used, the dusted items should be placed in a container, such as an envelope. The placing of the items inside the envelope should be conducted away from the location where the plant will be exited, otherwise the powder will carry freely and contaminate the entire area, leading to the possibility of an innocent person accidentally getting some on his hands or clothing. Where powders have been used, this is a point usually brought up in court at the trial. The defense will seek to show where the defendant could have picked up the powder by accident through contamination. Also, it is a good idea to test cleaning solvents used on the premises to observe what color they fluoresce under the light; then purchase a color that is radically different from that of the cleaning solvents. Most cleaning materials, solvents, soaps, detergents, etc., will fluoresce a shade of orange.

PROSECUTION POLICY

The company should establish a firm policy, in advance, determining the disposition of individuals apprehended for theft of company property. Some concerns insist on prosecution for every incident without exception; however, it can be argued that this is sometimes unfair and unwise. Other alternatives exist. For example, an employee who steals a small tool, such as a screwdriver or wrench, should not have his future working career jeopardized as a result of the incident being made a matter of record with the authorities. Simple termination, or possibly a first-time warning, would be more consistent with the seriousness of the offense.

Policies should be established based on the value of the items and/or repetition of the act, and they should be uniformly enforced. The value of having a preconceived policy is that it ensures that all personnel will be treated fairly and in a consistent manner.

Note that in several jurisdictions throughout the country, theft by employees is an accumulative crime, pertaining to the value of the stolen merchandise. Thus, if the line between a felony and misdemeanor is $400, three petty thefts of $150 each, totaling $450, would amount to a felony charge, subjecting the thief to serious penalties.

EMBEZZLEMENT

The embezzlement of company funds is usually conducted at a higher level of the management structure, although it has been known to occur at an accounting level or among employees having access to sums of cash.

Embezzlement is simply the removal of cash with an attempt to cover the shortage by manipulation of accompanying paperwork. As an example, one of the most common methods of embezzlement occurs within the payroll department of a large firm, where the payroll clerk or paymaster carries extra, nonexistent employees on the records. Checks are drawn to the fictitious persons, then cashed with false identification. Other methods of embezzling funds (although the methods appear petty) include the submission of falsified petty cash vouchers or falsified expense account receipts.

Collusion in this area can be extremely serious. For example, an outside supplier may ship only a portion of an order but charge for the full amount. An accomplice within the purchasing department may be involved with the supplier, clearing the paperwork and furnishing false inventories—sharing in the overpayment with the supplier.

The most successful deterrent and preventive measure to frustrate this type of activity is frequent audits of every department and employees' books, where cash or the transfer of funds is handled. The internal auditor and his aides should be high on the list of personnel who must be cleared carefully through a background investigation by the security department. It may also be wise to have an audit conducted on an annual basis by an outside accounting and auditing firm.

In most instances, careful audits will also pinpoint the source of an embezzlement. Once a suspect has been identified, it is necessary to conduct a careful investigation and, in particular, a credit check to determine whether the suspect has been living beyond her normal income, has paid off any unusual amounts, or has been laboring under any particular financial stress. If it is determined that the suspect has no legitimate outside source of income, such as stocks, income property, a second job, etc., then her activities can be placed under surveillance to obtain additional proof of the activity.

PROCEDURAL CONTROLS

Security devices and systems such as locks, alarms, guard patrols, and CCTV are not the only means of protecting a company against loss. Procedural controls are also an important defense against internal dishonesty.

The business procedures in various departments of a company can and should incorporate controls that minimize the potential for employee dishonesty. Every business utilizes a number of forms and reports—such as inventories, requisitions, purchase orders, receiving slips, shipping orders, sales orders. Too often, these forms and reports are never examined from a security point of view. Properly used, they can provide a means of establishing accountability and noting any discrepancies or violations of procedures that could be indications of dishonesty.

To prevent the use of forms in employee diversion schemes, the forms used in procedural control systems should be prenumbered, and all numbers must be accounted for. Any gaps in the numbering sequence require investigation. In addition, the person who made the count or recorded the information should sign all forms.

Accountability is an essential principle in a system of procedural controls. Accountability requires that all materials that are counted must undergo a second, independent count that is then compared to the first. Material counts and other information will be compared at various critical points that can be determined through a security survey.

The principle of *separation of responsibility* is also important in establishing procedural controls. A single employee should not be authorized, for example, either to order and receive merchandise, or to handle cash and keep the records of cash receipts and disbursements.

Specific procedural controls will vary with the type of business or industry and the operation of the various departments within the organization. Whatever the procedural controls are, they should be explained fully to all employees. Each employee should understand his individual responsibilities, the importance of his functions, and how they fit into the overall system of accountability.

The following control procedures are typical of those that might be established in three specific departments: purchasing, shipping/receiving, and accounting.

Purchasing Department

1. All purchasing should be done through a centralized purchasing department.
2. Each purchase order should be numbered sequentially and coded to indicate the department being serviced. All purchase orders out of sequence or missing should be accounted for.
3. Purchase orders should be checked carefully against the packing slip on incoming orders, and the order themselves checked on arrival to ensure all items purchased are in fact delivered.
4. Purchase order forms should be printed on unalterable paper on which any erasures or other alterations will be recognized easily.
5. Duplicates of purchase orders should be delivered each night to the auditing department so that all copies cannot be maintained and later destroyed by a dishonest employee. One method of theft is for a clerk in the purchasing

department, working in collusion with a supplier, to order items, then destroy the paperwork on the order and delivery. As a result the supplier is paid from an open account on merchandise not actually delivered.

6. Frequent audits, internally controlled, should be made of the purchasing department's activities and procedures. These audits should be conducted quarterly.
7. An annual audit should be made of the purchasing department accounts.
8. Any imbalance or shortages should be investigated immediately.
9. Suppliers' bids and the methods of purchasing agents in selecting supplies should be reviewed periodically. It is possible that a purchasing agent may be receiving a kickback from a supplier who may in fact be charging more than a competitor.
10. Purchasing agents should not be allowed to accept gifts from suppliers or salesmen.

Shipping/Receiving Department

1. Packing slips and order forms should be cross-checked and compared carefully.
2. All items being shipped and received should be inventoried and compared with proper order forms. These procedures should be supervised by a security officer assigned to duty at a post in the shipping and receiving dock area.
3. If company trucks are used, security seals should be utilized on the truck door, ensuring that the driver will not be able to stop en route to unload a portion of the contents. The seal should be checked at the receiving end of the shipment.
4. A long-term undercover agent should be employed in the shipping/receiving department. The agent should submit daily reports of the employees' activities and should also comment on conditions that might indicate hazardous activities which could lead to accident, fire, or waste.
5. A closed-circuit television camera should be installed on the loading dock, not only to act as a deterrent factor, but also to provide actual surveillance of the area.
6. Loading dock doors should be closed and secured when the dock is not actually in use. This should prevent someone from driving a private vehicle up to the dock and loading it with merchandise.

Accounting Department

1. The company controller and senior accountants should be cleared very carefully through pre-employment investigation by the security department.
2. An independent accounting firm should make annual or semi-annual audits.
3. The company controller should be required to present a monthly financial report to the board of directors or president of the company.
4. All accounting department employees having access to cash, billing, or payroll procedures should be bonded.

REVIEW QUESTIONS

1. What measures might be taken to prevent employees from carrying pilfered items out of the plant in their lunch pails?
2. How can an undercover investigation be of value in controlling internal theft?
3. Discuss the arguments for and against prosecuting all apprehended employee thieves.
4. Explain the principle of separation of responsibility as a method of preventing theft.
5. How can numbered forms provide a procedural control in purchasing?
6. Discuss the physical security procedures that should be used for a loading dock.

Chapter 14

Retail Security

Charles A. Sennewald, CMC, CPP

As indicated in the Preface, there are certain areas of specialty that the author felt could be addressed more appropriately by an expert who concentrates on and is known for his or her work in that particular field. Charles Sennewald is such a person for the field of retail security.

Mr. Sennewald began his career as a military policeman serving in the U.S. Air Force during the Korean War. Following the service, he joined the Los Angeles County Sheriff's Department; then, upon invitation, transferred to the Bureau of Investigation of the Los Angeles County District Attorney's Office. Finally, a stint as chief of campus police for the Claremont Colleges ended his law enforcement career as he joined the security staff of the Broadway Department Stores, where he remained for eighteen years, ultimately attaining the position of director of security for that major retail business. In 1979 he became a security consultant and continues his practice to date.

Mr. Sennewald is the author of several books, and the third edition of his popular text, Effective Security Management, *has just been released. He is also not only a founding member, but the driving force behind the formation of the International Association of Professional Security Consultants and a recognized expert in the field of retail security.*

It has been my honor, during the past couple of decades, to consider Chuck both a colleague and a close personal friend. It is also my pleasure, to present him as a guest author for this chapter on retail security.

—David L. Berger

The student of security will soon discover that of all the various industries and environments in which security professionals play an important and active role, retailing far and away dominates the field. Think of it this way: How many hospitals will you find in a given community versus the number of retail stores? Or banks and other financial institutions, or hotels, transportation companies, manufacturers, or amusement parks? So it makes sense that in just sheer numbers, if each facility hired by one security person, there would be more retail security employees than any other security specialists.

Further, how many crimes occur in a given industry or business on a day-in day-out basis? Again, considering the number of stores and considering the never ending phenomenon of shoplifting the "crime clock" for larceny beats steadily. Thefts occur in every environment but certainly not as frequently as in retailing.

With respect to the risk of employee dishonesty, what other business or industry subjects its employees to such a wide array of tempting items which can so easily be stolen, or to the handling of so much money, with so little supervision?

Aside from shoplifting and employee theft, retailers are leading targets for armed robbery, nighttime burglaries, bad checks, counterfeit currency, forgery connected with stolen or lost credit cards, pickpockets, quick-change artists, and fraud applications for credit.

A retail security practitioner will be exposed to and involved in more crime, more arrests, more investigations into loss in 2 years than his or her counterparts in other industries will experience in 10 years. Hence, if a person is standing on the threshold of a career in the security industry, the door marked "Retail Security" is where the action is. And not only is this the most active security discipline, it's where growth and opportunity for advancement awaits the achiever, because of the sheer size of the industry.

INVENTORY SHRINKAGE

Inventory shrinkage, also known as inventory shortage, is a term used in retailing that is frequently interwoven with the mission of the security department and/or is used as a tool to measure the effectiveness (or ineffectiveness) of the security program or strategy.

Inventory shrinkage really reflects the difference between the "books" and what's actually present and accounted for in an inventory taking process. Simply stated, if the store buys 100 red widgets, that is recorded in the book. Each red widget sold reduces the number in the book. So if 90 are sold the book inventory reflects 10 left. At the end of the year all the red widgets still on the shelves in the store are physically counted. If the count is 5, then 5 are missing. Five missing, represents a 5 percent loss. Different kinds of retailers have different kinds of loss experiences, that is, full line department stores might average between 1.5 and 2.5 shrinkage whereas a specialty store for consumer electronics would be below 1 percent.

This interesting "inventory shrinkage" figure reflects four sources of loss. Most recent figures, 1977, reflect those sources and the estimated percentage of contribution as follows:[1]

Employee theft	41.4%
Shoplifting	35.1%
Administrative error	17.6%
Vendor fraud	5.9%
Total	100%

Such calculations obviously give direction to the strategies employed by the security department. For example if a large retail chain has 100 security employees and 90 are used exclusively in shoplifting detection and 10 are used to detect dishonest employees, the deployment and utilization of resources isn't taking into account the source of loss, as represented by the above figure.

As interesting and helpful as this inventory shrinkage figure may be, it fails to reflect all the losses caused by crime in retailing. If an employee, for example, slips $50 out of the register and pockets it, that loss (and all cash shortages) is not factored into the shrinkage figure, nor are loses caused by robbery, bad checks, or credit frauds.

So despite the long-standing tradition of equating security's effectiveness with the inventory results, one should look more broadly at the whole cost of crime in retailing as a total bottom figure, year by year:

Inventory shrinkage	$$
Known merchandise losses	$$
Cash shortages	$$
Credit losses due to crime	$$
Bad checks	$$
Other crime losses (robbery, etc.)	$$
Security Department budget	$$
1999 Total Cost	$$$$$$$$

Shoplifting is best defined as a theft of merchandise that belongs to the store by a customer or person who appears to be a customer during the hours the store is open to the public. That means that a variety of other types of thefts, such as a customer stealing packages that belong to another customer, or an employee coming to work in the morning without a bra and then putting on a new one without paying for it, are not acts of shoplifting. Acts of theft, yes. Shoplifting, no.

During the 1960s, as the security manager of the Broadway Department Stores, I was responsible for the shoplifting detection activities of this large chain. I was proud of the outstanding results of those who were specifically and exclusively charged with catching shoplifters. Our arrests in this area numbered in the thousands! We were among the best, in my view, when comparing our numbers with other major stores. But all of a sudden our inventory shrinkage shot up over 3 percent of sales, despite all of our arrests!

Prior to this I had always taken the position I could increase shoplifting detections if my budget was increased, that is, the more store detectives, the more arrests. That almost suggested there was an endless supply of shoplifters out there.

Now, faced with the reality that despite all the arrests, losses were still mounting, I reached a new level of professional maturity, with the reality that I couldn't catch them all. The company couldn't afford to hire an army of detectives, but I indeed could stem the tide by discouraging and preventing a lot of the shoplifting acts with an untried new strategy. The strategy was based on a known phenomenon, a phenomenon that was seen as a curse to store detectives: "burning" what would otherwise be a successful shoplifting arrest. "Burning" meant making eye contact with the shoplifter before they left the store, or by the would-be shoplifter being approached by some helpful employee who

inadvertently "spoiled" or scared the thief into purchasing the item or otherwise dispos-
ing of the item (rather than stealing it).

It was also a known reality that each time a shoplifter was detained, the store
detective was removed from the selling floor, sometimes for hours, completing the
paperwork and waiting for the police to arrive. All that while, other shoplifters were
browsing the store with no or fewer professional eyes to spot them.

I implemented the following radical program at no appreciable increase in costs:
Only the very top and most productive store detectives continued in their detection
roles. The rest of the detectives, about 85 percent of them were issued red blazers bearing a gold "security" patch on the breast pocket and their new role was to simply patrol
the store making eye contact (with a pleasant expression on their face) with as many
customers as possible. The results were predictable, but also startling. Agents reported
time and again that "customers," when looked at by a "red coat," reversed direction and
disposed of articles hidden in their clothing or bags or purchased the item(s) or simply
threw the article down and departed. These "burns" were memorialized reflecting the
productivity of the agent, which also gave the agents a sense of achievement in this
strange new way of dealing with theft.

For those thieves who thought the program was dumb because they could see the
"red coats" and went ahead with their shoplifting, the best detectives picked them up.
Those shoplifters then cried "foul" because we had tricked them into thinking that prevention was all we were doing.

In three years the inventory shortage dropped from over 3 to 1 percent, which represented millions of dollars saved.

Many major retailers recognized this prevention strategy, however it's not generally practiced as the principal strategy for a number of reasons, including corporate
management's insistence on seeing positive results from the dollars spent on security,
which includes arrests!

EMPLOYEE THEFT

As the reader now knows, employee theft is the largest source of loss experienced by
the retailer. And that makes sense when you consider the employee, subjected to all the
temptations, coupled with an infinite number of possible sources to rationalize "taking"
something, and once starts stealing, successfully, continues until caught, is it any wonder they take more than a shoplifter? A shoplifter hits one store today, another store
next week, and so it goes. But the employee is there every day!

Books on how to investigate and detect dishonest employees are available in our
industry, just like books on shoplifting, including mine.

My intent here is to proactively approach this employee problem. That's to say, if
we know employees steal, and we do, then what do we do to discourage that conduct?
My approach has been one of being absolutely up front about the problem of employees
succumbing to the temptations of theft and the ultimate consequences of being caught!

When I first entered the retail industry in 1961, and an employee was caught stealing, the prevailing attitude in management was to keep that fact a secret, that is, not

ever let it be known an employee was caught and terminated (or sent to jail). Interestingly, real thieves who were fired were thought of as "victims" of an insensitive management who had really caught them chewing gum and wanted to fire them, or for some other flimsy reason got rid of a good employee. That bred mistrust of management, which can lead to rationalizing theft (getting even with mean management).

I prevailed over time with a new and better strategy. When an employee was caught stealing and was terminated (and possibly jailed), the store executive would talk to that employee's supervisor advising that one of his or her employees had just been caught and was terminated, without using the employee's name. (The supervisor knew or soon did learn the identity of the now gone employee.) The executive would challenge the supervisor with the question "What could have gone wrong that would allow one of your employees to go bad?" Not accusing the supervisor of poor supervision, but setting a climate wherein all employees and all supervisors are responsible, in some measure, for what takes place around us.

This of course is in reaction to dishonesty, which is important, but more importantly, what can be done to prevent it in the first place?

Following is but an abbreviated listing of things that can help prevent employee dishonesty.

Every applicant must be screened, including verification of past work history. Newly hired employees must be exposed to a presentation during their orientation session about the reality of employees succumbing to temptations and the consequences of being caught, including police involvement, and the reality of what do they put down on the next application for employment, after being fired? Do they put down they worked here but was fired for theft? Or do they thereafter lie on every application.

All employees must be trained to understand that the margin of profit in retail is very low, typically. Around 1 to 3 percent and stores go under because of such small margins. They typically have the mistaken notion big companies make big profits and can stand a little theft here and there.

All employees should be trained to identify with company goals. If a company is profitable, it can expand and grow. With company growth comes new supervisory and managerial positions room for promotions.

Employees must understand that when one employee steals, most coworkers fall under suspicion. And that should outrage them! If they don't understand that, they will look the other way and avoid getting involved.

Employees should have a legitimate way to advise management of their knowledge or suspicions about employees who are stealing that guarantees anonymity. Such programs are sometimes called "Silent Witness" programs.

The key strategy in effectively addressing the issue of internal dishonesty is communication, talking about it and not hiding it under the rug, so to speak.

MISCELLANEOUS OTHER CRIMES

Mention has already been made of numerous other crimes that retailers experience, such as robbery and burglary, etc. One's imagination should soar beyond the typical expectations of crime involving a store. Here's a sampling of the types of crimes and misconduct, retail security practitioners have dealt with:

Indecent exposure to children inside the store.

Indecent exposure to female customers in the store's parking lot.

Theft of vehicles, vehicle parts, and contents from vehicles in the lot.

Drunks causing a disturbance in and outside the store.

Lewd phone calls to female employees.

Lewd sexual misconduct in the men's rest rooms.

Purse snatches in the parking lot.

Counterfeiting of company negotiables (like "Mickey Mouse money") including gift certificates.

Intentional destruction of merchandise with sharp instruments (e.g., razors blades) and chemicals.

Intentional setting off of "stink bombs" or smoke bombs to disrupt business.

Intentional breaking of windows and doors with gunfire or slingshots during the night.

Intentional setting off of fire sprinkler heads with small fires.

Use of counterfeit credit cards and currency.

Extortion of executives.

Fraudulent refunding, for example, purchasing distressed or freight-claim goods and returning them to the store for full retail price/value.

Employee impersonations, for example, during hectic holiday sales when new and part-time employees are used to relieve them for a break. When the employee leaves, the impostor empties out the cash register and disappears.

The list could go on and on and is only meant to offer some insight into the wide spectrum of retail security and its many challenges.

SAMPLING OF TOOLS AND STRATEGIES

Retail security departments, often called Loss Control Departments, can't really "prevent" the myriad of crimes and misconduct that occurs regularly in the industry, and hence have at their disposal a range of tools and strategies to cope. Some include:

Computer software programs, which include such data as the frequency of point-of-sale terminal (cash register) shortages by amounts, dates, times, employees on duty at the time, etc.

CCTV for floor surveillance, with emphasis on shoplifting detection.

CCTV installations for specific suspected internal theft surveillance, such as in a receiving and shipping dock area.

Electronic systems that monitor employees at the register, wherein the actual transactions are visually displayed, for example, the investigator can see via camera a "customer" present a leather coat to an employee and then see the employee ring the transaction as $4.

Various types of electronic article surveillance (EAS) tags which, if not removed at time of sale, will activate an alarm.

Use of "integrity shoppers," that is, specialists who pose as customers and make purchases to determine if the employee rings the correct amount, underrings the amount (and pockets the difference), fails to ring the sale at all and pockets it all, or rings it all and then subsequently voids the transaction and pockets it all.

Use of undercover agents in the workforce. These "spies," unknown even to management, work right alongside of all other employees and report daily, by various means, what is happening in the workplace as it pertains to supervisory practices, use of alcohol or drugs in the workplace, sexual harassment, employees that are stealing or talking of stealing (and when and how).

The acquisition, use, oversight, maintenance, and management of these various tools and the effectiveness of their use rests with sound retail security management. The improper use, for example, of CCTV and the video recording of a suspected shoplifter who later files a civil action against the company only to discover the videotape wasn't retained, could lead to charges of spoliation of evidence, a serious charge indeed! The mishandling of information obtained from an undercover agent or the giving of improper instructions and directions given to an undercover agent that leads to entrapment and/or false accusations of dishonesty could have its own serious consequences.

SUMMARY

Retail security, then, is truly the core discipline/industry because of its size in terms of the number of retailers across the land and the number of specialized security employees required. It also is the industry that is victimized by the greatest number of criminal acts representing the widest possible range of types of crimes and generates the greatest number of arrests.

The retail security industry is in part driven by and measured against such quantitative tools as annual inventory shrinkage results. Such results can shape, year by year, security organizational design, allocation of resources, strategies, focus, and goals. Yet the method of analyzing all protection costs and losses is still not the custom and practice today. Genuine efforts to prevent shoplifting, as opposed to the common and popular strategy of detection and detention, has but limited application. In sharp contrast, more is done today in terms of working with employees to discourage and prevent internal dishonesty.

The scope and range of problems that the retail security practitioner must deal with seem almost boundless. Yet, various modern tools and long-standing strategies are available, but require good management practices to ensure they don't create more problems than they solve.

NOTES

1.   *National Retail Security Survey, Final Report* (Gainsville, FL: University of Florida, 1977).

Part IV

EXTERNAL THREATS AND SPECIAL PROBLEMS

Chapter 15

Perimeter and Exterior Protection

External controls form the facility's first line of defense against entry by unauthorized persons. These controls, including physical barriers, lighting, guard posts, and patrols (supplemented by alarm systems, CCTV, and other electronic protective devices), serve not only to detect any attempt at unauthorized entry, but also to deter would-be intruders by making evident the company's determination to protect itself. Computer systems are available to integrate the above techniques into the company's total access control program.

BARRIER PROTECTION

Fences and other physical barriers serve to define the perimeter of a facility. Their fundamental purpose is to deny or impede access by unauthorized persons. Almost any barrier can be climbed or otherwise penetrated by a determined intruder, but the presence of the barrier provides both a delaying factor (making entry more difficult) and a psychological deterrent.

In some situations design and construction of a facility will take advantage of natural barriers such as rivers or other bodies of water, cliffs, canyons, and other physical obstructions. These may make access control easier, eliminating the need for some other type of barrier. It is a mistake, however, to rely too much on natural barriers. Most are overcome relatively easily and must be supplemented by other protection.

Fences, block walls, building perimeter walls, and other structural barriers commonly form the basis of perimeter protection—supplemented by some form of surveillance (guards, CCTV, and alarm systems), and security lighting.

Fences

The most common type of security fence is the chain link design. It should be made of at least 11-gauge wire with mesh openings not larger than 2 inches square. The chain link should extend to within 2 inches of the ground or, if the soil is soft and easily moved, the mesh should be extended below the surface. The mesh should be tightly drawn and secured to rigid metal posts set in concrete. Although many existing industrial fences are 6 feet in height, security fencing should be a minimum of 8 feet high overall, including 7 feet of chain link mesh extended another foot by three or four strands of barbed wire angled outward at the top.

An installation that, under many conditions, may be more effective or appropriate than barbed wire topping is coiled barbed tape, or razor ribbon. It consists of a single helical coil of stainless steel barbed tape, 18 inches in diameter, which is mounted on top of the fence, attached to the top strand and leaning away from pedestrian traffic. While this barbed tape significantly extends the delay time in attempts to climb the fence, it should be noted that many penetrations involve cutting, breaching, or going under the fence.

It is also possible to alarm a fence so that any attempt to scale or penetrate it would be detected immediately at a central security control station. The fence should be lighted at night to make the areas both inside and outside, as well as the barrier itself, visible to roving patrols, and to act as a deterrent.

Masonry Walls

Masonry walls should also be an overall minimum of 8 feet high in perimeter barrier configuration, with a barbed wire top guard or broken glass or pointed barbs embedded on top of the wall. While such barrier walls deny the opportunity for an outsider to look into the protected property, they also provide cover for a potential intruder. In this respect the chain link fence offers better opportunity for security guards to observe any external approach to the perimeter. The fence also permits area police patrols to visually inspect the inside of the perimeter for intruders.

Openings in Perimeter

Openings in any perimeter fence or wall should be kept to the minimum necessary for carrying out the business of the facility efficiently. All openings should be guarded, locked, or secured in some other fashion. Gates and doors not in use should be locked. Windows and all other openings in exterior perimeter walls of buildings should be covered in such a way as to deny entry, by means of bars, grills, or other barriers. This includes vents, pipes, conduits, and any other openings. In high-security areas, all openings should also be alarmed.

Clear Zones

Clear zones should be maintained on both sides of the perimeter barrier. Shrubbery and weeds that could provide cover for an intruder, or for the hiding of stolen goods, should be cut away, preferably for a distance of 15 to 20 feet. Stored materials, boxes, or trash of any kind should not be allowed to pile up near the barrier, offering places of concealment. Particular attention should be given to neighboring structures, trees, utility poles, or other aids that might make it easier for an intruder to circumvent the perimeter barrier.

Signs

The fence should also have signs posted approximately every 30 feet indicating that the property is private and that trespassers will be prosecuted. The sign could also state that other measures are present, such as armed guards, alarms, or guard dogs.

Building Walls

If the facility consists of a single structure, the exterior walls of the building itself may form the perimeter to be protected. Whether or not the perimeter is fenced, the exterior of the building should maintain a certain degree of protection, such as protective gratings or metal bars over the windows and alarm protection of windows, doors, vents, and other openings.

All doors, with the exception of the main entrance, the employees' entrance, and the loading dock area, should be kept closed and locked. These doors should be equipped with panic hardware and both audible and wired alarms to the security alarm control panel. Thus, if an emergency arises, such as a fire, the employees can leave by that door easily. Any doors and windows no longer needed for any purpose can be permanently closed with bricks or cement blocks.

OFFICE BUILDINGS

If the business is located in an office building, the building provides the basic door hardware, which is compatible with the building's master key control system. This technique permits access at times when the offices are normally closed, such as at night, for cleaning crews and other emergency entries and service or repair people.

Because the preceding situation does obviously compromise the security of the business, there are options. (1) Make certain that all confidential materials are carefully secured in a strong safe or vault, which is also alarmed. The alarm may be connected to the building's security console where the officer on duty can respond to the area or call the police. (2) The alarm can be connected to a central station or (3) the business can retain an in-house officer to remain throughout the night hours and days when the office is closed. (4) Historically, night cleaning crews sometimes are the source of petty theft and, where that is not the case, they are always considered suspects. Arrangements may be made with most building management offices to take the company's office doors off the building's master key system, and install special locks.

That being the case, the company must provide keys to the premises for emergencies, and arrangements must also be made for office cleaning either in-house or under supervision.

The preceding options are necessary only when the business has high exposure to loss of property or proprietary information. Most businesses, located in large office buildings, rely on the building's security force, and any special patrols required, or other unique arrangements, may be made with the building management.

RETAIL STORES

Stores and shops should secure all doors, except for the main entry, from the inside when closing. This is most appropriately accomplished with the utilization of panic hardware. The panic bar locking device is simply an interior deadbolt that has no exterior keyway nor any other means of opening the door from the outside. Usually, there is no doorknob or any other hardware on the door's exterior. On the inside of the door, attached to the deadbolt, there is a horizontal bar, designed to be pressed, to activate and open the lock and door. This device is required by fire departments and building and safety codes as a safety measure to permit instant escape from the area in case of fire or other emergency, even in a "panic" situation.

If the store is located in an urban location, it is best to leave interior lights on, permitting passing police patrol cars to view the inside for any intruders or other signs that the establishment has been entered. If the store maintains a safe, that safe should be in plain view with a strong light overhead.

Lights should also be placed over exterior doors. The outside lights must be contained in tamperproof housings, high on the building walls. Finally, any windows should be protected, by barring or sealing in the rear and sides of the building and using heavy plate glass, well lighted, in the front.

Consideration may also be given to retaining a private patrol to check the business throughout the night and weekend hours and/or an alarm system covering both burglary and fire.

If large amounts of cash are kept on hand or, if for any other reason such as the nature of the inventory, the business is subject to armed robbery, a "panic alarm" should be installed. This alarm is simply an activation device, such as a button concealed under a counter or on the floor that, when depressed, silently notifies a central alarm station that the proprietor, or clerk, is the victim of an armed robbery.

ALARM PERIMETER PROTECTION

Various types of electronic sensors are on the market that are designed to detect the presence of an intruder in an exterior area. Not all are applicable to all situations, and each facility will have to be evaluated individually. For example, nearby vehicle traffic may cause false alarming in microwave detectors. Heavy fog, rain, snow, or dust may interfere with the operation of infrared systems.

- *Fence disturbance sensors* detect an intruder climbing over, cutting through, or lifting up a chain link fence. The sensors are designed to discriminate between the higher frequency vibrations caused by an intruder and the lower frequency vibrations caused by wind.
- *Microwave or infrared systems* send an invisible beam of microwave or infrared energy from a transmitter to a receiver and detect an intruder moving through the beam.
- *Buried pressure sensors* detect the pressure of an intruder passing over a buried cable.
- *Electrostatic fences* utilize an electric field generated along a series of wires that comprise a fence. When an intruder's body changes the electric field level to a certain degree, an alarm is activated.
- *Ultrasonic systems* emit patterns of radio-frequency (RF) waves, and alarm when the signals are altered by the presence of an intruder.
- *Ferrous metal detectors* are sometimes used in high-security government installations within an "inside" perimeter where metallic objects are not permitted. Buried in the ground, the detectors react to metal objects carried by an intruder.
- *Personnel metal detectors and X-rays* can be used. Similar to those units installed at airport entries to boarding areas, units are utilized at the entry doors to high-security areas to ensure that no firearms, weapons, or explosives are brought onto the property where they are prohibited.

These methods are expensive and are necessary only in companies maintaining maximum security projects. The alarm products themselves should be examined and rated to determine whether they are applicable to each individual situation. All alarm systems are subject to false alarm potential. The major cause of false alarms is malfunction due to a mechanical defect in the alarm hardware or wiring itself. The second major cause is use of a system that is not compatible with the environment, such as using certain types of motion detection units in areas where large animals are likely to enter the field, or ultrasonic units in buildings too close to railroad tracks with heavy traffic.

LIGHTING

Lighting is one of the "best buys" in security. Relatively inexpensive to install and maintain, lighting not only provides security guards with personal protection (by eliminating shadows and other areas of cover for intruders), but it also functions as a psychological deterrent. No intruder welcomes crossing an open, well-lighted area, particularly if it is known to be under surveillance. The now famous Oakland, California, burglary prevention ordinance noted that "three out of four commercial burglaries are committed against buildings that either have no lights or inadequate lighting."

Types of Protective Lighting

There are five basic types of protective lighting:

1. *Continuous lighting.* Fixed units located so as to light a given area continuously during hours of darkness.
2. *Standby lighting.* Units not turned on continuously but activated (automatically or manually) when an alarm is given or a guard notes suspicious activity.
3. *Movable lighting.* Rotating searchlights or spotlights, usually manually operated, that can be turned on as needed or set to operate continuously.
4. *Entry lighting.* Lighting for doorways, personnel, and vehicular entrances where identification is checked, and parking lots.
5. *Emergency lighting.* Backup equipment, including an on-site power source, in case regular lighting systems are inoperable due to power failure or other emergency.

The protective lighting system may be turned on and off automatically (by controls that respond to changes in the light passing through a photoelectric cell, or by timers) or manually.

Types of Lighting Equipment

The preceding distinctions are based on types of use. Security lighting may also be distinguished by the types of equipment selected (streetlights, floodlights, Fresnel lights, searchlights) and by the different light sources, or lamps, used. The most common light sources include the following:

- *Incandescent.* The most familiar lamp of this type is the standard light bulb.
  Advantages: low cost, good color rendition, instant turn-on.
  Disadvantages: relatively short life, low efficiency (i.e., relatively low lumens per watt), high operating cost because of the short bulb life.
- *Fluorescent.* Most widely used in interior lighting in offices and factories.
  Advantages: good color rendition, high efficiency, low operating cost.
  Disadvantages: length of the fluorescent tube and its fixture, relatively short range of coverage.
- *Mercury vapor.* Gaseous discharge lamp, blue-white color.
  Advantages: more efficient than incandescent lamps, longer life, low operating cost.
  Disadvantages: slow warm-up and recovery (many gaseous discharge lamps require from 2 to 5 minutes to recover after a power failure).

- *Sodium vapor.* Gaseous discharge lamp, produces a golden white or yellow light. Both high-pressure and low-pressure types are available. High-pressure sodium vapor lights are more popular at this time, although both types have their uses.
  Advantages: high efficiency, low operating cost, long life.
  Disadvantages: slow warm-up and recovery for high-pressure units (low-pressure types recover quickly), relatively high initial cost of installation.
- *Halogen.* Form of incandescent light. Generally brighter. Used in fixtures where beam control is important.
  Advantages: good color rendition and controllability.
  Disadvantages: relatively low efficiency with regards to lumens per watt.
- *Metal halide.* High-intensity discharge (HID) as in the mercury vapor and sodium gas lighting.
  Advantages: best color rendition of any HID; high efficiency, long lamp life.
  Disadvantages: long start-up and restart time; high initial cost of installation.

Among the different types of equipment available, both conventional streetlight fixtures and floodlights are widely used in industrial settings. *Floodlights* are particularly valuable in that they can be directed to flood a particular area with light, or to cast a focused beam of light over considerable distances. *Streetlights* are fixed lighting units designed to illuminate the immediate area. *Fresnel lights* are used primarily in glare projection applications. Their wide beam lighting strip is directed outward to illuminate the clear approaches to a facility. They are not used in situations where glare could be a problem. The familiar *searchlights* are usually employed as supplementary lighting, especially in emergency conditions. They may be either fixed or movable.

Standards for Protective Lighting

Guidelines have been established over a long period of time for effective security lighting in different applications. Those standards are usually established by the I.E.S. (Illuminating Engineering Society) and, depending on the advancement of technology in the lighting industry or changes in the requirements which enable individuals to "see" under different conditions, the standards can be modified at any given time. As an example, a few years ago in an area of medical research, ophthalmologists determined that older persons required more light, enabling them to see better as the functions of their eyes deteriorated through the normal aging process and grew weaker. As a result, lighting in and around retirement homes, for example, were increased in order to accommodate those elderly individuals and make those areas safer.

The I.E.S. does produce a manual defining those standards but, as that manual is updated frequently, it is probably better to have a lighting expert determine the needs of any installation being considered by the company. Not only will the expert have access to the I.E.S. standards, but they are also aware of any local "codes" which must be met in order to insure the lawfulness of the installation. Incidentally, many times, the I.E.S. standards exceed the requirement of local codes or regulations.

Security consultants who design security systems or function in a forensic capacity (expert witness) are capable of determining whether or not security lighting is adequate or not only in a general observation based on prior experience. Usually, if there is any question relating to standards and codes, the consultant will recommend a lighting specialist, considered an illuminating engineer, to take light-meter readings using grid patterns to evaluate any given area. Security consultants use only basic tests, such as: the ability to read a license plate in a parking lot at some given distance or whether they are able to read a newspaper under the existent lighting.

As a general rule in security lighting, the highest levels of protective lighting should be at entry doors and gates where identification of persons is required. Vehicle entry points need maximum levels of lighting, also, with lower levels of illumination for general surveillance only. Light in areas where CCTV is utilized for surveillance should be increased unless "low light level" lenses are utilized on the cameras. Hotel hallways many times do not have lighting sufficient enough to enable guests to identify persons at their door through the security peephole. The same is true in apartment house hallways and front doors of single family homes.

Secured industrial facilities should also consider adjacent areas to the targeted area of illumination. For example, 25 feet on either side of a pedestrian entry, 50 feet on either side of a vehicle entry, 40 feet from a building face within a fenced boundary, etc. Each area should encompass that additional area of similar illumination.

Lighting and Surveillance

Lighting is only as effective as the surveillance it makes possible. Perimeter lighted areas should be under continuous or periodic guard surveillance. Within the perimeter, specially sensitive areas should be both lighted and observed by security guards.

Placement of lights should be designed to direct the light down and away from the protected area. There should be a minimum of shadows, and the intent is to direct glare into the eyes of any intruder while eliminating glare for the protective force.

Lighting fixtures should be positioned so as to produce overlapping beams of light; thus a burned-out lamp does not leave an area of total darkness.

Perimeter lights, as already mentioned, should provide illumination both inside and outside the perimeter. The extent to which light can be allowed to extend into the approach area beyond the perimeter is dependent on neighboring buildings, roads, and other adjacent occupancies.

Lights should be placed high enough and enclosed in vandal-proof housings to eliminate the possibility of tampering or damage. A light is of little value if it can be knocked out with a stone. If possible, light posts should be installed inside the protected area.

Entry Lighting

All gates and doors should be equipped with night lighting. In fact, the entire exterior of the building should be well lighted at night, with at least one strong light at every corner of the building. Lobbies and display areas visible to the street should also be well illuminated.

Lighting for Safe Environment

Companies have a legal as well as a societal obligation to provide a safe environment through adequate lighting. Although there have been numerous cases over the years in the civil courts relating to "lighting" as a relevant issue in security-related matters, an early Illinois case reported in the Private Security Task Force Report on Private Security *(Faucil vs. G.S.E. Foods, Inc.)* that a police officer's widow filed a wrongful death suit against a store owner who had disconnected a rear entrance light even though he had been burglarized several times and the police were known to check his store regularly. The policeman was shot and killed by a burglar hiding in the dark area behind the store. In finding for the officer's widow, the court supported the view that the store owner was negligent in failing to provide adequate lighting.[1]

CLOSED-CIRCUIT TELEVISION

It is also possible to maintain strategically placed closed-circuit television cameras covering the exterior of the plant. Exterior cameras should be of the "low light level" type to enable them to adjust from bright daylight to nighttime lighting. The cameras should also be equipped with pan, tilt, and zoom features so that they can be controlled and directed from the main security control and used to sweep areas for full observation. The cameras should be placed high and in housings that are resistant to both weather and tampering.

Closed-circuit television systems are discussed in greater detail in another chapter of this book.

GUARDS IN EXTERIOR PROTECTION

The uniformed security personnel assigned to exterior posts or patrols in large complexes not only perform tasks that make penetration more difficult for an intruder, but they also act as a deterrent to the opportunist who might be assessing the facility's vulnerability. Industrial plants, shopping centers, and residential complexes are examples.

If the officer is not properly trained and equipped, however, she could be in danger of becoming the intruder's initial target. There have been many instances where an understaffed guard force, utilizing only one officer, has had that officer overpowered by a burglar who decided on that course as opposed to attempting to bypass the officer by stealth.

The number of security officers needed for exterior posts and patrol depends on many factors, including the following:

- The type of facility, its location, size, and layout
- The types of activities conducted on the premises
- Hours of operation
- Number of persons employed at the facility
- Number of pedestrian and vehicle gates
- Number of visitors admitted daily
- Alarm systems and other electronic protective devices in use.

Main Gate Post Officer

If the property is encircled by a fence, the main entrance to the facility should have a guard post that is manned during each working shift when the gate is opened. The officer at that post should have both telephone and radio communication with the security control inside the building. A telephone check should be made with the officer at regular intervals to ensure his safety. The manner of checking by telephone should follow an established procedure; any deviation from that procedure will be the officer's way of indicating trouble at the post. The post should also be checked hourly by a supervisor in person.

An exterior post of the type just mentioned should be housed in a small structure where the officer is protected from inclement weather and can maintain communications and records necessary to perform his task. The structure should afford the officer good visibility in all directions. Consideration may be given to installing one-way glass windows or windows that are heavily tinted, so the officer is not visible from the exterior. First, he is not a target and, second, when the booth is not occupied, such as in a parking lot, a potential car thief must still consider the possibility that someone is in attendance. It is most important that an officer standing post duty be given an environment that is safe, comfortable, pleasant, neat, and functional. It is also important that the officer be relieved every 2 or 3 hours simply to break the routine either of boredom or heavy traffic. Regular relief periods extend the officer's efficiency and minimize fatigue, and in addition afford another officer the opportunity to maintain familiarity with that post should emergency relief be necessary due to the primary officer's absence.

The main gate post officer has two major functions. First, he is to permit access to the property only to authorized persons and vehicles bearing proper identification. Secondly, he acts as the primary receptionist for visitors and guests, directing them to the proper parking area and entrance to the facility. The officer's role in access control is discussed in detail in another chapter.

Because the main gate post officer is the first contact a visitor will have with the company, his appearance and courteous manner are very important. First impressions establish the foundation for the guest's relationship with the company. For that reason alone, the main gate post officer should be chosen very carefully and impressed with the importance of his public relations image.

Exterior Patrols

Patrols of the exterior of the premises have two major functions. First, they are used to ensure that all locking devices and access control systems are in order, as well as to observe any activities that violate laws or company regulations; second, they provide a deterrent factor and discourage any potential criminal activity.

Exterior patrols should be established on an hourly basis but should not conform to any set time pattern. The uniformed officer's appearance should not be predictable by virtue of a regular or rigid schedule.

If the security force is large enough, two patrolmen should be dispatched for patrol during night hours for safety. The possibility of arming the night patrol should also be considered, again for the officer's safety. A second benefit to arming night and early morning patrol officers is that the protection and psychological support the weapon provides gives the officer more confidence, enabling him or her to enter darkened and remote areas that might otherwise be avoided. The officers should also carry walkie-talkies or have other communications with the interior control station, and be required to check in with the control officer at regular and frequent intervals.

In smaller facilities, where the officer is working alone, such as in an office building, a cellular telephone should be provided.

The officer should be instructed to patrol and cover all areas of the exterior, but be cautioned to vary his routes with each patrol and not to establish a fixed pattern.

All doors should be inspected, not only to ensure that they are locked and secured, but also to detect any signs of attempted prying or other methods of forced entry. Windows should be examined in a similar manner.

Fences should be checked carefully for any signs of attempted scaling. Such signs include bent upper wire strands, damaged main mesh linkage, or boxes and other debris piled against the fence.

The night patrol should report any lights that are not on and functioning properly, and those lights should be replaced as quickly as possible.

Night officers should accomplish their patrols as quietly as possible, so as not to announce their approach. If the officer is quiet and alert, he may be able to hear unusual activity prior to actually seeing it.

Both day and night patrols should pay careful attention to the parking areas and be alert for car prowlers and strippers as well as employees sitting in their vehicles using narcotics, concealing stolen company property, or simply "goldbricking."

Where company property is extensive and covers large acreage, it probably would be more practical to provide the officer with a patrol vehicle. The patrol vehicle should be equipped with two-way radio and spotlight.

Guard dogs may also be considered and utilized on premises where exterior grounds are extensive. Properly trained dogs not only function extremely well and eliminate the necessity of a second patrolman, but are formidable deterrent factors in themselves. When using guard dogs, it is necessary to use the handler-dog concept rather than allowing a dog to roam free. A free-roaming dog does not permit legitimate pedestrian traffic, because the dog cannot distinguish between individuals and will only respond to the handler.

One word of caution. Night patrol duty can become extremely routine, and after a period of time the guard becomes complacent and less alert. For that reason alone, guards should be rotated on a regular basis and given more active tasks to perform when they are not on patrol. Rotating assignments enable all officers to become more versatile and capable of taking over other assignments in case of absence or emergency. Officers should be required to maintain a log of patrols and the activity conducted on each tour, such as doors found open and persons contacted. Whenever an incident occurs, such as contact with someone or a door or window is found unsecured, a narrative "incident" report should be completed. Logs and reports are not only necessary to maintain documentation of events but they keep the officer alert.

The officers on patrol duty must remain alert, for their own safety and that of the company. They must be prepared for that one incident . . . which just may occur on the next patrol.

PARKING AREA CONTROLS

Parking areas pose special problems within the subject of exterior protection and deserve separate discussion. Facility parking areas are normally divided into four separate areas in larger facilities:

1. *Executive parking section.* A section for administrative and executive parking is normally set aside from the balance of the employee parking, due to the necessity of these persons frequently leaving the premises during normal working hours, or arriving later than the production force. Spaces in this section should be numbered and assigned to ensure the space will be available to the individual when needed.

2. *Employee parking section.* The employee parking section need not have assigned spaces, providing there are sufficient spaces available. This area should be far enough from the business entrance and exit to discourage the employees from carrying contraband to the vehicles without the chance of being observed by a security officer or other employee. If possible, the employee parking area should be outside the perimeter of the facility, requiring the employees to pass through a guarded entry.

3. *Visitor parking section.* The visitor section should be close to the main entrance of the facility, not only as a matter of convenience but also to ensure the occupant will not drive to an obscure area where a confederate within the plant could transfer contraband to the visitor's vehicle.

4. *Delivery and service section.* A separate section should be placed near, but not directly adjacent to, the loading dock or delivery entrance to afford easy access for small deliveries, contract workmen, etc. This area should be under the direct observation of security control, either through a guard stationed in the vicinity or coverage by a closed-circuit TV camera.

Each classification of parking should have a color-coded window sticker indicating the level of parking permitted. In the case of deliveries and visitors, temporary window passes can be handed out by the security guard at the main gate for placement on the dashboard.

It is necessary for the exterior patrol to check the parking areas on a regular basis to inspect the area for unauthorized vehicles, improperly parked vehicles, and any possible car thieves or vandals operating in the area.

During the night hours, the entire parking area should be well lighted and patrolled at regular intervals. It is also possible to have the area covered by a closed-circuit television camera to scan the sections. Should any unusual circumstances or persons be observed, a security guard should be dispatched to the scene.

It might also be advisable to have a temporary parking section for employees who are either picked up or delivered to work by a family member or friend.

Consideration must also be given to the potential of sabotage or terrorist activities, the threat being dependent on the nature and type of business or industry. Security officers assigned to a gate entry post or front door of the facility should be able to observe the entry point to the business. Note that the occupant of a vehicle, particularly a van or small truck, actually enters the facility from the visitor and receiving areas. Be alert and constantly aware of the potential for a vehicle containing high explosives to gain access to the property.

REVIEW QUESTIONS

1. If "almost any barrier can be climbed or otherwise penetrated," of what real security value is a perimeter fence?
2. Give two security reasons for providing a clear zone on either side of the perimeter boundary.
3. Describe four different types of perimeter alarms.
4. Under what circumstances might a glare-projection perimeter lighting system be installed? What type of equipment is best suited to this application?
5. Describe an effective guard post station in terms of its function and its physical characteristics.
6. What is the purpose of varying the routes and schedules of an exterior patrol?
7. Give at least four examples of things the officer on night patrol should look for.
8. For optimum security, where should the employee parking lot be located? Why?

NOTES

1. *Private Security: Report of the Task Force on Private Security.* National Advisory Committee on Criminal Justice Standards and Goals (Washington, DC, 1976), p. 183.

Chapter 16

Executive Protection and Terrorism

During the 1970s executive protection came into its own as an aspect of private security—as an alarmed response by business and industry to the plain fact that, around the world, terrorism, hostage-taking, and kidnapping had become a "growth industry."

In the beginning such acts of terrorism were principally political, and as such were directed primarily against government agents, diplomats, and political figures. But as these targets have been progressively "hardened," and as terrorist successes mounted, new principal targets had been found, none more tempting than the businessperson. Even more recently, in the 1990s, foreign and domestic elements have been attacking and bombing both government and private structures.

One reason is that kidnapping a business executive has proved to be profitable. While the U.S. government has discouraged kidnapping of its officials (though not entirely) by a firm policy of conducting no negotiations and paying no ransom to terrorists, U.S. and foreign businesses have been understandably reluctant to adopt such a stand because of the human factors involved. Exxon paid $14.2 million to rescue refinery manager Victor Samuelson in Argentina in 1974. An Argentine conglomerate, Bunge and Born, paid $60 million ransom for the safe recovery of two key executives (still the highest known ransom paid to this date). In some countries, such as Italy and Colombia, kidnapping and other terrorist attacks have become an accepted fact of life—the primary source of income for many political groups and common criminals.

When *Industrial Security* was first published in 1979, the author reported that "In the United States, there were a record 1058 bombings reported in 1977." The most recently available Bureau of Justice Statistics Sourcebook reveals that bombings in 1994 had increased to a new record of 1916. The upward trend was reversed, slightly, in 1995 when the bombing incidents dropped to 1562; however, while it is impossible to make predictions of trends in this area, most security experts, government and private, do not find future prospects reassuring, particularly in view of the recent development of chemical and bacteriological weapons. Both dissident groups and criminals have shown a quickness to copy the successes of others in different parts of the world. The fact that kidnapping and hostage-taking have proved to be "successful" elsewhere has the predictable effect of encouraging more such actions—and in new, more fruitful territory such as the United States.

This hard reality has not been lost on U.S. business and industry. Virtually all major multinational companies such as General Motors, ITT, Xerox, General Electric, as well as oil companies and large banks, have instituted extraordinary measures for the protection of key executives, both abroad and in the United States. Moreover, it is estimated that at least "80 percent of major U.S. firms have either started executive protection programs or are considering doing so."[1] Executive protection programs, executive training to reduce the risk, ransom insurance, defensive driving courses, crisis management teams, and increased physical security both for company facilities and residences became part of the security picture beginning in the late 1970s. This type of protection planning *must* be a consideration for any company, large or small, that has operations overseas, and it is becoming increasingly accepted in this country as well.

KNOWING THE ENEMY

Who are the terrorists? In many countries terrorist organizations have become more notorious than their counterparts in the United States. Among the best known are extremists of the Palestine Liberation Organization. One specialist in executive protection, Fred Rayne, has described five categories of terrorists:[2]

1. The *politically motivated* terrorist, whose primary goal is to bring down the government or to effect dramatic changes in society by creating chaos.
2. The *minority-group* terrorist, acting from an outraged sense of injustice.
3. The *criminal* terrorist, adopting the tactics of kidnapping and extortion as a good way to get big money.
4. The *mentally deranged* terrorist, who often acts from an irrational sense of having been wronged.
5. The *religiously motivated* terrorist, who adopts criminal actions from a sense of high purpose.

For all of these, with the exception of the third category, terrorism is a form of "theater." Publicity and media attention, with the attendant sense of power, may be as important as monetary gain, and a large, highly visible corporation or prominent individual ideally fills the terrorist's needs.

A 1995 Department of Justice report on domestic terrorism[3] identified terrorists as follows:

1. *Left-wing terrorism.* The change in the structure of the Soviet Union has deprived leftist groups of the ideology that precipitated their activities, thus their threat has lessened considerably.

2. *Right-wing terrorism.* Usually antigovernment and racist groups feeling displaced by changes in the U.S. economy and by cultural changes. These groups many times refer to themselves as "militias."

3. *Special interest extremists.* Antiabortion groups are an excellent example of this category.

4. *International terrorism.* Foreign nationals who consider the United States as their enemy, for one reason or another, and who live in and travel throughout our country.

5. *State sponsors of terrorism.* The recognized state sponsors of international terrorism, Iran, Iraq, Syria, Sudan, Libya, Cuba, and North Korea, continue to maintain diplomatic facilities in this country.

6. *Formal terrorist groups.* Such groups as the Al-Gama'at Al-Islamiyya, HAMAS, and Hizballah have supporters in the United States believed to be engaged in criminal activity, including military-style training.

7. *Loosely affiliated extremists.* Unilateral radicals, adhering to the worst excesses of hatred born of various international conflicts.

Unfortunately, the mobility of modern society, along with an active spirit of cooperation among dissident groups throughout the world, has put sophisticated weaponry into the hands of terrorists—even the individual or small group with minimal resources. At Rome in 1973, five Palestinians who tried to shoot down an El Al jet were using man-portable Soviet SA-7 surface-to-air rockets. Another Palestinian damaged a Yugoslav aircraft at Orly Airport in 1975 with an antitank weapon. The kidnappers of Italy's Aldo Moro were armed with modern automatic weapons manufactured in Czechoslovakia when the attack was made. In the 1990s the terrorists arsenal has been upgraded to include nuclear, chemical, and bacteriological weapons. Terrorists, in fact, have little difficulty in obtaining automatic weapons or the ingredients for a Christmas catalog of bombs.[4]

Even in the United States there is considerable interaction among radical groups. One radical magazine in Wisconsin published a list of the "Top 40" executive targets for kidnapping. Various publications, both underground and above ground, have offered advice on how to build a bomb. And a terrorist manual written by the late Venezuelan terrorist called Carlos, entitled *The Mini-Manual of the Urban Guerrilla,* has been widely distributed in America as well as Europe and South America.

And with all this, the threat to the average executive in the United States from the so-called "ordinary criminal" may be even more probable than that offered by organized terrorism. Because kidnapping, once regarded as solely a crime against the wealthy, is now beginning to be perceived as an easy, less dangerous source of money than many other criminal acts. Even the smaller businessperson or company executive, from whom relatively small sums may be extorted, can be a victim.

RISK ASSESSMENT

Not all industrial concerns will accept the fact that they or their executives may be credible targets. Moreover, the costs of a formal executive protection program beyond normal physical security measures may seem prohibitive. The first step in executive protection planning, then, is the same as it is for all security programs: evaluating the risk and determining whether a need for the program exists.

The first part of this assessment is an analysis of the specific company's vulnerability. Is the company—because of its location, activities in foreign countries, position or philosophy it expounds in a publication or network television, the products it makes or for any other perceptible reason—a potential target for political or otherwise motivated terrorist attacks?

Commonsense evaluation as well as intelligence offered by cooperative local police agencies will contribute to this analysis. But there may be other signs that company security should be aware of, such as open demonstrations, dissident employees, "crank" calls or letters, published attacks against the company or its policies in radical publications, bomb threats, or actual bombs. Any escalation in such activities should be perceived as increasing the probability of actions against company property or its people.

If the company is doing business in a high-risk country, such as Colombia, or Iran during the turmoil accompanying the takeover by the new revolutionary government early in 1979, for example, the threat to prominent company representatives is high. Even in the United States, factors that may increase the perceptible threat would include the political climate of the area, any recent history of attacks, social unrest, and a rising crime rate.

The other side of risk assessment is an evaluation of existing protection, both inside and outside the company. As a general rule, government agencies, including law enforcement, simply cannot protect individuals or company executives. Even in foreign countries that ostensibly try to provide police or army protection for prominent U.S. executives, that protection is generally considered to be undependable. In most cases, the company or the individual must provide the protection.

The degree of protection offered by the company can only be determined by a systematic security survey of both company facilities and residences of key (target) executives. Along with evaluating the risk and the existing security measures, threat assessment must also consider the cost of additional protection. An extensive executive protection program can be expensive. Major private security firms such as Pinkerton's, Burns, and Wells Fargo offer sophisticated executive protection programs, as do a host of smaller firms specializing in this area of security. There are also several individual sole practitioners who do nothing else but executive protection, some having served in various law enforcement agencies of the federal government, including the Secret Service.

Obviously, budget limitations will help determine how much protection an individual company can provide for its key personnel. Absolute protection is impossible at any price; some minimum protection through training programs and existing physical security can be provided at low cost. The degree of risk and the budget available for protection must be assessed by each company, and, as always, the security program will be a compromise. Each company management must finally determine how much risk is acceptable—and how much is unacceptable no matter what the cost.

A complicating concern in this assessment is the human factor. Property loss is a serious concern for any company. But when you are talking about executive kidnapping for political or monetary gain, you are contemplating human loss—assessing the cost of a human life. As a matter of policy, in order to reduce the temptation of repeated attacks, nations may make it clear that under no circumstances will they negotiate with terrorists or pay ransom, either in money or in the form of releasing political prisoners. Few corporations are willing to adopt such a stand, with its implicit acceptance of the necessity to "sacrifice" any hostage. An additional complication in this respect is the fact that the executive is not the only target; his wife and children are equally tempting—and usually more vulnerable—targets. When an executive's family is held hostage, the level of personal anguish is increased, along with the compulsion to negotiate at any cost.

PRACTICAL EXECUTIVE PROTECTION

When realistic threat assessment establishes that some degree of executive protection is desirable or necessary, the first stage in the development of such a program is selling management—and the top executives themselves—on the need. Even more than other security programs and policies, the personal protection program simply cannot work without total conviction, commitment, and support on the part of top management.

Unless there has been an actual incident within the company or close to it, few executives readily accept the necessity for measures to protect *them.* How can I do my job, the executive will ask, with bodyguards cluttering up my life, restrictions on my movements, constant changes in my habitual way of doing things, and the inevitable invasion of my personal privacy that a protection program entails? The normal reaction is that "It won't happen to me." Only if top level management openly supports the program will it be accepted by all executives as a "necessary evil."

Only top management, moreover, can establish firm policies regarding ransom payments, instituting expensive new procedures, establishing authority for carrying out the program and responding to incidents, secret board meetings, special travel arrangements, and other procedures that may be part of the program.

The case of Aldo Moro provides an unhappy object lesson in what can happen when an executive (or politician) either fails to accept the necessity of security procedures, or relies too heavily on a single line of defense (in this case, bodyguards). Even though Moro had been threatened many times and was a highly visible figure in the midst of a virtual epidemic of kidnapping and other terrorist attacks, he consistently violated some of the fundamental principles of safety. He refused to ride in an armored car, although such protection had repeatedly been offered to him. He failed to change his routine, going to church every morning at the same hour, and then following the same route on the way to his office, although specific plans called for varying his route. He rode in a government limousine with prominent insignia and license plates. The result was that his kidnappers were able to carry out their attack with military precision, killing his five bodyguards, at a known time on a known route against a known vehicle that was vulnerable to attack. Moro was held prisoner 54 days then executed after the Italian government refused to release 13 members of The Red Brigade from prison. This 1978 case is still studied by specialists in executive and heads of government security.

Key executives, then, must be impressed with the necessity for carrying out sensible precautions, for their own self-protection and that of their families, as well as for the company's well-being. And every effort should be made so that essential personal safety procedures interfere as little as possible with normal activities.

Preplanning

The importance of advance planning in executive protection applies as much as it does in emergency and disaster situations already discussed. As with general emergencies, there must be a clearly defined line of authority extending downward from the top officer of the company. When a crisis occurs, there is no time for deciding who is in charge, who should be notified, who has the authority to authorize negotiations, ransom payments or any other response, who should contact outside agencies (the police and the FBI) or the nearest U.S. State Department official in a foreign country.

At all times either a top officer of the company, or someone reporting to him, should be able to respond swiftly to the personal crisis situation. The security director may be in charge of carrying out the details of a planned program, but a higher officer may be designated as the director of executive protection (or crisis management, a term that is becoming more widely accepted). Some decisions, such as those involving calculated risk to a hostage or the payment of large sums of money to meet terrorists' demands, require approval at the highest possible level. As with emergency plan officers, there must also be backup responsibility designated in the plan.

Kidnapping in particular, but also serious assaults against property, creates emotional situations, and in such an atmosphere sound policy decisions are difficult to arrive at. All such policies should be determined in advance, when there is time for a wide range of input and for objective discussion and decision. Those involved in the response program will then be able to act quickly and responsibly in a crisis.

Advance basic planning should also include provision for prompt communication with corporate officers and outside agencies. How extensive the protection should be and who is to be protected are other preliminary decisions that affect the entire program. Keep in mind that the handful of officers at the very top of the company are not the only potentially attractive targets to the kidnapper. At the same time resources may limit the number of people who can reasonably receive special protection.

Reducing the Risk

Some aspects of an executive protection program can be carried out by *any* company, regardless of its size or budget. The advice of protection specialists in this field for reducing the potential risk through the executive's own actions can be of value to any executive or key manager in industry, as much as for the supermarket or bank manager who may also be threatened.

Maintain a Low Profile .   Executives should be educated to understand the ways in which their own behavior can unwittingly call attention to themselves as potential terrorist targets. Executives should not advertise their identity, position, and importance. Suggestions for maintaining a low profile include these:

• Do not put name on mailbox, door, or parking space.
• Avoid personalized license plates.
• Have an unlisted telephone number and release it only with discretion.
• Avoid company logos on vehicles or corporate aircraft.
• Keep travel itineraries and business or personal schedules confidential.
• Use a shredder or other secure means of disposal when discarding confidential letters, documents, travel plans, etc.
• Avoid publicity (including photographs) about social and recreational activities, vacation and travel plans.
• Exercise discretion on the telephone and in conversations that could be overheard.
• Register the executive's vehicle in the company's name rather than the individual's.

Avoid Predictable Movements .   The kidnapper's job is made much simpler if the executive and/or members of his or her family follow an unvarying daily pattern so that they can be found in the same place day after day at the same time. Variations should be introduced into the pattern of the executive's route and time of travel to and from the office, for the morning jog, an evening session at the gym or afternoon tennis game, business lunches at a favorite restaurant; and any other regular actions. This applies to the spouse's and children's activities as well.

Anticipating Danger .   The executive and members of her or his household should make an effort to be observant and alert to any possible dangers. Strange persons or vehicles in the area of the executive's home or place of business should be noted carefully. If they appear to be loitering or conducting surreptitious surveillance, authorities should be notified. It is common for kidnappers to watch their victims for several days before taking action.

At home, family members and servants should be instructed not to open the door to strangers and not to accept delivery of packages unless the sender is known. The identity of repairmen and telephone or utility company servicemen should be checked before they are granted access. A phone call to their employer can verify their authenticity.

School authorities should be instructed never to release children from school without verified parental consent. Parents should know their children's whereabouts and companions at all times.

In general, the executive and his or her family can reduce the risk of personal attack by following the old military dictum of staying below the horizon line, offering no clearly visible target but blending unobtrusively into the background. Conversely, the executive—and those close to him or her—should cultivate the habit of being conscious of what is going on around them at all times.

Hardening the Target

Even if a company is unable to do more than train its executives in the awareness of risk and everyday actions that can reduce the risk, and tighten up its physical security, these two aspects of a protection program will add a practical dimension of personal security.

As a general rule, industrial facilities have an advantage over many other terrorist targets in that they are already committed to physical security measures and to the use of a guard force. As one government analysis of the terrorist threat puts it, "Limitation of access through physical means and controlling the accessibility of dangerous devices and materials is necessary. Fences, guards, various sensors, closed-circuit television, metal detectors, tags for explosives, secure communications means, etc., are elements of a growing *counterterrorism technology.* . . . Deterrence of future terrorist acts, though a subjective matter, is undoubtedly enhanced by reducing target vulnerability."[5]

When executive protection becomes an added security consideration, then the first priority at the facility (or facilities in a larger company) should be an evaluation and upgrading of physical security as necessary. It is true that basic measures of this kind— fences, guards, alarms, patrols, etc.—are primarily designed to keep out the curious intruder and the conventional thief. They may not keep out a more determined, well-armed group of terrorists or kidnappers. Nevertheless, a well-maintained and well-lighted fence, intrusion sensors, alert security patrols, and closed-circuit television surveillance do "harden" the target, making surprise attack more difficult. Access controls, not only at the perimeter but also at building entrances and executive offices, are especially important.

The vulnerability of the executive's residence should also be surveyed. Here again, enhanced physical security in the form of perimeter security, intrusion alarms, better lighting, CCTV, and guards may be considered. Guard dogs are a relatively inexpensive and effective form of protection. In high-risk situations where budgetary considerations permit it, experts recommend the creation of a "safe room" in the executive's home, a highly resistant sanctuary where the family can withdraw to hold out until help comes.

Special problems arise for the executive living in rented housing (especially in a foreign country) or in an apartment building, where neither the executive or the company has direct control over security. As a practical matter, a key executive should not live in an apartment building that offers little or no physical security. Access controls, surveillance systems (such as CCTV), and intrusion warnings should be minimum requirements for any residence.

Personal Protection

One of the "growth trends" in private security in recent years has been in the hiring of bodyguards. There is nothing new about the use of bodyguards, but there has been a dramatic increase in this type of personal protection for executives as well as political figures. Bodyguards, whether hired directly by the company or executive, or supplied by a contract agency, may be essential for the high-risk executive who travels extensively or works in a foreign country. Even where this level of personal protection is not considered essential, many experts recommend that the executive's chauffeur should also be a bodyguard who is well trained and armed.

Other aspects of personal protection that should be considered in the planning stages are bulletproof vests and related protective equipment, armored vehicles, personal communications equipment, and personal weapons. (Whether or not the target executive should be armed is a highly debatable question that should be a matter of specific company policy.)

One other conventional security measure that has not been mentioned is personnel screening. Anyone working or acting in proximity to the target executive should be the subject of a thorough, in-depth background investigation. This would apply to company personnel and also to anyone working at the executive's home, such as servants, chauffeur, gardener, and others.

Another recommended practice is the maintenance in a highly secure location of a personal file for each executive, including such details as a photograph, fingerprints, voice tape, handwriting sample, and personal information an outsider could not reasonably be expected to have. (Use of the personal file in crisis situations is discussed later in this chapter.)

Protection in Vehicles

Evasive driving tactics and other aspects of vehicle and transit security are an important part of even the most basic executive protection program. The executive is most vulnerable in his automobile. Security specialists point out that "90 percent of all assassination and kidnapping attempts have taken place while the victim was either entering or leaving his car, or on the road. Moreover, 80 percent of such auto ambushes have succeeded, because the attackers have the advantage of striking while the victim is relatively isolated from help."[6]

West German industrialist Hanns-Martin Schleyer was abducted and murdered by terrorists in 1977 after his driver stopped in front of a vehicle blocking the road. With proper evasive maneuvers, he might have escaped.

Professional training in evasive vehicle maneuvers is recommended for company chauffeurs or for executives who drive their own vehicles. Several schools have been established for evasive driving instruction. Companies can spend about $1200 to train their drivers to execute abrupt turnabouts and high-speed getaways, to run through barricades and ram past blocking autos.

To ensure that the vehicle will be capable of performing such maneuvers—and that it will not break down on the road—it should be kept in excellent condition, with regular maintenance and servicing. The gas tank should be kept at least half-full.

Vehicles can be armored to withstand attack by most weapons. The cost is high, however, and the fully armored vehicle is too heavy to execute evasive maneuvers. A compromise is the installation of armor plating around the engine and passenger compartment and the use of bullet-resistant glass in the windows. A high-powered engine compensates for the added weight.

Protection of the executive on the road should encompass more than evasive driving skills. A fundamental rule is this: Never follow the same routes at predictable times. Taking the identical route in Rome every day, as already noted, was one of Aldo Moro's fatal mistakes.

Alarm systems are available that will sound an alert if there has been any tampering with the hood or doors of the vehicle. As a protection against a vehicle being wired with explosives, a device can be installed to start the engine and turn on the car's electrical system from a safe distance. The vehicle should have a key-locked gas cap.

The driver or passengers should look inside the vehicle before entering and should not enter if anything suspicious is observed, such as an unfamiliar parcel. In addition, a walk-around check of the car should be made to observe any evidence of surreptitious entry, blockage of the tail pipe, or planting of explosives. All vehicle doors should be locked as soon as persons enter. Should the chauffeur be under duress from attackers, he should be instructed to give a prearranged "trouble" signal to warn the executive against entering the vehicle.

Driving should be confined to well-traveled streets and daylight hours when possible. Traveling in convoys of two or more cars is an added precaution. Where there are two or more lanes in one direction, the executive's vehicle should use the left, inner lane to avoid being forced to the curb.

Distress situations along the road, such as apparent accident scenes or motorists stranded by broken-down vehicles, may be traps. The driver should evaluate such situations carefully rather than unhesitatingly stopping to offer assistance.

Two-way radio or telephone communication can be helpful in an emergency. If the executive's car is being followed, the police or company security can be contacted for assistance, noting current location, direction of travel, and description and license number of the pursuing vehicle. Other protective equipment includes an electronic "beeper" that can be installed on the vehicle to emit a radio signal so that a receiving unit can keep track of the vehicle's direction of travel and distance away. If the vehicle is attacked and escape is impossible, the driver should sound the horn or vehicle alarm to attract attention.

Special Situations

It is impossible in a brief chapter to cover all of the details that must be included in executive protection planning. However, in addition to making the executive less vulnerable at the office, at home, and while driving, extra precautions must also be considered for a variety of special (but common) situations. These include visiting public places, such as restaurants or country clubs; attending conferences or sales meetings, often held at major hotels or other meeting places; and general traveling, whether on business or vacations.

The principle of maintaining a low profile applies especially when vacationing or going into public places. Such commonsense practices as not announcing travel plans in advance, obtaining tickets or reservations in the company name or a false name rather than in the executive's name, not sitting at a "favorite" table in a restaurant, avoiding crowds wherever possible, and being alert if not outright suspicious of friendly strangers should become a routine part of the executive's life. For an executive with a family, it is also important that someone in the family know where each member is at any time.

In the case of company meetings or conferences attended by one or more executives, consideration should be given to security inspections of the location beforehand, upgraded security especially during arrival and departure times, and debugging of meeting rooms if the threat of electronic surveillance is a credible possibility.

Protecting the Executive's Family

The need in some situations to extend protection to the executive's family has already been mentioned. Any executive (and hence her or his company) is at least equally vulnerable to extortion demands when a spouse or child, rather than the executive, is the victim of kidnappers. Realistically, of course, the more persons who are protected under the program, the more difficult and costly it becomes. Nevertheless, especially in high-risk situations, planning should provide for the safety of the executive's family both in the home and in their everyday activities. Awareness of risks, being alert to the presence of strangers or unusual activity in the neighborhood, the use of a trained chauffeur and even bodyguards—all of these fundamental aspects of the safety program for the executive should also be considered for the executive's family.

If an executive should be kidnapped, immediate concern should be given to the family. They should be provided with additional high-level protection for the duration of the crisis.

THE CRISIS RESPONSE

Response to a crisis situation cannot be the same for all companies. Those in defense-related industries working on government contracts may have to coordinate their actions with the official agencies involved. An organization with access to nuclear materials or other sensitive targets (such as weapons) will not react in the same way to extortion demands as one whose only target asset is money. A corporation whose kidnapped executive is the principal stockholder is in a far different position than one whose stock is widely held among the general public.

All such variations, however, are part of preplanning. Such circumstances are known, and it is possible to determine policies in advance of a crisis. As a general principle, executive protection plans should anticipate any contingency; the real time for decision is *before* something happens. The response is then preconditioned. Responsible company officials can act confidently and quickly, and decisions will not be a reaction to extreme stress or emotional turmoil.

The late pioneering security consultant, Don D. Darling, outlined steps that should be taken when a company executive has been taken hostage and ransom demands are made. Those basic steps include the following:[7]

1. Make certain the person allegedly kidnapped is actually missing. Try to locate the missing person face-to-face. Extortionists have sometimes tried to exploit the absence of an executive who is only off on an unexpected trip or a clandestine visit with a girlfriend.
2. Report the kidnapping to key corporate officers as outlined in the basic plan.
3. Anticipate the fact that criminals other than the kidnappers may try to cash in on the crisis. When a contact is made, insist on proof that the person kidnapped is in the hands of the callers. This is one of the primary purposes of the personal file mentioned earlier. It can enable you to verify a handwriting sample, voice tape, or other identifying personal information.
4. Once a kidnapping has been verified, establish a secret code word or phrase with the kidnappers for use in subsequent contacts. One person should be designated as the contact for the company.
5. If a decision is made to pay ransom money demanded, the payoff should be handled by preselected company employees or trained contract agents. They should preferably be young, cool-headed, and reliable.
6. Ransom demands generally require negotiation. The company negotiator should try to obtain as good a "deal" as possible, with primary emphasis on the safety of the hostage.
7. Avoid publicity at all times.

Other generally recommended procedures include activating a tape recorder to record all calls from the kidnappers, maintaining a log of all events, notifying police and the FBI promptly when the first contact with kidnappers is made (if the abduction occurs in the United States), taking prompt action to safeguard the missing executive's family, and avoiding recriminations or emotional reactions in dealing with kidnappers. The attitude during all contacts and negotiations should be calm and cooperative.

The point about contacting law enforcement agencies immediately should be emphasized. Generally speaking, it is a mistake to try to handle the crisis secretly and without professional help. Police and the FBI have access to informants and other intelligence, and they have the equipment, experience, and expertise to provide the kind of help and advice that can increase the chances of the safe return of the hostage. In all such situations there are no absolute guarantees, but it is essential to take advantage of every edge you can find.

CRISIS MANAGEMENT TEAMS

Many large organizations, particularly those that are multinational or are considered to be target industries, have embraced the concept of the crisis management team to coordinate the company response to a kidnapping or other terrorist incident. This is an extension of the emergency team that deals with natural disasters and other general emergencies. The team should be small, but it should have full authority to take any action necessary to handle a crisis.

The crisis management team should include the following people: a senior executive capable of acting for top management, a lawyer skilled in tough negotiations, a finance officer who can obtain large sums of money on short notice, the security director (corporate security director in a large organization) whose responsibilities may include intelligence as well as liaison with law enforcement or government authorities, a public relations officer, through whom all request for information by the media should be channeled to maintain a "low profile," and the personnel director. Other officers of the company (or outside specialists) can be substituted for those just listed, but the *capabilities* suggested should be essential for the team. It should also be able to call on any other needed skills, such as expertise in communications or electronics, and couriers to be involved in possible ransom payoffs.

The advantages of such a crisis management team are many. The unit can be trained in advance (even including mock "abductions"). It can act quickly and responsibly. It facilitates preplanning, and it fixes responsibility and authority for action during a crisis. It effectively shortens communications lines within the company, and it creates tighter control over such things as publicity and relations with outside agencies.

Because many such teams are composed of people who are executives themselves, most will be strong men or women with forceful opinions. For this reason alone, it is essential that the team leader, normally the senior executive involved, be capable of exercising strong leadership. Otherwise the cohesion and control offered by the team concept will disintegrate into time-wasting debate and delay in making hard decisions.

REVIEW QUESTIONS

1. Describe five categories of terrorists and the motives of each.
2. Discuss the factors that must be analyzed in assessing a specific company's vulnerability to terrorist attacks.
3. Why is preplanning especially important in a kidnapping situation?
4. List six practices that can help the executive maintain a "low profile."
5. Discuss the role of physical security in an executive protection program.
6. Describe the contents of the personal file that should be maintained for each executive and its purpose.
7. Where is the executive most vulnerable to attack?
8. Outline seven basic steps that should be taken when a company executive has been taken hostage and ransom demands are made.
9. List the skills required by the members of the Crisis Management Team.

NOTES

1. *Time* (July 10, 1978), p. 54.
2. Fred Rayne, "Doing Business in a Terrorist World," *Security World* (November, 1977), pp. 22–23.
3. "Terrorism, Current Threat" (Washington, DC: U.S. Department of Justice).
4. Robert H. Kupperman, "Facing Tomorrow's Terrorist Incident Today" (Washington, DC: U.S. Department of Justice, Law Enforcement Assistance Administration, 1977), pp. 4–5.
5. *Ibid.*, p. 5.
6. *Time, op. Cit.*
7. Don D. Darling, "Action Security for that 'Crisis Situation,'" *Security World* (November, 1974), pp. 15–16.

Chapter 17

Specific Crime Problems

Businesses can become the targets of almost any type of criminal attack. The most common, employee theft, was discussed in Chapter 13. Others include burglary, robbery, kidnapping, industrial espionage, sabotage, and on-the-job gambling and narcotics and alcohol abuse.

Although most crimes are potential problems within a business, certain violations will be more prevalent due to the environmental risks of opportunity, temptation, and external criminal intent created therein. Investigative procedures must therefore be carefully established; however, the first line of defense against such criminal behavior is the careful planning of deterrent and preventive measures.

SURVEILLANCE AND INTELLIGENCE

Deterrence is divided into two major functions: surveillance and intelligence. Surveillance is established through those processes that afford physical control of personnel and observation of movement throughout the facility. Note that the "surveillance" identified here, is visible, as opposed to the surveillance conducted secretly in an investigative process. This category would include:

1. Guard and patrol
2. Alarms
3. Closed-circuit television
4. Key control and access limitation
5. Inventories and inventory control
6. Close scrutiny of merchandise and stock movement and storage
7. Accounting procedures and audits.

Each of these controls is discussed separately in this text.

The intelligence function, although not as extensive as surveillance procedures, may be the most significant aspect of crime prevention, along with investigative processes following any incidents. Intelligence gathering is a very sensitive process and must be handled with great discretion, because much of the time information is obtained of a personal nature that has no bearing on company business and is totally irrelevant to a pending investigation. That personal information must be discarded and in no way disseminated through normal channels or maintained in records or files of any kind. That type of information could easily be considered a violation of an individual's right to privacy and may result in an otherwise competent investigation being compromised.

Intelligence is gathered through covert penetrations and planned operations such as undercover investigators carefully planted in sensitive areas of the working force. These investigators are placed specifically to obtain information in areas where crimes are statistically out of proportion with the norm and in an effort to determine the source of the activity.

Much valuable intelligence is also gathered through the security force's everyday rapport with other employees, *if* they are sufficiently aware of the value of the information they receive and recognize its potential.

Several years ago, an investigator was eating in the employees' cafeteria of a large company with several other employees who were discussing a coworker who happened to be off sick that day. The conversation related to the coworker's sudden change of habits and temperament, along with mention of a new sports car he was seen driving to work. Because there had been recent thefts in that employee's department, as a result of that conversation he was added to the list of suspects and, in fact, did turn out to be the thief. Intelligence combined with recognition of a change in a normal pattern plus an investigator's instinct led to the solution. Not that the solution would not have been arrived at ultimately, but alertness and awareness of possible indicators of theft did speed up the process, saving more loss of property and man-hours expended on the problem.

The final source of intelligence is the informant, the individual who possesses information pertaining to a crime or potential criminal activity and who, for one reason or another, deliberately reveals this information to a security officer. Many employees feel it is their duty to pass on information of this nature, either because of loyalty to the company or a feeling of moral responsibility dictated by their own conscience. Sometimes their motives are revenge, reward, or a simple dislike for another individual. Regardless of the motive, the information should always be acted on and thoroughly investigated.

Specific security procedures can be exemplified in an examination of some of the more prevalent crime problems, the basic deterrent factors which can be established, and the investigative and follow-up procedures after an incident occurs.

EXTERNAL THREATS

Burglary

A burglary, or penetration of the premises by external elements, can only be protected against by means of a competent alarm system covering all areas of access to the building or property, combined with thorough patrol procedures on a 24-hour basis with particular emphasis on the night hours. The locking and securing of valuables, either cash, property, or company secrets, should also be accomplished whenever the valuables are not in use and under direct supervision.

Major pieces of company machinery and equipment should also be stenciled with identifying markings or numbers to aid in recovery should they be taken. This is also an excellent deterrent to theft. The fact that machinery and "other company property" is so marked should be posted on the exterior of the property along with other warning signs.

The marking or stenciling of private property, such as televisions, computers, and stereo systems, is also a good idea in apartments, condos, and single-family houses. In the residential environment, the driver's license number should be stenciled on the items. Local law enforcement agencies, who handle burglaries, find it very difficult and time consuming to obtain Social Security identifications from the federal government, whereas, driver's licenses can be obtained on their patrol car's on-board computer instantly. This time element could prove very important, because police officers may observe a suspicious individual walking down the street with a television set and wonder if its theirs. When questioned, a suspect might states that he is taking his sister's TV down the street for repair. If the set has been properly stenciled, his story can be checked immediately.

Should a burglary occur, it is most important that both the point of entry and the immediate area of the actual theft be preserved as carefully as possible for the authorities, in case they have to dust for latent prints or examine for other identifiable evidence such as pry or chisel marks.

The police, along with the insurance company, should be provided with accurate descriptions of the items taken, serial numbers, identifying marks, and photographs if the item is unusual in construction. This implies that all company property be catalogued, with identifying numbers, description, and photograph where desirable. The same would be true for private residences.

Note that the term *burglary,* as it is used in this chapter, refers to the "entering for the purpose of stealing personal or company property." In its legal definition, however, the term *burglary* extends far beyond the crime of theft and refers to the breaking into and/or otherwise entering any private property with the intent of committing *any* felony or petty theft.

Robbery

Armed robbery in a business is rare where large amounts of cash and other negotiables are not maintained on the premises. Some companies still pay their employees in cash; thus a great deal of money is readily accessible. The normal danger areas under those circumstances are the accounting office where the money is maintained, the payroll office where the money is distributed to the employees, and, of course, the time when the money is transferred from the bank to the company by armored vehicle. The safest manner to protect the cash is to keep it and distribute the payroll in an interior portion of the facility, complemented by armed personnel and outfitted with special panic alarm units to notify security control of an armed robbery in progress. Security control in turn notifies the local authorities. Even safer, of course, is to pay by check.

Retail establishments are also subject to robbery due to the fact that cash does change hands frequently during the day. Fast-food businesses, convenience stores, and small motels located within immediate proximity to a freeway are also frequent targets for robbers. The locations, near a freeway, imply an immediate and fast route for escape prior to the police arriving. Also, transients driving through the area may seize the opportunity which conveniently presents itself.

Advance planning is vital in protecting against a possible armed robbery. The employees directly involved in the cash transfer should be advised not to offer any resistance but to observe as carefully as possible for accurate details of the incident and, in particular, descriptions of the suspects. A certain amount of marked money should be maintained with the serial numbers listed so that, when an apprehension is effected, the money can be identified as being taken in the robbery. Possession of marked bills would be important evidence leading toward a conviction and full recovery.

Armed personnel should be careful not to position themselves, or to attempt to fire their weapons, in such a way as to endanger innocent company employees or other persons. Their weapons should be used only in a defensive posture, should the robbers begin harming and endangering the lives of company employees, guests, or patrons. Absolutely no firing should take place if hostages are taken. Security personnel should limit their activities to observing—particularly the description of any vehicles used in the getaway.

Industrial Espionage

Espionage activities may be conducted by a foreign element if the company is engaged in the manufacture of a product under strict military or government secrecy; however, most instances of this crime involve a competitor within the same industry.

The most frequently utilized method of learning company secrets is the placement of undercover agents whose task is to infiltrate sensitive areas of the company for the purpose of removing plans, designs, actual finished products, customer lists, bidding schedules, future product designs, or any other materials that could be utilized to the competitor's benefit. The undercover agent secures information through microphotography, document reproduction, and the actual theft of material.

Of particular concern should be the protection of computer data. Any confidential entries should require an access code, and those codes should be maintained in the strictest of confidence. When employees having access to computer data leave the company, for any reason, that entry codes should be changed. Also, the system should list those employees gaining access to confidential areas along with the date, time, and length of access.

Other methods of securing information are through burglaries, wiretapping, or the planting of electronic listening devices, and the solicitation of company employees for the purpose of paying for information.

A Case History

One of the cleverest operations by an industrial espionage agent occurred in Los Angeles about 25 years ago. A major industrial firm was engaged in the production of an item distributed on an international level. The design of new products was very carefully protected; however, the firm's major competitor, an Eastern-based firm, always seemed to produce a similar item that would appear in the retail stores shortly prior to the appearance of that of the Western company. The product was inferior, but its early marketing cut deeply into the Los Angeles company's sales potential.

An investigator hired by the Los Angeles firm had his attention drawn in the early stages of the investigation to an ad in the help-wanted section of a major Los Angeles newspaper where the advertiser was seeking designers in that particular industry. The company employee who brought this ad to the investigator's attention had no idea of its significance; however, the salary the advertiser was offering was much too high and totally unrealistic to be legitimate. Also, the ad stated that the advertiser's representative would be in the Los Angeles area for 3 days only, staying at one of the more expensive hotels, and that any interested parties should call for an appointment at that time.

Arrangements had been made for an adjoining room, and agents placed the advertiser's representative under surveillance. During the next 3 days approximately 50 percent of the Los Angeles company's designers appeared for interviews, along with other designers from other companies and several investigators hired by the Los Angeles firm. The advertiser's representative interviewed each caller very carefully and listened as they tried very hard to sell themselves in an effort to obtain the high-paying position. Their conversation included a great deal of bragging about the products they were currently designing, which the representative probed carefully and with the thoroughness of a true professional. A tape recorder took down every word, even though the "applicants" in some instances provided samples of their work through sketches and, in a couple of instances, actual blueprints taken from the company. Later interviews of the Los Angeles company's design employees produced some very red faces and terribly embarrassing moments. They did not realize they had compromised the company to the extent they did, and without exception cooperated fully in the ensuing legal action, which the advertising company lost to the tune of several million dollars. Investigators working undercover in the Eastern facility of the advertiser determined that the position described in the Los Angeles help-wanted columns did not in fact exist.

SOURCES OF INFORMATION

It is amazing how the collection of little scraps of information over a period of time can develop a total picture of a company's most carefully guarded secrets. Undercover industrial espionage agents are trained to collect such scraps of information. They periodically raid the trash, picking out notes and correspondence, secretaries' shorthand pages that have been thrown away, etc. For that reason, all paperwork should be carefully destroyed through a shredder prior to being thrown in the trash. Along with that, carbon ribbons and single use cassettes from typewriters can be removed and read like ticker tape. Typewriters using that type of ribbon should be fitted with a security lock, preventing removal of the ribbon. The actual removal should be supervised and the ribbons shredded. All paperwork and documents should be secured in locked file cabinets and safes each night and protected as previously indicated in earlier chapters. Finally, all computer terminals should require access codes for entry, and any attempt to activate a terminal should be indicated both at a manned security console and/or in the data system and this information should be reviewed daily.

Employees should be cautioned not to discuss their work with anyone, and to report to security anyone who makes a deliberate attempt to learn information of any kind regardless of how innocent it may appear.

An espionage agent employed as a secretary could easily make an extra carbon copy of a document being typed and remove the extra copy. The more clever operatives will place a new carbon paper in between a particularly sensitive piece of material and its copy, and simply place that piece of carbon paper in a pocket or purse. It is therefore strongly recommended that carbon paper be eliminated totally, replaced by NCR or similar reproducing papers where possible. It is also an easy task to make just one extra copy on the copy machine. For the above reasons, it is important to account for paper goods used and carbon paper issued. If an inordinate amount is being used by one secretary, security should be notified and the employee should be placed under surveillance to determine if he or she is in fact engaging in that activity. Also, a careful count should be maintained of copies turned out by the machine and the user held accountable. Maintaining "counts" of paper, carbon, and copies also acts as a deterrent to that activity.

WIRETAPS AND BUGS

On a regular basis, possibly as frequently as once a month, or prior to each sensitive board meeting, electronic sweeps of security areas should be conducted by a specialist in electronic countermeasures to determine if any listening devices or phone taps have been installed. This is a highly technical procedure and requires an expert in that field. The larger security forces should have someone trained in that area with the proper equipment. Smaller concerns can retain a specialist, working independently.

It is also possible to purchase equipment designed to frustrate listening devices and telephone taps when turned on during sensitive conversations. These units are on the open market and can be found advertised in any good security trade magazine. Usually the security departments will be contacted by salespersons from companies that manufacture countermeasure equipment.

SABOTAGE

An act of sabotage is any intentional and malicious damage to machinery, tools, property, or production procedures that is designed to disrupt or destroy a company's ability to produce. Sabotage is not limited to the actual destruction of property causing a mechanical breakdown, but also includes the intentional feeding of misinformation or viruses into computers, accounting procedures, bidding lists, etc.

During wartime, the most prevalent source of sabotage is enemy agents or sympathizers. It is not uncommon, however, for a business to become the target of sabotage by terrorists, competitive organizations, disgruntled employees or former employees, or mentally deranged individuals who for some reason bear a grudge against the company. Sabotage may also occur during labor disputes when emotions are running strong. In any case, sabotage is an act of extreme violence and can be disastrous to a company financially or through the loss of lives.

The primary defense against sabotage is the vigilance of the security department and the proper establishing of procedures for surveillance, access control, and liaison with law enforcement agencies. Long-term undercover operations are also valuable in this area, because they can reveal internal conditions within the workforce that might indicate emotional stress in a group or individual, which could conceivably lead to an act of sabotage. With this intelligence, the security force can increase its surveillance in that particular area.

Sabotage from external forces cannot always be predicted; therefore, the basic intrusion detection procedures, including alarms, patrols, and CCTV, along with careful access control, must be employed constantly to their fullest capability.

The mere threat of violence can be considered psychological sabotage; it builds tension, fear, and apprehension among the employees, creating low morale and stress sufficient to affect production. Bomb threats, which were discussed in Chapter 12, are included in this category.

Should an act of sabotage occur, the local authorities should be called immediately. If the company maintains a government contract, the FBI should be contacted as well. With the exception of immediate emergency measures (such as extinguishing fires, evacuation procedures, flood control, and removal of conditions or obstacles that create an immediate hazard), the area of the sabotage or attempted sabotage should be cleared and preserved for laboratory analysis by the authorities.

Many company security departments maintain a file of "crank" letters and make accurate reports of any unusual or threatening phone calls received at the facility. These files are maintained for reference and many times reveal the source of an act of sabotage, particularly if it stems from an internal problem or a mentally disturbed individual.

A particularly vicious act of sabotage was instigated several years ago by a factory employee who bore the company a long-lasting grudge over a minor wage dispute. The employee, who had suffered extreme stress and pressure stemming both from family and financial problems, irrationally blamed the employer for his troubles when he was passed over for a raise in salary. In addition, he had disputed the amount of a check from the company, believing he was entitled to more. His anger grew well out of proportion to the situation and developed into a maniacal desire to retaliate.

One evening, prior to leaving work, the disgruntled employee placed a lighted cigarette behind the last row in a book of matches and threw the matchbook into a trash container of discarded oily rags, paper, and other combustibles. When the cigarette burned down to the match heads, the matches ignited, in turn igniting the trash and causing a potentially serious fire. An employee on the next shift spotted the fire, pulled the proper alarm, then proceeded to grab the closest fire extinguisher. The employee did not check the safety seal securing the release pin on the extinguisher. He began to empty the extinguisher's contents onto the fire. Earlier, however, the saboteur had replaced the water in the extinguisher with gasoline. The resulting explosion killed the helpful employee, injured 14 others, and ultimately consumed about a third of the factory.

That tragic example illustrates not only the potential danger from internal forces such as the disgruntled employee, but also the absolute need to educate and provide proper training in fire control and its inherent safety procedures.

NARCOTICS, ALCOHOL, AND GAMBLING

The use of narcotics and consumption of alcoholic beverages have long posed problems for businesses due to their effects on the company's daily business activity, production, relations with clients and customers, and the creation of safety hazards to other employees. The use of narcotics or alcohol on the job should be prohibited.

Drug Addiction

Drug addicts are not reliable on the job, particularly if they are performing hazardous duties such as operating machinery where they could pose a danger not only to themselves but also to others. Moreover, if their need for drugs becomes great enough and extends beyond their ability to support the habit, they may turn to theft of company property in an effort to increase their income, or become susceptible to blackmail from others desiring access or information from the company. Espionage agents many times identify addicts, then use them to help in their espionage activities.

If dealers in narcotics and dangerous drugs are identified through undercover operations or other intelligence sources, they should be reported immediately to the authorities. All possible cooperation should be provided to the law enforcement agency in obtaining sufficient evidence to effect an apprehension.

Alcohol Abuse

The use of alcohol is another problem altogether. Excessive consumption of alcohol can greatly demoralize an individual and his or her coworkers, in addition to creating a work slowdown. However, an employee who suddenly develops a drinking problem is usually manifesting other underlying personal problems, which may be more serious in nature. An immediate supervisor, or possibly even a higher ranking company employee within the personnel department, should attempt to counsel the employee who has a drinking problem. It is worthwhile for the company to make an effort to salvage that

employee, who is already trained and in whom the company has a considerable investment. Possibly some financial stress can be solved with a loan from the credit union,
pension plan, or an advance in salary. It may be that all the employee needs is someone
to talk to who can offer sound, objective advice in a sympathetic atmosphere. In any
event, the result may be to instill a stronger feeling of loyalty in the employee, simply
because the employer showed genuine concern. Both the employer and the employee
may profit from the experience.

Gambling on the Job

Gambling activities within an industrial facility can also pose a problem to management, particularly if they become organized and regularly scheduled events. Not only
does gambling interfere with the normal work schedule, but it may create emotional
problems among the losers, especially when they are unable to withstand the financial
losses.

Paycheck pools, betting on football, baseball, and basketball games, and cards and
dice should all be discouraged. If undercover and intelligence sources reveal evidence
of gambling activity, security officers should enter the scene immediately, advising par-
ticipants that the activity must cease and that any further repetition will result in dismissal.

REVIEW QUESTIONS

1. As defined in this chapter, what is surveillance?
2. Discuss the problem of personal rights of privacy in the context of company intelligence gathering.
3. What are the two primary protective measures against burglary?
4. Why is it important to shred or otherwise destroy such things as carbon typewriter
ribbons, carbon paper, and shorthand notes?
5. Describe three measures of defense against industrial sabotage.

Part V

ELECTRONIC AIDS
IN SECURITY

Chapter 18

Closed-Circuit Television

The use of closed-circuit television as a tool of the security profession goes back more than 35 years. The author, who spent many years in the broadcasting industry, both in radio and the early days of television, participated in 1961 in one of the earliest applications of CCTV to premise protection. A self-contained, closed-circuit television system was developed for a large office building in Los Angeles. The basic techniques used in this successful experiment are for the most part still in use today; only the technology has improved, greatly extending the operational scope of the installations and increasing the coverage potential.

The value of CCTV for security is immeasurable. CCTV's potential has remained consistent over the years, as illustrated by the following comments published 30 years ago:

> Can you justify cost? Actual cost savings realized from installing a closed-circuit television system are due primarily to the fact that manpower can be effectively replaced by electronics.
>
> Example: In a Los Angeles commercial structure, building management required a level of security to be maintained which would have necessitated hiring at least four security guards per shift on a 24-hour schedule.
>
> Installing a closed-circuit television system, in coordination with other alarms and communications, replaced two of the officers. The two officers cost approximately $14,000 per year. The total installed system cost approximately $65,000 initially. This means that the system will pay for itself in a period of five years: Further savings in terms of losses, damage, etc., prevented by the tighter security afforded, are impossible to calculate at a fixed dollar amount, but quite likely could be greater than the initial cost of the entire system.[1]

Although the cost factors have changed over the years since the appearance of the above article, the theory still holds.

Many volumes have been written on the subject of CCTV and all of the tangent elements of the systems, circuitry, hardware, and so forth. This chapter is intended to cover only the basic elements of the equipment and suggested techniques of installation, leaving the technology to the suppliers and manufacturers of equipment along with security consultants skilled in designing the systems and specifying the equipment. Current technology utilizes computerized systems management, combined with other efforts in the alarm, access control, and communication programs as well.

LOCATING THE HARDWARE

The primary task of the security director in planning a CCTV installation is to select the proper locations for camera placement in order to provide maximum coverage of the most sensitive areas. The areas to be covered are (1) those which require continuous surveillance, (2) multiple areas which require close inspection but would prove too heavy a burden in terms of patrol activity and man-hours expended by security officers, and (3) those which require additional coverage, expanding the total protection of the premises both through the observation and deterrence value of CCTV.

Those areas most frequently selected for CCTV coverage include the following:

1. Interiors of highly sensitive areas such as file rooms or rooms containing vaults with classified materials
2. Loading docks (interior)
3. Shipping rooms
4. Stock and storage areas
5. Interior hallways that terminate at secured doors leading to the outside
6. Cashier windows and booths, or rooms containing large amounts of cash or other valuables
7. Exterior perimeters and parking areas; in particular, individual levels of parking in subterranean garages and structures
8. Exterior views of loading areas, showing trucks and loading activity
9. Any other area considered sensitive enough for constant surveillance. Various types of businesses have unique areas within their structures that require special surveillance, such as drug storage or pharmaceutical areas of hospitals, casinos, remotely activated access doors in apartment houses, etc. These specialized security concerns must be determined on an individual basis.

It is important that no camera be placed in personal areas utilized by the employees, such as locker rooms, lunchrooms, or restrooms.

The advisability of placing cameras in manufacturing sections or directly on the production line, for the purpose of personnel surveillance, is questionable. That decision must be made by weighing the actual need for such surveillance against its adverse effect on morale. Many times union contracts with companies forbid their use in production areas.

In any event, the location of the camera and its immediate environment will determine the type of camera to be purchased for that particular installation. No single camera, fitted with the same hardware and accessories, will be suitable for all situations.

CAMERA HARDWARE

Horizontal Resolution

After determining the location of the camera, the second most important factor to be considered is the degree of clarity or detail needed from the camera. This factor is known as *resolution,* and in television cameras it is measured by the number of lines of *horizontal resolution.* The image on a television monitor is actually composed of hundreds of horizontal lines. The average home television receiver has a minimum of 380 horizontal resolution lines for the older models; the newer sets vary from 650 to 800 lines. Closed-circuit television receivers also begin at that point, and increase from there—the more horizontal lines, the more detailed the picture. The better cameras will transmit more horizontal lines, and the better receivers are sensitive enough to receive those additional lines in order to preserve the clarity of the image. It should be emphasized that the more horizontal lines of resolution, the more expensive the television camera. Note also that present-day technology is such that matching the camera's resolution with that of the monitor is not as significant as it formerly was.

The degree of resolution necessary depends on the purpose of the CCTV installation. In numerous installations, for example, a CCTV system has been utilized in controlling entrance to a facility. The caller is first identified on the TV monitor, then admitted by activation of an automatic door. The installation may also be equipped with an intercom for communication with the caller. In a situation such as this, a 1000-line horizontal resolution camera may be utilized because of the high degree of detail necessary for identification purposes—not only to observe the caller, but to enable the security officer to "zoom" in to the caller's identification card or driver's license with the necessary clarity.

The same facility might have several cameras at fixed locations in hallways, on the other hand, where it is necessary only to detect movement with good, but not excellent, resolution. In those areas, minimal-line horizontal resolution cameras are perfectly satisfactory. These cameras cost only a few hundred dollars compared to $1500 for a more sensitive unit. The savings could be put to better use in other equipment.

Low Light Level Cameras

Wherever cameras are utilized on the exterior of a building, they should be fitted with *low light level* lenses. This simply means that a very small amount of light at the source will be sufficient to reproduce a normal image on the monitor screen. Low light level lens cameras are equipped with automatic apertures that open and close the lens to compensate for the light difference between day and night hours.

Low light level cameras can also be used in interior areas where coverage is needed but lights must be turned down at night to save energy. Current technology enables the cameras to automatically adjust the lens iris depending on the level of illumination available.

Motion Features

Other features available on CCTV cameras are those that effect the movement of the camera in order to select the direction, height, and specific area to be viewed.

Pan. The pan feature, by operation of a switch at the control monitor, will rotate the camera from right to left. Many units have a feature that allows the camera to pan automatically from side to side. The panning motion can be stopped if more careful examination of an area is desired.

Tilt. The tilt feature, usually operated by the same control as the pan feature, raises or lowers the lens of the camera.

Zoom. The zoom feature selectively brings distant images closer, like a telephoto lens, or reverses the operation for a more distant wide-angle image—maintaining a constant focus at all times.

All three features, used in conjunction with each other, can enable the camera to effectively scan a large area such as a parking lot.

Tamperproof Housing

Cameras, particularly those installed outdoors, should be fitted in *tamperproof* housings, eliminating the possibility of the units being intentionally put out of commission. The housings will also act as weatherproofing, providing additional protection for the camera against natural elements.

It is also recommended that the cameras be placed high—as additional protection against tampering and, more importantly, because the added height provides a better visual angle for viewing a large area.

Monitors

The appropriate size of the monitor actually depends on how many monitors are planned for the console. There are two basic approaches to monitoring. The first is to use a single monitor (or possibly two) that automatically switches from one camera location to another. Such a system normally allows the officer to hold any one view if unusual activity has been detected during the sweep, and to switch to and hold any camera location if an additional alarm indicates trouble in that particular area. When such a system is utilized, a larger screen, such as a 19-inch or 24-inch screen, should be considered.

The second monitoring approach is to use one monitor for each camera. This system is generally preferable. When an individual monitor is used for each camera location, it is possible for the officer on duty to scan and study each individual image of his or her own choosing, based on the activity being projected. The officer can still be aware, through peripheral vision, of any movement on other screens, or check other screens with a quick glance. If the one monitor for each camera is utilized, another larger screen monitor can be mounted above the lower, individual screens where any of the views may be selected to appear on the larger monitor. A VCR may be connected to the larger monitor to record any activity on that screen either automatically or by manual operation.

The use of a single monitor on a rotating sequence could allow sufficient time between successive views from one camera for some important activity to be missed. In larger installations, cameras and the monitoring systems are coordinated with the alarm activations. Thus, if an alarm is activated in an area where a closed-circuit television camera is focused, both the alarm will sound and the camera will "lock" on that view. Additionally, if so programmed, a VCR will also be activated, recording the incident.

The use of one monitor for each camera does have its limitations. Tests have provided convincing evidence that no more than 10 monitors can be scanned effectively by a single individual assigned to monitoring duty. (To achieve this rate of effectiveness, the monitors must be placed in the proper configuration, a problem discussed later in the Fatigue Factors section.) When the one-camera, one-monitor system is used, it is probably better to use smaller screens, such as a 9-inch screen, in order to avoid spreading the officer's scanning range too far. The monitor should be placed on a console, slightly below eye level. The screens of the monitors should be angled so as not to reflect the overhead light, and they should be fitted with filters, further eliminating reflection but not lowering the intensity of the light and picture on the screen.

FATIGUE FACTORS

In the very early 1960s, during the infancy days of CCTV and after it became apparent the technology was here to stay, the author placed 20 television monitors of the 9-inch size on a table where they were watched continuously by security officers. Under close observation, the officers recorded their ability to concentrate, observe, function effectively, and maintain their posts for long periods of time. The screens were fed with simulated views and situations to which the officers had to respond. The monitors were moved continuously, changing position and configuration, in an effort to find the most effective pattern.

The objective of the tests was to increase the officer's ability to function over long periods of time without undue fatigue and with greater efficiency. Based on those studies, the following are some suggestions concerning the design of the CCTV console:

1. The monitors should be placed in a curved configuration directly in front of the officer, who is seated in the center of the arc. In this arrangement, the officer's eyes are continuously equidistant from every screen. If the monitors were placed in a straight line, the officer would have to refocus her eyes continually from (as an example) 4 feet for the first screen on the left, to 2 feet for the closest screen in the middle, then back to 4 feet for the last screen on the right. Constant refocusing of the eyes causes headaches and fatigue and has an almost hypnotic effect after a period of time.

2. The officer's chair should be comfortable—one that swivels from right to left, rolls freely, allows his feet to rest comfortably on the ground, leans back on a moderate spring tension, and adjusts in height so that he can select an eye level of approximately 6 inches above the monitors.
3. The monitor screens should *not* be tilted upward, because this will catch the reflection of overhead lighting, superimposing a lighted image on the projected picture. Such reflections also cause eyestrain and are disorienting.
4. A polarized filter should be placed over the screen to further reduce reflections of light. Most of the new monitors come equipped with this feature.
5. The stacking of monitors should be avoided if possible. Rather than stack monitors, it might be preferable to use a single monitor that switches from one camera location to another, as discussed earlier.
6. Screens should be placed in a sequence providing a logical continuity with relation to the location of the cameras.
7. Officers assigned to console duty should be given additional tasks to perform, such as log entries, communications, or emergency phone call response for the purpose of calling municipal emergency services or dispatching patrol units. Keeping the officer active will increase their efficiency and eliminate the hypnotic effect created by constant staring at the screens.
8. Consideration should be given to assigning female officers to this post when possible. Tests show they function more effectively than men at this assignment.
9. Officers at this post should be rotated, for two reasons: first, to allow all personnel to become familiar with the equipment, which forms the nerve center of the entire security system; and, second, to give the officers a break in routine from what could develop into a monotonous task.

VIDEOTAPE RECORDERS

The videotape recorder, or video cassette recorder (VCR), is an extremely valuable aid in three major areas of the security operation. It can be used to preserve visual evidence for use in:

1. prosecution, when criminal activity has occurred;
2. defense, in civil litigation alleging inadequate security; and
3. arbitration, when an employee has been terminated for violation of company rules.

It is, of course, possible to have a VCR connected to each of the monitors on the console; however, this is an extremely expensive procedure. Many of the new systems have, in addition to the usual monitoring receivers (10, for example), an extra monitor of a larger screen size, mounted above the regular scanning screens. At any given time, at the operator's discretion, any one of the normal images on the 10 monitors, or the one rotating view unit, can be thrown onto the large additional unit and held. The VCR can be connected to this special screen and can be activated by the operator when any activity occurs that requires visual recorded documentation.

Another potential use of VCRs is in the area of evidence gathering. Let us assume that we know a theft or series of thefts is occurring in the loading dock area. A specially marked item is "planted" in hopes that the thieves will remove it in an unlawful and unauthorized manner. A camera and monitor equipped with a VCR can be trained on that location. The problem is that no one knows precisely when the theft will occur. An officer would have to watch that screen 24 hours a day. Even then, the theft might occur so quickly that the officer might not be able to activate the VCR in time to record the event.

Time lapse photography could be used, but it might miss the precise move desired for evidence, and it is expensive. A continuously running VCR is hard on the equipment and requires someone to review the tape each time it is changed.

The answer could be to install a 30- or 60-minute continuous *repeating* cassette in the VCR unit. Thus, every hour (or 15, 20, or 30 minutes, or whatever time element is desired), the tape repeats the circuit, erasing the preceding time element and rerecording another on the same tape. When the theft occurs, the tape will reveal the entire sequence covering the period of time necessary to establish full details of the activity.

When utilizing a repeating cassette, it is important that cassettes of sufficient length be used in order to avoid erasing a portion of the tape, which should be preserved for evidence. For example, in the situation described where planted evidence is under surveillance, if the plant is to be checked by a security officer every 45 minutes, a 1-hour repeating cassette should be used. As long as the plant remains undisturbed, the tape can simply repeat. When the officer finds the plant missing, the past hour of tape can be reviewed.

Some large cities are using this technique at major intersections, which are particularly prone to vehicle accidents. A 15-minute repeating tape cassette is attached to the system. Reports of accidents usually come much more quickly than 15 minutes. Thus, immediately upon receiving a report of a collision, the police department stops the VCR, removes the tape, and retains a full video record of the incident.

Finally, it is advisable to utilize a VCR system with the capability of showing a time and date superimposed on the video image on replay. If the tape replay is to be introduced as evidence in a court of law, proof of when the tape was obtained is important. Some state courts currently require this time–date feature (in each picture and/or picture sequence with VCR, and in each frame with 16mm motion picture film) in order for the tape or film to be admissible. Since this requirement appears to be reasonable, it seems probable that all states will have a similar provision in the future. There is no other method of ensuring that the tape was obtained at the exact time a crime or other incident occurred, except for testimony, which can always be challenged.

VCR AS A TRAINING AID

VCRs are also extremely useful as training tools. Not all security officers can be present at a training session; some will be working on their shift or absent due to illness or vacation. It is a simple matter to record a training session on videotape to be played back at the convenience of the other officers. Libraries of tape instructions can be accumulated and used for new personnel as they are hired.

For example, a videotape could be made of a security officer as he moves through his rounds in a facility, showing all the proper procedures to be followed on that particular tour. The tape can then be played for all new officers working that patrol.

REVIEW QUESTIONS

1. What is the primary long-term economic advantage of CCTV?
2. Give five examples of areas where CCTV might be used effectively and efficiently for security purposes.
3. Give an example of a situation where (a) a TV camera with average horizontal resolution would be satisfactory and (b) where a high-resolution camera would be desirable.
4. What is the major advantage of a television console providing one monitor for each camera? What is a disadvantage?
5. What is VCR? Give an example of its use in security surveillance.

NOTES

1. David Berger, "Watch It!" *Buildings, The Construction and Building Management Journal* (September, 1968), p. 87.

Chapter 19

Communications Systems

Communications are vital to any organizational function; they are crucial to a function that must frequently deal with emergencies and other threats requiring a swift, coordinated response at any hour of the day or night. In addition, security's protective role requires extensive reporting and record keeping.

Communications are usually divided into two categories: written and oral. Written communications were discussed in Chapter 4 in the sections on Forms and Report Writing. Effective oral communications require knowledge of the methods of transmitting, the facilities available and their limitations, and plans for their use.

ADVANTAGES OF TWO-WAY RADIO

The two-way radio, in particular, the miniaturized walkie-talkie or handheld radio unit, is the security officer's most convenient tool while on field duty. It provides immediate communications directly from a problem area, quicker and more accurate response to emergency situations, and a manner by which directions can be given and executed in all situations where time is of the essence.

Every officer assigned to patrol duty, whether inside or on the exterior of the premises, should be equipped with a walkie-talkie. Additionally there should be a base station at the main security control dispatch station, with remote facilities located wherever dispatching or response might be necessary, such as at the fixed post locations.

Various systems of radio frequencies are currently in use. Based on the potential limitations, and relative cost of each, it is up to the individual security department to determine which system should be utilized.

TYPES OF SYSTEMS

Citizens Band

The citizens band (CB) frequencies currently operate on 40 channels. About the only advantage of the CB system is its cost; units can be purchased for as little as $30. The primary disadvantage of the system is "overcrowding" of the frequencies by literally millions of people, ranging from truckdrivers to preteenage children playing with the new 100-milliwatt handie-talkie Uncle George got them for Christmas. Most of the users are unlicensed and untraceable individuals with no regard for the manner in which the system is used.

CB systems broadcast on a very low frequency, resulting in a limited "line-of-sight" transmission with very little, if any, ability to penetrate solid objects such as buildings. The Federal Communication Commission (FCC) has limited the power of the units to 5 watts; unlicensed users, however, operate pirate stations with as much as 100 watts, interfering with the frequencies to such an extent that it is virtually impossible for a legally licensed operation to maintain effective transmission.

FCC regulations state that the CB radio cannot be used as a commercial enterprise and can be used only for limited business purposes.

Note, however, that CB may very well be applicable for a security department with a limited budget if its facilities are located in outlying communities where smaller populations do not overcrowd the CB frequencies and where building structures are not dense enough to inhibit the transmission. CB is better than nothing at all.

Low-Band FM

The 30- to 50-MHz range is a low-band frequency-modulated (FM) system. The average transmitter usually operates at around 60 watts. This system is rated fair for mobile use (base to car, car to car). For security purposes it is not normally used by in-house guard forces, however, because walkie-talkies are difficult to obtain on this frequency. The units are too big and the antennas too long to be carried on patrol practicably. Remember that, basically, the lower the frequency, the longer the antenna necessary both to receive and transmit on that frequency. The low-band FM system has only moderate range, providing the transmitter tower and main antenna are placed high enough. Penetration is only fair. This system is utilized primarily in mobile units and would probably be ideal for a private patrol company operating in a limited area or a small town.

Because of its low frequency, the system is also subject to skip conditions, which at times interfere greatly with emergency communications. *Skip* is a term used for radio transmissions that, although normally out of range of the company's receiver, may be received at times as clearly as one of the company's mobile units a block away. The condition is caused by sunspots or atmospheric conditions, causing transmissions from hundreds of miles away to bounce off the ionosphere and be deflected great distances. A mobile unit in Los Angeles once responded to a fire emergency at a certain address on 6th Street, only to learn that the call emanated from a private patrol station in Ann Arbor, Michigan. The Michigan dispatcher thought it was his unit answering the call when the Los Angeles unit responded.

High-Band FM

The high-band frequencies in the 150-MHz ranges are probably the most widely used in the security industry. The units have excellent range, and good power is available for transmission. Walkie-talkies are miniaturized with loaded antennas of only about 1 to 6 inches. Penetration is good, but subject to limited interference.

Like all radio frequencies available for business use, high-band FM frequencies are shared with other users. In large metropolitan areas, the frequencies are becoming congested with users including taxicab companies, trash pickup trucks, and construction firms. Most of the major communications manufacturers equip their units with a special automatic and coded squelching circuit that prevents the "voice transmission" of other stations from being heard on the units. This feature (called *PL*) does not eliminate the other station's "signal" (RF), however, and if another station sufficiently powerful or very nearby is transmitting at the same time, the effect is still to block out communications. With congestion of the frequencies, this could happen frequently, particularly if the security department is operating from a base station with master transmitter and external antenna. The interference would not be so great simply from walkie-talkie to walkie-talkie.

The most current technology has expanded the available frequencies and created circuits that greatly limit interference from other stations, but there are still enough of the older units in circulation that the above critique has been retained in this chapter for reference.

Equipment is available with sufficient sensitivity to eliminate the interference; however, the user should expect to pay about $200 to $900 per unit. In electronics, especially, the old adage holds true: You get what you pay for.

The high-band FM station is the most practical, durable, and efficient that can be used by a security department. Unless special penetration problems exist, such as high-rise construction (30 or 40 floors or more), several underground levels such as parking structures, or high-density steel and concrete construction with possibly some leaded areas, the high-band FM frequencies would be the most functional on which to operate.

Ultra High Frequency

The ultra high frequency (UHF) bands, operating around 450 MHz and above, are extremely functional and contain probably the most efficient channels available. It is particularly necessary to go to the UHF band when structural considerations require heavy penetration. The range is greater and the units are usually constructed more efficiently and are smaller in size. They are only a little more expensive than the high-band FM systems.

Cellular Telephone Combinations

Combination units are currently being marketed that are comprised of a two-way radio and cellular telephone. These units are especially effective for security officers working either alone or with a second officer in a small complex such as a shopping mall or residential area. The cellular telephone number is used by the residents, or store owners, to summon the officers, plus the officers may still maintain contact between themselves.

POWER

The base stations of all of the units just discussed operate on normal 110-volt power. The walkie-talkies operate on batteries of varying voltage. Two power considerations are very important in planning the purchase of a system. First, rechargeable nickel-cadmium batteries should be used. This saves the cost and storage problems of normal batteries. When nickel-cadmium batteries are used, the walkie-talkies normally come with recharging stands. When finished with the radio, each shift places the unit in the charging stand so that it will be fully charged and ready the next time that shift comes on duty. It normally takes approximately 16 hours to recharge a unit; therefore, sufficient extra batteries or units should be purchased to enable use during one shift while the other shifts' batteries are charging.

The second important consideration is to establish a regular charging *schedule* for the batteries, ensuring each battery sufficient time to be fully charged for use. In this way, the batteries will last longer and provide more constant power to operate the units. When properly drained and recharged, a nickel-cadmium battery should last 2 years or more.

A good system of battery charging would be as follows. Assume there are 12 units in the field—4 per shift. Basically, only 4 radios are required, with 12 batteries. The batteries can be color-coded for each shift: *red* for days (8 A.M. to 4 P.M.), *green* for nights (4 P.M. to 12 midnight), and y*ellow* for mornings (12 midnight to 8 A.M.). Within each color, the batteries can be numbered 1 through 4. It is then easy for each shift to use its own battery—leaving it in the charger for a full 16 hours while that shift is off duty. The radios, too, should be numbered 1 through 4.

It is also wise to retain an extra battery or two, as well as a couple of extra walkie-talkies, for emergency use in case one of the primary units requires repair or additional units must be issued for one reason or another. Note also that there are "quick charge" battery chargers that can replenish the battery in 0.5 to 2 hours. Tests show, however, that the long charge does extend the life of the battery and is more efficient with regard to the time the battery will last between charges.

RADIO PROCEDURE

Voice communications by radio should be maintained in a formal and concise manner. Proper transmission procedures are necessary for clarity; in addition, the radio user never knows whether other persons may be monitoring the transmissions, either utilizing another receiver tuned to that frequency, or merely standing near an officer with a unit. The security department's radio transmissions should reflect at all times the organization's professionalism.

Coding of messages has two purposes: (1) to enable the message to be brief, to facilitate understanding under emergency situations where speed is essential, or when static and other interference may garble a long detailed message; and (2) to create some degree of confidentiality from those persons, unfamiliar with radio procedure, who just happen to tune in on the frequency and are curious regarding the communications.

The standard, international ten-code is utilized by most security and law enforcement agencies. It is designed to transmit numbers that represent various phrases and can be easily understood even under conditions of moderate radio interference. That portion of the ten-code that is normally utilized by security and law enforcement agencies is reproduced here.

10-1	Reception is poor.
10-2	Reception is good.
10-3	Stop transmitting.
10-4	General acknowledgment.
10-5	Relay (also used to indicate a stake-out).
10-6	Station is busy.
10-7	Out of service.
10-8	In service.
10-9	Repeat last transmission.
10-10	Out of service. Radio still on.
10-13	Advise weather and/or road conditions.
10-14	Convoy or escort detail.
10-15	En route to jail with prisoner.
10-16	Pick up papers.
10-17	Pick up prisoner.
10-19	Go to office (or communications desk).
10-20	Location.
10-21	Phone office.
10-22	Cancel last message.
10-23	Stand by.
10-24	Trouble at station.
10-28	Check for full information on vehicle or subject.
10-29	Check for "wants" on vehicle or subject.
10-33	Emergency traffic on air.
10-34	Clearance for emergency traffic.
10-35	Confidential information.
10-36	Correct time.
10-47	Go to location.
10-87	Meet officer or unit.
10-97	Arriving at location of call.
10-98	Last detail completed.
10-99	Emergency—all units copy.

The ten-code is adaptable to individual situations. There are also sufficient numbers not in use that can be added to indicate any meaning or message that may be unique to the company's circumstances.

The alphabet should be used phonetically in radio transmissions in order to avoid any misunderstanding of the proper letter. The armed forces utilize a phonetic alphabet that has never been adopted by local authorities, in order to make a differentiation between civil and military transmissions. A simple phonetic alphabet follows.

Adam	Nora
Boy	Ocean
Charles	Paul
David	Queen
Edward	Robert
Frank	Sugar
George	Tom
Henry	Union
Ida	Victor
John	William
King	X-ray
Lincoln	Young
Mary	Zebra

Utilizing the above code, it is virtually impossible to mistake one letter for another; whereas, for example, D and T might easily be mistaken for each other under adverse transmission conditions where there is static or a very weak signal.

STATION CALL SIGNS

The base station will be identified by a series of call letters and numbers that are assigned by the FCC at the time the station license is issued. It is proper to use those call signs either at the conclusion of every conversation or transmission by the main base station or at least every hour, on the hour.

Each permanent station should have a determining unit call identification. The main base station should be identified as "security control" or "base one," or some other similar identifying title. Each other permanent unit, such as stations at the employees' entrance and fixed posts, should also be identified as "control two," "base three," etc. Each officer carrying a walkie-talkie should also have an individual identification. This can be done in one of two ways: either numbering the unit by virtue of the assignment, such as "patrol one" (where "one" indicates patrol route number one), or assigning a permanent number to the individual officer, such as his or her badge number, time card number, or employee's ID number. Either system is satisfactory, depending on the individual circumstances.

INTERCOMS

The security department should be aware that radio transmissions are always subject to monitoring by individuals who know the proper frequency. The motives of such persons are unknown; they may have improper or criminal intentions. For that reason, each permanent station should also be equipped with an intercom station, with slave stations at other sensitive areas of the company. Intercoms should be in the main office, communications center, file room, permanent posts, etc. They should be utilized for normal and confidential traffic that is intended to be received at a specific location only, where it is not necessary to go on the air for all units to receive the message.

Intercom units are also very valuable when located at each CCTV camera location. These units should be installed utilizing a loudspeaker unit capable of picking up sound from a distance of several feet. The unit should be activated from the security console; in that manner, the console operator can challenge an individual observed on camera, carry on a conversation with him, give proper directions, etc. A unit of this type is necessary in a smaller installation where a single officer at a central control station is monitoring entrances and exits during night shifts when the staff is down to minimum personnel. The operator can observe an individual approach a door, speak with him as well as observe him on the TV monitor, then open the door with a remote door-opening switch once proper identification is made.

PAGING SYSTEMS

Many plants will be equipped with paging systems, music systems, or a combination of both. The security department can make excellent use of this system for announcements in emergency situations, particularly where evacuation is necessary.

The location of the main amplifier should be known to the security department or, preferably, should be within the security office facilities. Immediately accessible to the amplifier there should be prepared scripts to be read by a security officer in case of emergency—or, better yet, prerecorded cassette tapes with instructions for the emergency. The tapes should be of the repeating type, which continuously broadcast the message in a clear, short, simple manner. The announcer's calm tone and the fact that a "plan" is in operation and leadership is displayed will greatly deter panic and encourage calm, prompt action by employees.

COMPUTERS

Finally, if the company is equipped with a computer system with terminals located throughout the facility, these units too may be utilized as a communication system simply by typing messages on the screen. Obviously, the computers may also be used to prepare reports and transmit emergency orders or warnings, all of which can instantly be filed and maintained for future retrieval as documentation.

CONCLUSION

A good communications system is a must for any security department. Technical specifications of equipment are beyond the scope of this text; this chapter has described briefly what is available, along with some limitations. It is up to the security department to determine its needs, environmental limitations, and available budget prior to making the proper selection of equipment. When the budget for communications equipment is being planned, remember that equipment of good quality will last for years; units of poor quality will give nothing but trouble and will fail when needed most.

REVIEW QUESTIONS

1. Is CB radio a good choice for security use? Explain.
2. What is generally the best choice for security communications: (a) low-band FM, (b) high-band FM, or (c) ultra high frequency?
3. In what circumstances would a UHF system be the best choice?
4. Give two reasons for using coded radio transmissions in security communications.
5. What is one advantage of an intercom system over radio transmission in an industrial facility?

Chapter 20

Alarms

An alarm is essentially an emergency notification of a condition or special situation that requires immediate attention and response. Nomadic tribes, whether in the Arabian desert or the American plains, kept dogs around the fringes of their camps to raise a clamor of warning against attack. In the modern industrial setting, mechanical or electronic alarm systems perform a similar function, warning of such diverse conditions as intrusion, fire, malfunction of equipment, or changes in the temperature or humidity of carefully controlled environments.

Alarm systems differ in the types of sensors used to detect the emergency condition, and in the methods used to transmit, receive, and annunciate the alarm signal. Any and all types of alarms may sound a warning at the location of the problem or transmit the message to another location, such as a security control center or central station.

Fire alarm systems were discussed at length in Chapter 11. Special use alarms that monitor machinery and equipment, or environmental conditions, are more properly considered as production and safety aids than as security devices. These may, however, be tied into a master console monitored by security, and in any event may involve security in the response. An alarm warning of the presence of toxic fumes, for example, may call for evacuation procedures and emergency access controls.

In this chapter, then, we are concerned specifically with intrusion alarms: systems that give warning of unauthorized entry of persons into a monitored location. (Intrusion alarms will react as readily to the *exit* of anyone through a protected area or barrier, such as the "hide-in" burglar whose presence is not detected until he is leaving with his stolen goods. For the purposes of discussion, however, intrusion alarms can be considered primarily as entry-detection devices.)

BASICS OF ALARM SYSTEMS

In any alarm system there are three fundamental elements:

1. The *sensor,* which is a means of detecting an alarm condition and triggering a signal
2. The *control unit,* which supervises the alarm circuitry and transmits the signal
3. The *annunciator,* which may be audible or silent, local or remote, depending on the application.

Sensors do exactly what the name implies. Mechanically or electrically, they function like human senses to detect intrusion by means of feeling (contact switches, pressure mats, taut wire detectors), sound (vibration and audio detectors), or sight ("seeing" the intruder by means of light beams, sound waves, microwaves, electromagnetic fields, etc.).

The control unit is the local brain of the system. It receives the first notification of the alarm condition from the sensor, sometimes interprets that condition to determine that the alarm is genuine, and either activates a local alarm or transmits the signal to a remote receiving station, on or off the premises. The control unit may also control the power to the system. In many situations one control unit may supervise a number of alarm circuits, and it may also perform other functions, such as automatically locking or unlocking doors and gates or activating closed-circuit television systems with a VCR capacity.

The third element of the system causes a bell to ring, a light to flash, dials a phone, or in some other manner "announces" the alarm, alerting a human response.

TYPES OF INTRUSION SENSORS

Circuit Breakers

One of the most widely used and simplest alarm systems for access control employs *contact switches* as the sensors. These magnetic or contact circuit breakers are attached to doors and windows and, when the system is turned on, become part of a continuous wired alarm circuit, or "loop." When the circuit or loop of DC power is broken, such as by a door opening or a window being broken, the alarm sequence is activated. These basic alarm circuits can be "open" or "closed," although the normally open circuit is not widely used in alarm applications because it is so easily defeated.

Figure 20.1 illustrates a simple open circuit. The open switch represents the sensors in the alarm system. When the switch is closed electricity is able to flow through

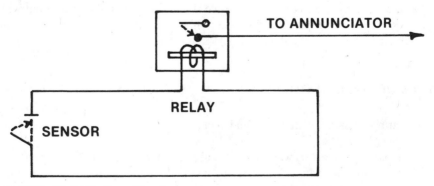

Figure 20.1   Normally Open Circuit

the circuit in a complete loop. The flow of electricity energizes the relay, triggering the relay switch and causing an alarm signal to be transmitted. The fundamental weakness of such an open circuit is that, being normally open, it can be cut at any point along the circuit without the break being detected. For this reason it is called an *unsupervised* circuit.

Most alarm circuits use the closed-circuit principle, a simplified form of which is shown in Figure 20.2. In this example, door contact switches are the sensors. These switches are actually small magnets. One is attached to the door jamb, the other to the door panel in a typical installation. With the door closed, the magnets are close enough to attract each other when the alarm system is turned on, the magnetic field acting as a continuous flow of energy to complete the circuit. The relay is thus continuously energized when the system is activated. When the alarmed door is opened, separating the magnetic switches, the circuit is broken. The relay switch (working in reverse of the previous illustration) is triggered when the relay is de-energized.

A closed circuit is said to be *supervised,* because it cannot be cut or interfered with without causing an alarm. The switches, however, can be shorted out or "jumpered" by a knowledgeable attacker, so this type of alarm cannot be said to provide the ultimate security. In the business setting, contact devices are a very common alarm application. They can provide effective auxiliary protection in a carefully planned and integrated system.

In some systems each breaker is wired independently, and the exact location of the break is recorded at either the central alarm station or security console. Many of the older types of alarm systems which employ the loop principle still form a total circuit of the entire building; they can determine only that the building has been penetrated, not the exact location.

The circuit breaker is generally utilized on the outside perimeter of the building, at normal points of access such as doors and windows, but these sensors can also be used on specific security areas of the interior, or on the doors of safes and vaults.

In addition to magnetic switches, *foil tape* can be applied to windows and doors near the edges, creating either a magnetic field or simply a continuous single connection forming a loop. When this field, or loop, is broken by an intruder, the alarm is activated.

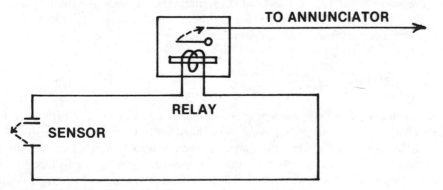

Figure 20.2   Normally Closed Circuit

Windows may also be fitted with *screens* that are, in effect, continuous carriers of energy (low voltage electrical or magnetic). Any breakage or penetration of this field will activate the alarm.

Single or multiple strands of *taut wire* can be stretched across openings of doors, windows, or hallways. When the wires are tripped by an intruder's body, the circuit is broken and the alarm activated. Taut wire detection systems are also an effective and low-cost form of outdoor perimeter protection. Here the wire is strung along the top of the fence or wall at a precisely measured tension. Any change in this tension—from being cut, direct pressure of an intruder's hand or body, or even movement in the fence itself—will touch off the alarm.

Vibration Detectors

The walls, floors, and ceilings of buildings, as well as perimeter barriers, can be fitted with extremely sensitive "contact" microphones as sensors. Any vibration resulting from an attempt to penetrate the barrier will be picked up by the microphones and an alarm signal transmitted. Vibration detectors are also used to protect security containers, such as safes and vaults.

Pressure-Sensitive Activators

Pressure-sensitive sensors in their most common application are planted under carpeting or padding, such as on a stairway or just inside of a doorway, and respond to the weight of a person stepping on them. They have two purposes: first, to be activated during night hours or at other times when no passage is intended in that area; and second, to be placed in an area where notification of a person entering is desired in order to have someone meet or attend to the visitor. This type of device is frequently installed in private residences for nighttime protection, and in retail establishments where the shopkeeper (who may be alone in the shop or in a position where he cannot monitor the entrance) wants to know when a customer enters.

Pressure sensors are also used in some industrial settings as a part of outdoor perimeter protection. Here the sensors are buried underground, usually inside the perimeter fence, and react to the weight of an intruder walking over them.

Motion Detectors

Motion detectors are rapidly becoming one of the dominant types of alarm system sensors. These are most commonly used in confined areas where no person should be present during the period when the alarm has been activated. Warehouses and storage areas are often protected by motion detection systems. They are especially effective in a room, which requires extreme protection because of the presence of high value or classified material in the area. Confidential file rooms, experimental laboratories, and vault interiors are examples of extremely sensitive areas where movement in any part of the room—-not only at the doors or windows—must be detected.

Ultrasonic alarm systems detect motion by impregnating an area with an extremely high frequency sound. The sound leaves a transmitter and returns after "bouncing" off a target of a given range. The distance of the sound's transmission and return is constant. Any solid body, which suddenly enters the field, changes the distance; the sound will then deflect back to the transmitter from the intruding object. The change in the constant flow of sound creates a "shift" in frequency, triggering the alarm. The principle is known in physics as the *Doppler effect,* named after its discoverer who initially applied the principle to light in the early 1800s. Alarm manufacturers refer to the phenomenon as the *Doppler shift.*

The *radar motion detector* operates on basically the same principle as the ultrasonic detector; however, the radar device emits energy consisting of a radio frequency. This unit measures the time required for an echo of the transmission to return to the origin of the transmission. Any change in the timing indicates a presence and triggers the alarm.

Microwave systems are also used to detect motion. Instead of high-frequency sound or radio energy, high frequency electromagnetic energy is utilized within the wavelength range from 50cm to 1mm. Here again, any body intruding within the impregnated area causes a shift in frequency, activating the alarm sequence. Devices on the market today protect areas as large as 100 feet long by 50 feet wide.

The motion detector systems described are called *active* motion detectors because they work by transmitting energy of one kind or another and measuring any change in that pattern. Two other systems are called *passive* motion detectors. These monitor not the energy they create but energy produced by an intruding body. *Infrared detectors* are able to sense the presence of an intruder by reacting to body heat. *Audio detectors* monitor the sounds made by an intruder in areas where such sounds should not be present. In addition to sending an alarm signal when strange noises are picked up, some audio systems also have a "listen-in capability," enabling a guard at a monitor panel, for instance, to continue listening for sounds of activity after being alerted by the first alarm.

A number of other sophisticated motion detection systems are in use for outdoor perimeter applications, usually in the zone just inside the fence or wall. These were discussed in Chapter 15.

Photoelectric Beams

The photoelectric alarm system utilizes a beam of visible or invisible ultraviolet filtered light traversing a specific area, such as across a doorway or in front of a safe or vault. When the beam is broken by a solid body or other object, the alarm is activated. The applications of this system in an industrial facility are limited; in fact, the photoelectric beam is primarily utilized in retail stores to announce the presence of a customer or to open doors automatically. Laser light is also utilized in the more sophisticated "beam" activators.

CAPACITANCE ALARMS

Specific objects to be protected against attack, such as safes, file cabinets, or vaults, can be equipped with a capacitance detector. This device emits an electromagnetic field of energy, usually extending over an area only a few inches from the protected object. Any solid body entering the field will activate the alarm.

This type of alarm permits employees in the general area to continue their normal routine and still provide protection for the object. In these circumstances the object must be clearly identified as being alarmed, in order to avoid accidental penetration of the energy field and resulting false alarms. Warning signs should indicate the extent of the protected area.

ALARM TRANSMISSION AND RESPONSE SYSTEMS

An alarm system, whether intrusion or fire, can be programmed to ring a loud bell or siren at the location of the problem, or to transmit the warning signal to another location. The latter is called a "silent" alarm because the annunciator is located away from the point of alarm and is inaudible to the intruder. The remote warning of an alarm condition may be a buzzer, a flashing light, a reading on a meter, or even a digital printout. Current technology utilizes computers to integrate alarms with other online security systems.

Under the conditions of fire, it is understandable that immediate notice must be given to surrounding personnel in the form of a local alarm, even though the signal may also be transmitted to a remote monitor. With intrusion, however, a choice must be made: Is it more advantageous to attempt to frighten away the intruder by a loud bell or siren, or to install a silent alarm (terminating at either central station or security console) and try to apprehend the intruder? The object of a local alarm, obviously, is not to catch the criminal but to scare him off. It is also possible to retain both silent and audible notification simultaneously.

Cost will be one consideration. A local bell, tone, or siren is the simplest and least expensive alarm system. Unless there is someone on the premises at all times, however, a local alarm is the least dependable in terms of response. All too often an alarm will be set off and the only one to pay any attention will be the intruder. A prime example of this is the vehicle alarm. There are so many . . . and they are activated so frequently that not many passersby pay any attention anymore. The local alarm could be effective in an area of single-family residences, where neighbors are sensitive to the neighborhood problems, especially where a *neighborhood watch* program has been organized.

The decision should also take into account the predictable response time of the emergency service involved. If the normal response time to the local police department, for example, assessed through statistical studies in the community, indicates that they will arrive in sufficient time to prevent the intruders from completing their entry and escaping, then the silent alarm system should be utilized. If not, a combination of silent and audible alarm signals should be considered.

If a "ringer" or siren is installed, it should be placed high and inaccessible enough to prevent tampering. It is not necessary for the intruder to disconnect the wiring or penetrate the sound-box. Many burglars come prepared with a large box, slightly larger than most alarm boxes, lined with heavy soundproof material. When this soundproofed box is placed over the alarm case, it muffles the sound sufficiently to render the alarm ineffective.

It may be more appropriate to place the sounding box inside the structure, against a high exterior vent. Even then the vent can be blocked, but the potential burglar would not easily be able to identify the location of the sounding device.

TELEPHONE DIALERS

In lieu of or in addition to a local alarm, alarm systems can be set up to dial a predetermined telephone number (or numbers) and to deliver a tape-recorded message. This system has the advantage of making use of ordinary telephone lines. A potential problem, however, is that the line or lines may be in use and the emergency call will not get through promptly. More sophisticated dialing systems use a digital dialer rather than a tape recording system.

The certainty of response is the primary concern with dialing systems. If the emergency call is made to the home of the plant owner or manager, for example, he may not be at home or his teenager may be using the phone. Problems also arise where the programmed telephone number is that of the police department. False alarm problems have made this practice unpopular, and in many jurisdictions dialers programmed to call the police directly have been prohibited.

OFF-PREMISE ALARM NOTIFICATION

For the smaller business or industrial facility where the company closes during night-time hours or does not maintain a 24-hour security system on the premises, contract alarm companies or private patrol services can be used to maintain alarm systems. These services charge the client a monthly fee plus installation costs for the equipment utilized.

When an alarm sensor on the company's property is activated, notification is received at the alarm company. A private patrolman or alarm company serviceman is dispatched to the premises and the proper authorities (police or fire services, depending on the emergency) are alerted. In addition, the alarm company should be instructed to notify a company executive of the situation.

The alarms installed on the company's premises are connected to the company either by private wired installation or by leased telephone lines. The system is normally protected against simple cutting of the wires by circuitry that will activate the alarm if the wires are tampered with.

In some smaller communities, it is still possible to arrange for the alarms to terminate directly at the local police or fire department. In larger cities, however, there are usually local, city, or county ordinances forbidding the practice. Such ordinances have been enacted (as with the prohibition of telephone dialers) in response to an excessive false alarm rate. In recent years, many cities have passed ordinances requiring special equipment and inspections of alarm companies' equipment to ensure that the false alarm rate will be kept at a minimum. Also, fines are levied after a given amount of false alarms. An alternative is a backup system to ensure the validity of the alarm prior to notification of the authorities.

It would be wise for a business to utilize the services of a *central station alarm* service, which indicates that the alarm company has met rigid standards established by the Federal government and/or the state. Such standards require U.L.-approved equipment and extraordinary building structural provisions for protection of wiring, records, and personnel against fire, intrusion, and other natural or man-made disasters such as earthquake or sabotage.

PROPRIETARY ALARM SYSTEMS

In proprietary alarm systems, the alarm signal is received at an alarm panel within the protected facility's property. If a proprietary system is utilized, the company should be large enough to maintain a security department on duty 24 hours a day, with three or more officers on each shift, and with constant monitoring of a security console or central control panel.

The location of the security console or control panel should be protected against intrusion and fire. The security officer on duty at that location should have, *at all times,* sufficient means at his disposal to communicate with the proper authorities (police, fire department, etc.) and/or adequate personnel to handle an emergency within the premises.

SECURITY CONSOLE

When a complete in-house alarm system is installed, it is important that the alarm panel at the console or security control center be "consistent" by virtue of geography. As in CCTV monitor placement (see Chapter 18), there should be continuity in the arrangement of light indicators on the panel. In other words, those lights, which represent alarm sensors actually located to the console operator's right, should be on the right-hand side of the panel. Those indicating trouble to the left of the operator should be on the left-hand side of the panel.

Many designs are now proving to be more efficient than the solid panel installation. Some consoles incorporate a large floor plan with lights actually spotted on the map in the location of the alarm which has been triggered. Intrusion alarms utilize blue bulbs; fire, red bulbs. Not only does this make it easier to dispatch an officer to the right location, without having to look up the exact area on a key sheet, but the display gives the operator an overview of the situation at a glance, including graphic illustrations of escape routes for evacuation, most direct routes for dispatching, and so on.

The computer systems indicate locations of activations on the monitor, along with instructions for approaching the area, emergency telephone numbers, and/or company personnel to be notified, along with any other information programmed into the system.

ALARM APPLICATIONS

Having a variety of sophisticated alarm equipment available does not automatically solve a security director's problems. In fact, it may compound them, making more difficult the selection of the right system, one that will be functional under any given set of circumstances. As with all security hardware, alarm equipment must be chosen on the basis of particular need—*not* because an alarm salesperson speaks eloquently of a system in glowing terms, or because it is the most elaborate and sophisticated on the market. You may not need a sophisticated alarm system.

How important is it to detect entry to the facility at the outer perimeter? If this is to receive priority, consideration should be given to alarm sensors located both on and inside the barrier. On the other hand, if the decision is to accept the presence of a fence and effective security lighting as adequate to delay and discourage a potential intruder, electronic protection may be used more effectively elsewhere. Moving inward from the perimeter, the next point of deterrence would probably be the access points of buildings, including regular entrances and emergency doors, windows, and skylights. And where there is high-value storage inside, interior space alarms may be advisable.

A completely integrated system, of course, can and often will use several types of sensors complementing each other. Taut-wire and infrared field sensors may guard the perimeter against intrusion. Contact switches and foil tape may detect unauthorized entry through doors or windows. And an ultrasonic or other space or motion detection alarm may detect and warn of movement in enclosed areas. The potential frequency of attack, the value of property being protected, and the cost of the alarm system will all be part of the equation that determines how much or how little protection is enough. The presence of other deterrents is also a factor; a 24-hour security force able to man all entry points might make an electronic warning system unnecessary.

Even when preliminary decisions have been made as to the need for particular kinds of intrusion alarm protection, there are other considerations. A variety of local conditions can give rise to problems, depending on the type of alarm to be used. Heat changes, humidity, electrical storms, thunderstorms, rodents or larger animals running through the field, the proximity of railroad tracks—all might be sources of false alarms.

Natural effects can trigger an ultrasonic unit, as opposed to the unauthorized intrusion it was designed to detect. Forced air from a heating duct has been known to activate an ultrasonic alarm; normal sounds from inside or outside the area, such as telephones ringing, can also be a problem. Noises and air movement will not affect a microwave system, but the waves are capable of penetrating many structures, including glass and many walls and doors. In these circumstances the system may react to movement *outside* the protected area. Similarly, audio systems may be upset by a passing train, thunder, or other natural sounds.

All of these sensors can be adjusted to be more or less discriminatory. The point is that great care must be taken both in the selection and installation of the system to reduce the probability of false alarms while retaining an adequate capability to detect real intrusion.

ALARM RESPONSE

Another vital factor in alarm system application is the type of response. If the annunciator is a local bell, who will hear it at three o'clock in the morning? If a telephone dialing system terminates at an answering service, a small private patrol service, or the plant owner's home, what is the predictable response time?

Even a central station alarm service can be highly variable in both response time and the nature of that response. Does the alarm service send its own personnel immediately to the scene when an alarm signal is received? Are plant personnel or management notified? Are the police also alerted? Where is the central station located in relation to the particular facility? Such services are "central" in relation to many clients. Obviously, they are not as close to some as they are to others. Finally, it should be recognized, not all such services are equally efficient.

An alarm system is no better or worse than the weakest of its components. The right system must make use of the appropriate sensors, it must make an effective choice between local or remote annunciation of the alarm, and it must produce a prompt and adequate response.

INSTALLATION AND SERVICE

Current technology has developed alarms that are totally wireless. Each activator on windows and doors, along with motion detection units, contains a small battery that can operate for several years before weakening to a point where it requires changing. There is, therefore, no wiring between the activator and the annunciator. A *signal* is transmitted between the two points initiating the alarm. Additionally, these systems are computerized and can be integrated with a company's main computer.

It must finally be said that a great many alarm systems look good "on paper," and even in their initial installation, but before many weeks go by they are subverted in their purpose for one reason or another. The problem may simply be mechanical, either through poor installation, defective equipment, or carelessness on the part of the user. Window foil is commonly found broken. Contact switches on a door may actually fail to make contact properly. An emergency exit that is supposed to be on alarm 24 hours a day may actually be propped open for extra ventilation or as a convenience to employees who want to go in and out; the alarm, clearly, must then be ringing all the time or shut off. User error, either in false activation of an alarm or failure to turn the system on at the right times, is also common.

If an alarm system is installed in any business or company facility, it should be subject to a regular program of testing and checking. This is most easily accomplished with a proprietary system, but if an outside service is used, proper testing and maintenance should be carried out as part of a regular, planned program.

REVIEW QUESTIONS

1. What are the three fundamental elements of an alarm system and what is the function of each?
2. What is meant by the expression *unsupervised* or *supervised* circuit?
3. Give an example of an industrial security application for each of the following: foil tape, pressure mat, taut-wire detector, ultrasonic alarm, vibration detector, capacitance alarm.
4. What is the *Doppler shift*?
5. Discuss the relative merits of using a local bell or silent alarm in intrusion detection.
6. What potential problems are associated with the use of telephone dialers?
7. Which is preferable for an industrial situation, (a) a direct-dial alarm system to a private patrol service or (b) a central station alarm service? Why?
8. What is meant by a proprietary alarm system?
9. Give an example of a potential cause of false alarms in each of the following types of alarm systems: ultrasonic, microwave, audio.

Chapter 21

Automatic Access Control

Although modern technology has developed the computer to accommodate security's needs regarding access control to company property, the author, who was involved with early development of the computerized systems, has experienced serious problems when the computer was "down." For example, one time an event occurred during the swing shift and the officers on duty, who were thoroughly familiar with the system, could not totally cope with the circumstances simply because they either forgot, or never were aware of, the basic principles of *access control*. This may seem incomprehensible to today's student or reader who has been raised with the computer; possibly even naïve; however, not only did this author experience the "breakdown" but the past 25 years as a forensic consultant and expert witness have proven this theory to be valid. On numerous occasions, while evaluating security officers' performance in litigation where "inadequate security" has been alleged, the system breakdown was directly caused by the officers lack of knowledge of *basic* procedures. Thus, those techniques many will consider antiquated, outdated, and useless, *will* be covered in this chapter.

Perimeter control, as we have seen in an earlier chapter, is the first line of defense against intrusion on the premises by outsiders. Similarly, personnel pre-employment investigation may be considered the first line of defense against surreptitious attack from within. The key element in both of these protective functions is the careful control of access to the premises through identification systems. The tasks that fall to the security department, therefore, are these:

1. Limit access to the facility to those who have business on the property by virtue of being an employee, customer, visitor, guest, or outside contracting agency. There are other categories also, such as various inspection teams (fire, safety, electrical, etc.).
2. Know who is on the premises at all times.
3. Know the whereabouts of persons who are on the property. Limitations on employee access may be enforced by color-coding of employee identification badges. Visitors, too, should wear color-coded badges. Sensitized proximity

activation badges are another option whereby alarms, door locking hardware, or other notification techniques are activated simply by the mere presence or absence of the ID badge.

4. Know why persons are on the property. In the case of visitors, know who they are there to see or do business with.

5. Know when outsiders are on the property and when they leave the premises.

Methods by which persons gain access to the premises are varied. During hours when the company is in operation and receptionists or security officers physically admit persons to the property, the procedures are precise (see Chapter 8). Identification can be made through personal contact with the individual.

There are times, however, when it is not always possible to have a security officer or receptionist physically present to admit an individual to the building or to some secured area within the building. At such times, various electronic and mechanical devices can be employed to control access.

Automatic access control systems are also utilized in smaller companies where security manpower is limited. They may also be used simply as a cost-saving method in facilities where an inordinate number of security officers would be needed to man all doors leading to secure areas.

The types of devices discussed here are applicable to any controlled entrance or exit, either on the exterior or interior of the facility.

MAGNETIC CARD ENTRY

Probably the most popular method of automatic access control is the magnetic card key system. Used universally on parking lot gate mechanisms, it can also be installed at any door. The system utilizes a plastic card which can be carried in a purse or wallet or worn as an identification badge. The card has a series of mini-magnets embedded within the plastic at one of the edges. When the card is inserted in a slot, the magnets make contact by means of a preset coded receiving mechanism, triggering the locking device and opening the door or swinging gate.

Two problems have become apparent with this system. The first is that, unless the card is in fact the identification badge and is worn at all times, the loss factor is high. The second is that the magnetic code location of the card is easily determined simply by sprinkling fine metallic shavings on the card. The shavings will adhere to the card at the location of each mini-magnet. When the excess shavings are blown off the card, those remaining form small circles around each magnet, identifying the location of each and making duplication simple. Use of this system in a high-security risk area, therefore, is not recommended.

There are card entry systems that do not utilize magnets and are instead coded in other ways that utilize computer chip technology. This entry technique is used mostly by the hotel/motel industry in guest room areas and, here again, the combination is changed after each guest checks out.

DIGITAL SYSTEM

In a digital system, the locking device is operated by a combination, which must be punched correctly for the door to open. Should an improper combination be pushed, the unit can be programmed to sound an alarm. When the proper combination is pushed, the locking mechanism is triggered electrically, permitting access.

Digital systems are more conducive to highly sensitive areas because the combination can be changed easily whenever circumstances dictate, such as upon termination of key personnel or some indication that the combination has been compromised. Many companies utilizing digital systems change the combination at regular intervals as a matter of course.

COMBINATION LOCKS

The primary difference between the combination lock and the digital system is that the digital system operates the lock and releases the mechanism electrically and remotely. For example, the digital unit can be placed on a wall adjacent to the door with electrical wiring running to the lock, triggering it automatically when the correct combination is pushed.

The combination lock operates on the same principle; however, the unit is housed in a single mechanism, the combination feature simply taking the place of a key. After the correct combination is pushed, the locking mechanism is released so that the individual can then turn the bolt manually. Here again, the combination can be changed whenever appropriate.

KEY LOCK ENTRY IDENTIFICATION

There may be areas of the facility where security or management wants to know who entered and when. For these conditions there are locking systems which record, on printed pressure-sensitive tape, the key that was used to enter and the exact time entry was made. This system might be employed in file rooms, parts departments, vault areas, engineering areas containing designs, etc. Special locks would have to be fitted where only a limited number of keys have been issued. Each key is coded so it is a simple matter to identify the user who was issued that particular key.

Recording lock systems are available on the market for sale or, should the need for that type of security be temporary (such as special contracts or limited projects), for lease.

REMOTE LOCKS

Most major security lock companies manufacture locks that can be opened and secured electrically from some remote location by a switch, button, or key. The system is most commonly used as a convenience factor when it is necessary to secure a door, which is frequently used at a location where it is impractical to maintain a full-time attendant just to open and close the door. The installation is also a high-security factor when it is not deemed appropriate to issue keys to the area and where individual identification is required each time someone desires entry.

For example, a receptionist seated at a desk in a lobby can clear a visitor for access to the main facility after he has entered an open lobby. Once identification has been properly made, the receptionist can simply push a button allowing the visitor access to the interior of the building. This system effectively isolates the lobby, which is accessible from the outside, and eliminates the possibility of someone simply entering and forcing access to the interior of the building.

Remote locking systems can also be utilized effectively in special high-risk security areas within the facility. The individual desiring access to an engineering lab or security control center, for example, can either be observed and identified through a door with a plate glass window or questioned through a two-way intercom before the lock is activated. This again eliminates the necessity of the room's occupant going to the door each time.

One of the most effective uses of the remote lock is in conjunction not only with the two-way intercom but also with a closed-circuit TV camera. With this type of entry control, an individual can approach an exterior door and be interviewed *and* observed along with proper visual identification, prior to admission. In this way, a single security officer at one central control station can control several, if not all, entrances to the facility.

SOPHISTICATED COMPUTERIZED ID ENTRY SYSTEMS

In extremely high-risk security facilities, newly designed computer systems are being developed every day. With one device, the individual desiring access places her palm in a hand-shaped receptacle. Her fingerprints and palmprints are "read" by a photoelectric mechanism and compared through a computer with exemplar finger- and palmprints already on file with the company and coded into the computer. In less than a second, a buzzer is heard at the door and a green light flashes on the entry unit to indicate the employee has been cleared. If an unauthorized individual places their hand in the unit, a red light flashes, stating "one moment please." A security officer can then come to the scene to investigate.

In another device, the employee places his company identification card, which bears his photograph, thumbprint, and signature, in a receptacle. The unit can compare any of the three items, as follows:

1. *Photograph.* A small CCTV unit is viewed by an officer at a remote location. One side of the split-screen monitor shows the photograph of the ID card, and the other side shows the individual standing in front of the unit.

2. *Thumbprint.* The visitor places his thumb in a receptacle. The officer or a computer unit compares the prints of the visitor with the one on the ID card.
3. *Signature.* The visitor signs his name on a sensitized plate, covered by a sign-in register log, and the signature is similarly compared with that on the ID card in the receptacle.

All of the these units are extremely fast, efficient, and effective. Currently, experimental units can read an individual's iris pattern, in the eye, simply by peering into a device that resembles a microscope. As with all mechanical devices, however, they will malfunction on occasion, so security personnel must be available to assume the access control post when necessary. Also, the units should be checked and maintained on a regular, frequent schedule.

When any mechanical system breaks down, that function must be assumed by a security officer. The first step should be to establish a *log* and to enter all persons entering and exiting the area. Maintain careful reports of any incidents in the area. Each area must retain a post order document, with careful instructions on how that area (or post) should be maintained and the requirements for entry, thus any security officer who is assigned to that location on an emergency basis, has complete and detailed protocol of their responsibility.

REVIEW QUESTIONS

1. In what way are perimeter alarms and employee background screening performing a similar security function?
2. When are automatic access control systems a cost-effective choice?
3. What special advantage does a digital combination lock have over a conventional lock?
4. Give two examples of security uses for remote locks.

Part VI

SECURITY AND SOCIETY

Chapter 22

Security Authority: Theory and Practice

"AUTHORITY"—A PHILOSOPHICAL VIEW

The role of the security officer is unique. He has "authority" within the confines of the company that employs him. He is charged with the enforcement of rules and regulations established by that company, along with normal statutory provisions, safety regulations, and civil procedures establishing liability. While on the property of his employer he may be armed, wear a uniform, issue instructions that must be obeyed, and assume the responsibility for the lives and property within the confines of that company. Those are the practical and actual functions of the security officer. Legally, however, the security officer is simply another employee with no more rights or privileges than any other citizen.

The truth is, it should seldom be necessary for the security officer to apply any of the authority, as limited as it may be, with which the officer is empowered by the company. An effective security program will place greatest emphasis on *prevention* of problems.

An example will illustrate the benefits of shifting emphasis from *enforcement* to *deterrence*. A major industrial firm called in a consultant to analyze its total security program and make recommendations for a more "economically acceptable" operation. The department was "effective" but costly. The effectiveness of the security department was defended angrily by the chief of security, who proudly pointed out that within the past 6 months alone, 40 apprehensions had been made, with an 80 percent rate of convictions; of the eight fires on the property, all had been extinguished prior to the arrival of the fire department; and, because of their accurate reporting procedures, the company's legal staff was fully prepared to successfully combat all pending civil claims.

The consultant's final report to the company recommended that the entire security department be reorganized, including the replacement of the chief. It was carefully explained, with supporting statistics, that a truly successful security department should have established sufficient deterrent measures to greatly reduce the necessity for making arrests, extinguishing fires, or defending civil actions. The company management agreed with what to them was a new principle. The change was effected and a totally new (to the company) concept of security was established, utilizing more appropriate procedures, modern equipment, and well-trained personnel. After the initial cost of installation, which would be paid for in 3 years, the total cost of operating the department decreased by 40 percent.

The consultant maintained a careful study of the company for the year following installation of the new department and learned that apprehensions had decreased to two. There was one minor fire and *no* civil action brought against the company for negligence.

The "authority" of the security department had been redirected from enforcement to establishing precautionary procedures and deterrence. There were also some apparent tangent effects of the new program. Company losses through theft were cut approximately 70 percent. Accidents and injuries causing lost man-hours, higher insurance rates, and low production efficiency were cut approximately 50 percent. Morale took a sudden upswing, also increasing production and efficiency of the total operation.

The "enforcement" authority had not been removed; it had simply been placed in a role of secondary importance. But what is that "authority"?

Authority is "the right to determine, adjudicate or otherwise settle issues or disputes; jurisdiction; the right to control, command, or determine."[1] With the exception of "adjudicate," this definition applies to the rights of a security officer *within the confines of the employer's premises*. That is the reason he was hired. The fact that he wears a uniform or carries a badge or other identification stating "security" is merely an indication to other persons that he is the individual who has been granted the proper authorization by the company to represent their interests in that manner. It also implies that the appointed security officer is a trained professional in that particular area and is knowledgeable in those skills for which security has jurisdiction. That, then, is the basic authority inherent in the position of security officer . . . from the standpoint of the company. But how is the security officer *legally* recognized?

THE LAW'S VIEW OF SECURITY

Police officers and the courts recognize the security officer as a private citizen who has been hired by a company to protect that company's property. When the security officer is trained and professional in his approach to his job and his relationship with law enforcement, he is further held with sufficient regard that his observations, reports, and intelligence are accepted as a basis for any action taken by the authorities. Additionally, most courts in the country will, upon proper foundation of experience and academic background, receive testimony of a security officer as a "reliable witness." Juries, too, will regard the officer's testimony as "authoritative" in many instances.

It is for that reason that the security officer must adopt and maintain a level of competency consistent with the law enforcement policies and procedures in the community. Observations, reports, investigative techniques, and preservation of evidence must be precise and accurate—always with the ultimate goal in mind of a successful prosecution or the necessity of defending the company in a civil lawsuit alleging "inadequate security procedures."

The authorities respect the security department that successfully deters crime at its facility, because they know that this is an area of their jurisdiction that is capable of "taking care of itself," relieving the police for other duties. This feeling will also promote an atmosphere of cooperation, with assistance provided, simply to maintain a well-run facility.

Deputizations

Some law enforcement agencies throughout the country will appoint security officers as "special deputies" or "special officers." There are two reasons for this procedure. In smaller communities, the "special deputization" in effect provides additional legal authority to the security officer by appointing him a reserve police officer. This activity usually occurs in communities with small police departments where the feeling is that additional law enforcement personnel, even though limited in their duties, are of value to the community. The deputies in those instances must be available, when not working at their jobs, to assist the regular authorities in cases of emergencies and civil disasters. Both the security officers and the police, therefore, benefit from the deputizations.

A few jurisdictions, such as in Las Vegas, Nevada, permit security officers to issue citations, on a limited basis, after receiving special instructions from the Metropolitan Police Department. In the case of Las Vegas, the authority is given to security officers at the state's major industry, the hotel/casino operations, and the violation those citations may be issued for is trespassing. Thus far, the program has proven to be very effective, relieving the local police officers of an extremely time-consuming response call, which enables them to be available for more important emergency assignments.

In larger cities, "special police" commissions are granted to those security officers who merely go through an extensive background investigation by the police department. This enables the police to ensure that the security officer has a clean record and is not an ex-felon who has access to a weapon and the means to gain access to secure or protected areas. It is simply a way to identify a security officer as one who has been properly cleared. It carries with it no additional authority or police powers.

Private Person's Arrest (Citizen's Arrest)

The laws concerning powers of arrest vary from state to state as well as from one country to another. The only fairly consistent factor is the differentiation between a felony and a misdemeanor; in this area of definition particularly, it is incumbent on the security officers to become familiar with the laws in their area.

Generally speaking, a security officer must make an arrest as a private citizen only. Usually, a misdemeanor arrest can only be made by a citizen who actually observes the crime committed; therefore, a security officer cannot arrest an individual simply on the word of another person who says he saw a crime committed. All the officer can do is investigate the circumstances and notify the authorities. Incidentally, even the police cannot make the arrest under these conditions. They must either ask the citizen who observed the crime to make a private person's arrest, *or* attempt to obtain a complaint from the city attorney or the courts.

Again, in most instances, a private person may make an arrest on a felony charge *if* he has direct and accurate knowledge that the felony has in fact been committed—and if he has reasonable cause to believe that the suspect has committed that felony. Even then, the citizen must call the authorities immediately. He may not transport the prisoner, nor may he use excessive force to detain him.

Because of all the differences in legal jurisdictions and the varying laws throughout the country, our discussion here will offer a philosophical theory of the security officer's responsibilities in apprehension—theory, which can be applied universally.

THEORY OF APPREHENSION AND ARREST

Arresting an individual literally means depriving him of his freedom. When an individual commits a crime, he legally becomes a "suspect" in the commission of that offense. The burden of proving him guilty of the crime rests with the state. The state, in this instance, is the people as represented by the criminal justice system: the authorities and the courts. The police or security officers are generally responsible for compiling the evidence to be used by the criminal justice system.

If the suspect is convicted in a court of law, his freedom is then strictly limited for a given period of time by virtue of being confined in a penal institution or placed on probation, which, in itself limits his activities. He may also be fined a considerable sum of money. Even after the fine has been paid and the prison sentence and subsequent parole time have been concluded, and even though he is legally considered to have paid his debt to society, the stigma of being an "ex-convict" or "convicted felon" still follows him for years thereafter, by virtue of criminal *convictions* being public record in most states. The doors of opportunity close in many cases, and in most circles he is viewed with suspicion. This may be one factor contributing to recidivism, as the ex-con desperately fights for survival, returning to illegal activities, as lawful endeavors become limited. Rehabilitation efforts by the community and the authorities are often ineffective, unsuited to some individuals, or simply nonexistent.

If the suspect is not convicted, or for some reason prosecution is dropped by the authorities for lack of evidence or some other technical reason, then the suspect *may* have civil recourse against the company, individual, or agency that effected the arrest. The resulting lawsuits are costly and time consuming.

The decision of whether to make an arrest is a tremendous burden to place on the shoulders of any person, particularly a security officer. The average citizen who has the courage to become involved takes action strictly on moralistic grounds; that may happen once in a lifetime, if at all. The security officer faces the potential need to make an arrest daily and is committed to becoming involved. The risk factor, then, is greatly in favor of his having to make that judgment frequently during the course of his daily routine.

But what is the obligation of the security officer? It is a highly arguable point; not so much the definition of his obligation, but the priorities attached to each element.

Security officers bear a responsibility to their employers to perform the task for which they were retained and are being compensated. But what of the employer who expects the officer to take unnecessary risks, extend the scope of their authority, participate in a program of "selective" enforcement (favoritism), or use the officer's position to exercise a vengeful arrest? Should the officer participate in such policies? Is the officer committing a fraud against the employer if the job is not performed in the manner that the employer desires and for which the officer is being paid? Is it up to the individual officer to make the decision as to the motives of the employer?

Security officers also bear a responsibility to their profession. They are expected to be loyal to the principles of lawful process in the performance of their duty. They are expected to have the expertise required to make sound judgments and maintain the professional standing they have attained. Functioning in this manner, they will earn the respect of their colleagues, law enforcement officials, and fellow employees.

But does not independent action of this type sometimes conflict with the desires of the employer? Is it not possible that the employer has assumed a position that may appear inconsistent with the officer's professional opinion and beliefs—but which may be totally valid based on other, unknown considerations? Does the officer's strict adherence to a professional code of ethics and behavior supersede the employer's wishes?

The security officer also bears a responsibility to himself and his family to avoid any activity that would threaten their future security. That responsibility also is what gives a person pride and dignity in knowing he is doing what he believes is right. But does he always know what is right? Has he considered the alternatives available to the company—alternatives of which he may not be aware? Does not stubbornness sometimes enter the picture, when an untrained executive of the company issues a directive that may be contrary to the officer's personal beliefs?

What should be the officer's priorities? Does the officer consider his unique position as one that obligates him to protect *all* persons equally, without prejudice, or must he obey his superiors even though their instructions may be inconsistent with that obligation?

The facts are that *no person,* security officer or not, is ever provided a totally free hand to maintain his or her own options, to function independently of any other authority, or to rely totally on his or her own judgment prior to making a decision—*without being held accountable for that decision to some higher authority.*

The fact is that, in industry, compromise is necessary. Exceptions are made, special considerations do exist from time to time, and—most importantly—the officer must deal with each situation separately, based on the circumstances at that time. To assume a posture of total rigidity regarding the enforcement of any rule, regulation, or law is destructive. It is also impractical.

The security officer's dilemma is illustrated by an incident that occurred at a manufacturing firm several years ago. Two brothers, one intoxicated, engaged in a fistfight over some personal family matter. The combat was broken up by two security officers and the shift lieutenant, who had observed the intoxicated brother strike the first blow.

During the course of the fight, the other brother was accidentally thrown to the ground by one of the officers attempting to separate the two and received a broken wrist. The lieutenant insisted on arresting the intoxicated brother for public drunkenness and assault and battery—crimes of which he was actually guilty.

Other employees on the scene, along with the foreman and the plant manager, attempted to talk the lieutenant out of the arrest, but he stood his ground firmly, stating that all employees should be "handled" in an equal manner and no one should be allowed to violate the law without facing due process, and punishment, if found guilty. The lieutenant also argued that neither he nor the company representatives were judges or juries; that his job was merely to enforce the law and permit the judges to make the decisions.

Management acceded to the lieutenant's judgment. After all, he was the professional and they could not negate his authority in front of the rest of the employees without seriously damaging the security department's standing and authority in the future.

The employee was in fact arrested and the police summoned. He was booked, fingerprinted, and placed in jail until the next morning. Later the next day, he was released by the city attorney when it was learned that the brother would not testify against the suspect, nor could any other witnesses be found who were willing to testify. Additionally, the other brother sued the three security officers involved and the company because of his broken wrist. The company's attorneys settled out of court for a considerable sum. "False arrest," "false imprisonment," and "unnecessary force" were among the terms used in the suit filed jointly by the brothers—and those charges may very well have been legally valid, although the case was never adjudicated.

Would not some other course, or choice of courses, have been more appropriate under the above conditions? There were other options open to the security lieutenant, as we shall see. In the long run, management could have made a decision that might not have been consistent with the lieutenant's professional beliefs but probably more consistent with good judgment and other management considerations.

A PRACTICAL APPROACH TO ARREST

Let us now view "arrest" from a practical point of view—not legal, not philosophical, and not moralistic—but *practical* from the standpoint of the security officer's realistic relationship with his employer and the employees over whom he exercises the limited authority discussed earlier.

Obviously, if a serious felony is committed in the officer's presence or is in the process of being committed, the perpetrator should be apprehended immediately, should be held, and the authorities called. An example of this would be a security officer chancing upon a burglary in process.

With most crimes, however, whether felonies or misdemeanors, there are both options *and* time. All crimes have statutes of limitations that provide sufficient time and opportunity to investigate, develop, and compile adequate evidence to ensure a conviction if the suspect is in fact guilty. If it turns out that the suspect was actually innocent, the company, the security officer, and the suspect have been done a great service by virtue of the patience shown on the part of the security officer.

Minor offenses need not always be solved by arresting the suspect. Other punishments, such as disciplinary proceedings or termination, are available at the discretion of management.

In any event, if the decision is made to make an arrest, the security officer must be certain that there is sufficient evidence to convict the suspect and that no mistakes have been made that could result in a costly civil lawsuit for false arrest and imprisonment.

When a security officer is talking to a suspect, unless an arrest is to be made, it must be made clear to the suspect, both by word and action, that the individual is free to leave at any time. If it can be shown that the suspect's freedom of movement has been impeded in even the slightest way, their civil rights have been violated and the officers involved in the detention will be subject to prosecution, criminally and civilly. Because the officer is the company's representative, the company too will be held responsible. If guilt is not certain, the suspect should be allowed to leave and the authorities notified immediately.

As of this writing, security officers need not read suspects their rights as proclaimed in the *Miranda* decision relating to peace officers. It is quite possible, however, that the courts will someday rule that security officers, too, will have to follow that procedure. It might be safer, therefore, to begin the practice now. It really cannot do any harm, and it just might strengthen the company's defense against any false imprisonment charges, should that company be the target of the supreme test in the courts.

If an arrest is made, the security officer must be certain to advise the suspect that he is under arrest, what the charge is, and the authority under which the arrest is being made (private person's or citizen's arrest). After the arrest, *reasonable* restraint is allowed to hold the suspect until the arrival of the authorities.

Regarding "reasonable restraint," it is universally accepted that "force" may be met only with equal force or sufficient extended force to control the suspect. If the suspect is weaponless, therefore, "deadly" force with a weapon cannot be used under any circumstances. Also, from a security officer's point of view, a deadly weapon should never be utilized under any circumstances short of the imminent defense of the officer's own life or that of another against a suspect armed with a deadly weapon.

The law is extremely complex in its statutory form; and it becomes even more complex due to ever-changing appellate court and Supreme Court decisions. It is not possible for a security officer to be aware of all the changes and subtleties, although it is incumbent on him to continually update his knowledge of the basic elements of crimes with which he may become involved at his place of employment. He should, therefore, utilize the company's attorneys or legal staff and the local authorities to provide advice and guidance in all situations.

DETERMINING THE LIMITS OF AUTHORITY

Upon beginning a new job with a new company, the security officer should make certain that the policies of that company have been put in writing. Additionally, the officer should have a frank discussion with his superiors to learn of the "political" climate within the company structure—and what exceptions are to be made to the established policy. He may find that some persons are "exempt" from authority simply by virtue of their position, rank, or relationship within the hierarchy. It may be difficult for the officer to tolerate those conditions, but that is the way some, if not most, companies are run. If the officer finds the situation intolerable, then he must secure new employment in an environment more suited to his moral and professional beliefs. In most situations, he is not going to change the company.

REVIEW QUESTIONS

1. What is the legal authority of the security officer?
2. Discuss the difference between "enforcement" and "deterrence" in the role of security.
3. What are advantages of special police commissions for security officers? Can you think of a possible disadvantage?
4. Generally speaking, when can a private citizen make an arrest in the case of a misdemeanor? Of a felony?
5. Discuss the author's argument that in some circumstances the rigid application of rules by the security officer might be impractical.
6. What is "reasonable restraint"?

NOTES

1. *Webster's Encyclopedic Unabridged Dictionary of the English Language,* Gramercy Books, 1989.

Chapter 23

New Directions in Security

In the opening chapter of this book, the discussion of security began with the consideration of the minimal needs of a small, independent "mom-and-pop" operation. In effect, a fictitious company was created, and subsequent chapters detailed the progressive security procedures that would accompany the company's development through its growing pains to the final stage where it could be considered a major industrial complex.

All of the steps necessary to develop the company's security program from the beginning to the ideal maximum-security operation have been outlined; the basic ideas and techniques are presented in substance. Most importantly, the *theory* underlying each area of coverage is emphasized. Before a successful security procedure can be implemented, it is essential first to understand the problem and to recognize the necessary areas of protection. Then, depending on the individual circumstances at the particular facility, it is possible to design, plan, and operate a functional system.

Each individual company will find itself at a different stage in the "evolutionary process" described. Each must determine to what degree an effective security program is desired and economically feasible. Then measures can be selected that are suitable and practical for the purpose.

The author also recognizes that advanced electronic and computer technology has allowed security systems to be developed that function at a level of extreme efficiency, reducing the staffing level and requiring a more technologically sophisticated security officer, one who is far more capable than the "retired old man" of barely two decades ago.

Systems continue to advance. Techniques are rapidly expanding and "systems" are being developed that, 10 years from today, may make current technology appear as antiquated as the "retired old man" does now. But what about *human* considerations? Will we deal differently with people simply because a computer supplies us with a printout suggesting someone's possible involvement in a crime? Are we to leave situations that require *tact* and *judgment* to a computer, which cannot be programmed to consider options based on exceptional conditions or human mistakes? And finally, how are the technicians supposed to program the computers without knowing the reasons "why" they are performing the functions they are expected to do? How can a programmer install "instinct," "professional conduct," and "consideration" into the formula?

"Security" is not a mathematical equation, which handles all situations in a precalculated manner depending on the input of data. "Security" involves dealing with people, with human beings who have feelings, tempers, bad days, good days; days when they're not feeling well; days when they're sick and need assistance. People require direction and sometimes a pat on the back. People need authority to define their limits in a very patient, subtle, and logical manner. People look toward security for protection and guidance in emergency and life-threatening situations. People, especially when under stress, need another human being to turn to—not a computer screen.

Computers perform mechanical functions magnificently. Their capabilities in storage of data cannot be touched by human effort, but the business of providing "security" requires the professional judgment of a human being. The security officer will never be replaced by a machine when it comes to dealing with other human beings and, for that reason, he or she must be knowledgeable of the principles of the profession along with being endowed with an ethical posture that completes his or her professional stature.

WHAT LIES AHEAD

No picture of private security today is complete without recognizing the rapid changes that are taking place and will take place in the immediate future. Security is fast becoming a full-fledged discipline. Someday, with increasing academic programs and universal criteria establishing standards and ethical behavior, it will ultimately become a true profession. It develops daily. University degree programs and graduate schools are more widely available and becoming more popular as a chosen career course of study. The technical aspects of the industry are also in a stage of explosive growth and change, becoming more sophisticated especially in the application of electronics, computers, and other sophisticated technology and hardware.

Security as it was known in the not-too-distant past will not be recognizable in the very near future. The "fat old man carrying a club and a rusty gun" has almost completely disappeared from the scene. Even his replacement, the larger force of slightly better appearing but minimally trained security guards, loosely accumulated to form a semicohesive guard "section," has in turn been replaced in many areas by the semiprofessional security department. And these semiprofessionals are developing finally into the electronically oriented, highly skilled, sophisticated, and totally professional security operation.

In an earlier chapter the entry problems presented by a totally safe structure—one with no doors or windows at all—were facetiously described. Consider now a much more realistic and practical hypothesis.

A manufacturing firm of several thousand employees, working three shifts, formerly was staffed by 75 security officers, not including the support personnel. Now there are 20 full-time, well-qualified, college-educated, skilled professionals performing the same tasks *more efficiently,* and receiving adequate compensation for their recognized contribution to corporate goals and profits.

The heart of this security operation is the security console and computer. Here one officer controls all access points to the facility (with the exception of the main lobby entry, which is covered by a receptionist not in the security budget), by means of a combination of closed-circuit television, radio communications, and automatic entry controls. All alarms are monitored at this central console and emergency communications are centered here. Nonsecurity personnel, especially the supervisory staff, are well oriented and sufficiently trained in emergency fire and evacuation procedures to be able to handle most situations with minimal help or direction. Employee morale is high and cooperation with security is excellent.

The officer at the console identifies a specific problem, such as an unlawful entry, by means of either CCTV or an alarm system, and is able to dispatch one or both patrolling officers on duty to the trouble spot. A shift supervisor who is also a trained investigator (as are the other officers) may also respond; he will also handle any follow-up required. The only other officer on duty is manning the main vehicle gate.

Extensive use of electronics, automatic hardware, and the security applications of minicomputers possible today make this picture not only possible but, in fact, a reflection of existing practice in some facilities.

In a facility so secured, situations need *never* arise in which extensive manpower is required to police an area and to effect apprehensions, to extinguish fires, to direct frequent evacuations, or to gather evidence for defense against civil lawsuits. Establishing effective deterrent and preventive measures that make full and effective use of the "state of the art" in security theory and technological practice will *eliminate* those functions.

"Never" and "eliminate" are, of course, expressions of the ultimate goals, which should continually be striven for even if they cannot be completely realized. More realistically, the situations described, and their manpower demands, should be "infrequent," and the proper protective measures will "minimize" these costly functions.

The key to effective security, then, is *deterrence*. The elements of deterrence are:

1. Properly trained and skilled personnel, present and visible
2. Effective modern equipment and electronic hardware
3. Responsible, understanding interpersonal relationships with management, nonsecurity personnel, coworkers, municipal and government agencies, emergency services, and the general public
4. *The ability to apply these elements properly.*

The tools and the knowledge exist. Their effective utilization, in the hands of trained protection professionals, is essential to the safety and stability of modern business and industry.

THE CHALLENGE OF SOCIAL CHANGE

Some of the ideas that have been expressed in these pages concerning the security officer's posture, the image he should present to the public, and his relations with other employees are at odds with attitudes commonly held in many parts of the security community. The alternative, however, of returning to security's "Stone Age" of only a few years ago is no longer acceptable.

Relationships among people of all kinds have undergone truly revolutionary change during the half century since World War II, a period that has also witnessed the explosive growth of the security industry. The courts, recognizing social change, have modified many of their decisions, much to the dismay of the law enforcement community and many law-abiding citizens.

Although many of these changes are arguably inappropriate and not in the best interests of society in general, the security community must recognize that change is a fact. There is no recourse but to adapt to new ideas, new attitudes, and new interpretations of law; working "within the system," even if it is with the hope that the pendulum will eventually swing the other way, in a direction in which individual rights will not be held above the safety of the beleaguered citizenry at large. Today's security officers must be flexible enough and intelligent enough to interrelate with the people they deal with on a daily basis if that officer is to win their cooperation and respect.

The authority of the security officer, as we have seen, is a regulatory authority delegated by an individual or corporate enterprise, which empowers that officer to ensure that its proprietary regulations are followed and that the company's premises are maintained in a safe, orderly condition, all toward the goal of efficiently producing a product, providing a service or an environment within a normal, profit-making enterprise in a free society. It is the ability of such companies to provide or produce, based on their technology and their relationships with employees and customers, which provides jobs for workers, improved products for consumers, and the very basis for the nation's economy.

Security's job is to support those goals. The security professional must carry out his function fairly and responsibly even in an environment that is restrictive of his actions and methods of enforcement. He must constantly recognize that he is dealing with human beings who are more independent, more aware of their rights, and more insistent on their privileges than their counterparts of 10 or 20 years ago. And security officers must also maintain their own awareness that *all* persons are entitled to be treated with equal dignity and respect. In time officers may also find that they, too, have changed.

REVIEW QUESTIONS

1. What are the four elements of deterrence?
2. Discuss the impact of "liberal" changes in the criminal justice system, emphasizing the rights of accused persons rather than the rights of victims or society, on the security officer.

Chapter 24

We Never Thought
It Could Happen Here:
Preventing Workplace
Violence

Steve Kaufer, CPP, and Jurg W. Mattman, CPP

On April 20, 1998, my wife and I arrived in Palm Springs, California, to attend the annual conference of the International Association of Professional Security Consultants. During that 4-day stay, I had the pleasure of meeting Steve Kaufer and Bill Mattman, two gentlemen whose reputation and work in the field of workplace violence had been known to me for several years. I had not only read some of their articles and heard of their exploits from other colleagues, but on a couple of occasions Bill Mattman was on the opposing side of a forensic assignment in the California courts. We had, in fact, spoken over the telephone on occasion. I also had the opportunity to attend a session, at the convention, conducted by these gentlemen who proved themselves to be worthy of the professional accolades extended by my colleagues. It was then that I decided it would not only add quality and dignity to my book, but it would be a wonderful, exciting addition to the text to have a chapter guest-authored by them.

Steve Kaufer is nationally recognized for his research and innovative approaches to combating occupational violence. He has advised a wide range of companies and government agencies, including Fortune 100 organizations. Steve, while still in school, earned spending money by setting up alarm systems for friends, family, and finally customers who heard of his skills. Following graduation, he began his own company in 1974, which ultimately developed into a well-known full-service security concern, with guards, patrol, and system design functions, along with the alarm business in Palm Springs, California. Then he formed Interaction Associates, a security systems design company where he also worked very closely with school districts and, finally, in 1993 formed the Workplace Violence Research Institute with Bill Mattman. Steve has spent his entire working and adult career in the security industry.

Jurg W. Mattman, president and senior consultant of The Mattman Company, is a native of Switzerland. He began his law enforcement career with the Immigration and

Naturalization Service with assignments in California and Texas. After 5 years, he was commissioned as a special agent of the U.S. Secret Service. Because of his foreign language capabilities and his knowledge of the customs and standards of most European, Middle Eastern, and African countries, Bill was given a 4-year assignment in Paris, France, from where he traveled extensively on both criminal and protective missions. In 1980, he entered the private sector and 2 years later formed his own company. Bill specialized in executive and VIP security but soon became involved in security design and risk management for major special events. He provided security for the Olympic Torch Relay, the 50-state tour of the Bill of Rights, and many other complex events. In 1993, Messrs. Mattman and Kaufer combined their expertise and experience in occupational violence and formed the Workplace Violence Research Institute.

Their manual on workplace violence prevention has since become the standard throughout the public and private sector. In addition, Mr. Mattman has served both plaintiff's and defense counsels as a forensic consultant and expert witness in well over 200 cases. He is the co-author and co-editor of Premises Security and Liability ... A Comprehensive Guide from the Experts, *which he wrote with Steve Kaufer.*

It is my extreme pleasure to present my guest authors and their chapter on violence in the workplace.

—David L. Berger

PART ONE: INTRODUCTION

Say the words "workplace violence," and most people immediately think of the mayhem that happened at post offices across the country. Others remember the headlines of disgruntled employees killing coworkers and managers at companies large and small in nearly every state of the union. Still others relate to the tragedies caused by dissatisfied customers who sought revenge by indiscriminately shooting the employees of the "guilty" firm.

While such deadly acts certainly pose a threat to the American worker, it must be noted that of the approximately 1000 deaths from violence that occur in the workplace each year, more than 75 percent are related to robbery. The berserk, disgruntled worker is the cause of a relatively small percentage of occupational deaths.

There are two definitions of workplace violence; one perpetuated by stories that appear in newspapers or on radio and television. We call it the Media Definition:

> "A disgruntled employee or client enters the workplace armed with multiple weapons and shoots selectively or indiscriminately at employees, supervisors and managers."

Studies have shown that the real threat faced by workers is more accurately described in the definition of the Workplace Violence Research Institute:

> "Any act against an employee that creates a hostile work environment and which negatively affects the employee, either physically or psychologically. These acts include all types of physical or verbal assaults, threats, coercion, intimidation, and all forms of harassment."

Each day thousands of American workers face threats, harassment, intimidation, and physical and verbal attacks. These are the true, and very serious exposures to workplace violence. An estimated 16,400 threats are made every workday, over 700 workers are attacked each day and nearly 44,000 are harassed. These figures from a study conducted by the Workplace Violence Research Institute of Palm Springs, CA, point out the real danger that workers face every day.

While the fatalities in the workplace attributable to violence are a tragedy, more workers suffer serious effects, both physically and psychologically, from the other elements of workplace violence. The cost of these various acts of workplace violence—threats, intimidation, harassment and various forms of violence to employers—is astonishing. Frequently, what at first seems to be a minor threat or act of harassment ends up as a major litigation and costs the employer thousands, if not millions of dollars in lost productivity, legal fees and other expenses.

Preventing workplace violence isn't just watching out for Bob, the disgruntled former loading dock worker, who might return to the workplace armed with a couple of semi-automatic weapons to get revenge for being fired. A truly effective workplace violence prevention program includes physical security, pre-employment screening, proper and humane termination practices, EAP, out-placement, and a host of other ingredients.

JUST HOW SERIOUS IS THE PROBLEM?

In addition to the Workplace Violence Research Institute's comprehensive study of the magnitude and true cost of occupational violence, there have been a number of studies examining specific areas of workplace violence, among them are:

Northwestern Life Insurance Company: one out of four full-time workers were harassed, threatened or attacked on the job; victims of these actions felt angry, fearful stressed or depressed; coworkers accounted for most of the harassment, while customers were responsible for more attacks; employers with effective grievance, harassment and security programs had lower rates of workplace violence.

American Management Association: 50 percent of the companies surveyed reported experiencing incidents or threats of workplace violence in last four years, 30 percent said it happened more than once; 25 percent reported the incident was by a current employee and another 9 percent by a former employee; 42 percent of companies who experienced an incident began training programs, compared with 18 percent with no incidents; 25 percent said the warning signs were ignored by the victim.

U.S. Department of Justice: On average, approximately 1100 homicides, annually, occur in the workplace. Approximately 60 of the homicides were committed by coworkers or former employees; on average, 43 were committed by customers, tenants or hospital patients. Seventy-five percent of workplace homicides are robbery-related.

CAL/OSHA: Workplace fatalities are increasing; in 1993 assaults and violent acts became the leading cause of death at work; workplace homicides increased over 25 percent from 1992 to 1993; taxi drivers, security guards, convenience store clerks, jewelry store employees and small motel desk clerks had the highest rate of death of all occupations.

The cost of workplace violence to American businesses and public organizations is staggering. While there has been a slight decrease in the years following the 1995 study by the Workplace Violence Research Institute the annual cost remains at over $30 billion. The calculations included the monetary cost of lost productivity, loss of life, injuries, counseling, legal fees, court awards, management time spent dealing with the crisis and a host of other factors that result in actual cash losses to a business that suffers from any type of workplace violence.

It is important to realize that these costs stem not only from cases where employees are killed or seriously injured, but most from those where no blood is ever shed. The costs of harassment, threats and intimidation that workers face each day greatly exceed the dollar loss of those cases involving fatalities.

OTHER THREATS IN THE WORKPLACE

Aside from the danger of violence from workers, former workers and outside factors such as robbery, another growing threat is domestic violence. A recent survey of 248 company security directors in 27 states found that domestic violence that spills over in the workplace ranked high on a list of security concerns and 93 percent of those surveyed said domestic violence is an increasing corporate issue.

In the case of domestic violence, often what starts at home is completed at work. Assaults by spouses in the workplace are common today. For those being stalked by a former spouse or other unwanted interest, the workplace is the one location where the victim can usually be found; they can change their phone number and move, but most cannot switch jobs to avoid the stalker.

In the case of domestic violence or stalking the potential liability exposure to the employer is often greater since the company is usually aware of the conflict between the employee and the person intent on revenge. Once on-notice, the employer must take reasonable precautions based on the threat to protect the employee and coworkers.

Today, 49 states and the District of Columbia have anti-stalking laws.

Recent legislation of a different kind has given concern to many involved in workplace violence prevention. More than forty states now permit the carrying of a concealed weapon. Conditions for permits vary but most include some form of a background check or other defined licensing and training process.

The availability of a handgun in or near the workplace dramatically increases the potential for an incident. Employers are strongly encouraged to review the impact of having armed employees on their property and develop a written policy on weapons. Most companies are adopting the stance that firearms are prohibited on the firm's property, with a violation resulting in termination.

If such a policy is adopted, it is essential that entrances to company property and buildings are clearly posted with a warning message prohibiting guns on the property. The vexing question facing employers is how to deal with guns kept in a vehicle parked on company property. The prohibition or permitting of weapons in cars creates two separate legal dilemmas, best addressed by the company's legal counsel.

LEGAL ISSUES OF WORKPLACE VIOLENCE

Aside from existing legal and regulatory obligations that employers have to provide a safe and secure work environment, recent legislation and landmark legal cases add more responsibilities to those already facing the employer. Many states have enacted legislation related to workplace violence.

CAL/OSHA, the state agency that monitors working conditions in California businesses, issued guidelines for workplace safety and a Model Injury and Illness Prevention Program. While businesses operating in California are not required to follow the plan, it seems that as the issue is further studied and accurately tracked, mandatory programs could be invoked.

Also in California, in response to the growing concern for the safety of health care workers, a law was enacted requiring hospitals, emergency rooms, home health services, long term care facilities and drug and alcohol treatment centers to increase security and worker safety. The law mandates that training be provided to staff, security officers be used, and an assessment of security procedures be conducted. This law also prompted CAL/OSHA to issue a detailed model prevention program. The Federal OSHA program issued a similar set of guidelines for health care facilities.

In addition, litigation has dramatically increased in the area of workplace violence. Example of jury awards include $5.2 million paid to a former supervisor who was shot and permanently disabled by a disgruntled fired employee; $5.49 million against a temporary employment agency who failed to adequately screen an employee provided to a client, after that employee fatally stabbed a worker at the client-company; $4.25 million against the U.S. Postal Service stemming from a shooting.

In legal action following an incident of workplace violence, the issues often involve:

Negligent Hiring: Failing to properly screen employees can result in a person being hired that the courts can judge had a history that should have caused the employee not to be hired.

Negligent Retention: Keeping an employee after the employer has become aware of the employee's unsuitability and failing to act on that knowledge.

Negligent Supervision: Failing to provide the necessary monitoring to ensure that employees perform their duties properly.

Inadequate Security: If security measures provided to safeguard employees, customers and members of the public at a business or place of employment are not consistent with the potential threat, and an injury results from the omission of proper security precautions, then a case can be made for this type of action.

While these are the most common elements of civil suits filed on behalf of those injured by an incident of workplace violence, many other factors can be drawn into a case. With the average out-of-court settlement of $500,000 and an average $3 million jury award, it makes sound business sense to reduce the potential for workplace violence and avoid exposure to litigation.

DEVELOPING A WORKPLACE VIOLENCE PREVENTION PROGRAM

Although acts of workplace violence have been reported in the media on a regular basis for many years and countless articles covering this subject have been published in virtually every trade and association journal, relatively few employers outside the Fortune 1000 companies have developed comprehensive plans to address workplace violence. Some have done so as a direct reaction to an incident, but since their efforts were crisis based, the plan lacks a coordinated effort necessary to be effective. It is clear that occupational violence which has potentially devastating consequences has become the number one human resource challenge. Not having a prevention program with appropriate policies and procedures is, from an ethical, moral, operational, and financial point of view, nothing short of organizational dereliction of duty.

When designing a Workplace Violence Prevention Program, it is important to realize that every organization, public or private, is different (demographics, products, services, clients served, stressors, etc.) and therefore requires a customized program. While some organizations need very complex programs which require the input and participation of representatives from many different disciplines, including unions, many others require only the basic elements listed below:

Forming of an executive committee, a.k.a. management team

Assessing current conditions (working conditions, organizational culture, existing security and access control programs, etc.)

Preparing and implementing policies

Establishing a Confidential Information Collection and Evaluation Center (hot-line)

Developing a training program for all employees

Providing supervisors and managers with conflict resolution training

Reviewing pre-employment screening practices

Reviewing the termination process

Preparing a crisis response plan

Testing and updating the program.

This list may make developing a program seem to be a daunting task, but most organizations have many of the components of an effective program already in place. These may include access control, security and asset protection programs, sexual harassment policies, minimum standards of conduct and employee assistance programs.

A strong and resourceful partner in the program development should be the Employee Assistance Program or EAP. An effective EAP program can deliver the help needed by many workers to face and resolve issues that affect work and create the potential for violence. Within established guidelines, EAPs can be an excellent source of information to help reduce the opportunity for violence.

Confidentiality is the cornerstone of any Employee Assistance Program. The Roper Starch Worldwide polling organization conducted a survey of 502 employees, finding that two-thirds of them said they would not discuss their personal problems with HR or other company personnel. However, 87 percent of the respondents said they would turn to an EAP program for assistance.

Surprisingly, many employees of organizations who do have an EAP program do not know or are not sure what services are available to them. It is, therefore, important that information on available EAP benefits be communicated to employees on a regular basis. In one study 71 percent of the responding companies offered assistance to employees with substance abuse problems, yet only 42 percent of the employees were aware of the help. Similar percentages were found with other programs, including domestic violence. This points out the critical need to clearly communicate this valuable benefit to all employees.

THE WORKPLACE VIOLENCE COMMITTEE

In order to begin, a committee must be established and charged with the responsibility for the program. This committee is typically composed of ranking representatives from human resources, employee assistance, legal, and security. In larger organizations, representatives from risk management, public relations, facility management, production, and labor unions may be included.

While smaller companies may not have distinct representatives for each area of responsibility, these functions, if they exist should be included. It is important that upper level representatives actively participate on the committee, since they are accustomed to interfacing with other department heads and have the authority to make policy decisions.

For the committee to be effective and consequently for the program to be successful, senior company management must endorse the program and telegraph their support clearly to all employees.

The next step is to assess any current programs, the physical security, any policy related to threats, harassment or unwanted behavior. The assessor should also take a critical look at the organization's culture, working conditions, both from a physical and operational perspective and exterior stressors facing the employees. The results of this evaluation will provide a baseline and allow the committee to identify existing strengths and potential vulnerabilities.

Often this step poses the greatest challenge to the committee. While its members have the best and most intimate knowledge of their company, they lack the benchmark to judge how their firm measures up to accepted standards. The solution for many companies is the use of a specialized consultant who can provide, with company input, an independent evaluation of exposures and vulnerability. The consultant can also assist in guiding the process as a facilitator of the planning committee.

POLICIES, TRAINING AND INFORMATION COLLECTION

The next three steps in the process are intertwined. Policies must be written to clearly define what is not acceptable behavior related to workplace violence; the employees must be trained on these policies and how to recognize potential violence; and finally a point of contact for employees must be established to allow workers to report behavior that may be symptoms of potentially violent acts.

Suggested text for workplace violence prevention policies can be found at the end of this chapter.

One of the most important elements in any prevention program is a written zero tolerance policy for threats, harassment, intimidation and possession of weapons. This does not mean that the offender is necessarily terminated for such an offense. It does mean, however, that some action will be taken if the prohibited activity is confirmed and verified. The personnel action may range from a verbal reprimand up to and including termination. Such a policy will help employees understand the elements of unacceptable behavior, the consequences of exhibiting such behavior, and provide legal support for termination, should that become necessary.

With a written policy and a schedule of disciplinary actions drafted, the next step is the establishment of the Confidential Information Collection and Evaluation Center or (CICEC), sometimes referred to as a "hot-line" or "tip-line." The CICEC is a place within your company that employees can, anonymously and without fear of retribution, report abnormal behavior or dramatic behavior changes by a coworker, or violations of the company's zero violence tolerance policy.

Once this information is received, it is evaluated and a response plan determined. Unless there is the possibility of immediate harm to an employee, the response must be benevolent. The only way employees will report information to the CICEC is if they see their coworker receiving help for the stress or other problem they are facing; a punitive response will quickly dry up the information pipeline.

The CICEC is particularly effective since the employee working alongside a coworker will sense changes in behavior that could signal the build up of stress that could lead to a violent episode. This behavior may not be noticed by a manager, human resource or security person who does not have daily contact with the employee.

The CICEC also serves as a conduit for information about weapons in the workplace, or employees that are harassing fellow workers. If there is no easy opportunity for employees to report what they observe without having to become closely involved, this information may not surface until after an incident.

The most effective prevention programs incorporate all employees in the solution. Employees trained to recognize the symptoms exhibited by a fellow employee who could potentially commit an act of violence greatly increases the odds that this behavior can be spotted, proper action taken to evaluate the threat of violence and that assistance can be provided the employee in dealing with issues that could be causing the suspect behavior.

Experience has shown that training at three levels is most effective. An orientation session is recommended for senior company executives, providing an overview of the issues of workplace violence, detailing the financial and legal consequences of not having an effective prevention program in place, and to gain their support for the program.

Next to receive training are department managers and supervisors. This training should include conflict resolution, background on workplace violence and how it affects the workforce, communicating with workers, stress reduction, and effective communications. These employees should also have a thorough understanding of the company's policies on workplace violence prevention.. Experience has shown that four to eight hours provides sufficient training.

A shorter training session, about two to four hours in length, should be given to all other employees. This training should include discussion of the company's zero tolerance policy, what constitutes threats, harassment and intimidation, and the warning signs that could be exhibited by potentially violent coworkers. Reporting this behavior and learning of the help that the worker who is displaying these behavioral flags will receive should also be a part of this session.

Another important element in employee training programs is conflict resolution. Providing employees the skills needed to work through and resolve workplace conflicts will dramatically reduce the incidence of more serious violence. An incident of unresolved conflict does not simply go away, it escalates and often leads to physical violence.

HIRING AND TERMINATION: TWO OPPORTUNITIES FOR PREVENTION

Human resources has an important role in reducing workplace violence. The hiring and termination process are two prime examples of the vital human resources link in the prevention program.

Hiring the right person is a critical part of a workplace violence prevention program. With the potential for overstating qualifications, inflating education, adding phantom job experience to the resume and forgetting to list jobs the prospective employee would rather you not know about, the potential for hiring the wrong person is great if the application is taken at face value. In fact, studies have shown that up to 42 percent of applications contain material misstatements of facts.

How do you increase the odds in your favor when hiring new workers? First verify everything on the employment application. Some firms undertake this investigation themselves, others use a professional service. This step will, at the least, ensure the person you interview possesses the skills, qualifications and job history claimed and meets the job's requirements.

In the past, when contacted about a former employee, most employers gave a "no comment" response or limited the information given to dates of employment and whether or not her or she was eligible for reemployment. To a lesser degree, this is still true today. However, recent workplace violence related litigations have brought important changes to what a former employer not only can but is expected to disclose when asked for information about past employees. Today, many states recognize a new tort doctrine called Negligent Referral which turns the table on old practices and provides employers with a better chance of learning about issues of concern. Under this source of liability, if an employer refuses or fails to reveal pertinent information about a former employee, such as incidents of workplace violence, the company can be sued for damages caused by that employee at the new firm.

A survey conducted by the Society for Human Resources Management indicates that the likelihood of gaining useful information increases with mail inquiries. The disparity found in the study shows that 81 percent of the firms questioned routinely requested information by telephone, however, less than 50 percent said they would give out information by phone. An effective strategy would be to make an initial phone call to obtain the correct address and name of a contact person, then send a written request to that specific person.

Equally important is the interview. Even for entry level jobs, potential employees should be interviewed twice, at different times, and in-person by a company employee skilled in the process. These two face-to-face meetings provide the opportunity to verify the information provided on the application. Often those who lie have trouble remembering the fictional tale they have woven. To be most effective, ask open ended questions to verify dates, job history and other information provided.

Some employers have attempted to use applicant screening tests to help judge the propensity to violence of the person seeking employment. With the advent of ADA laws, (*Americans with Disabilities Act*) such tests may be illegal if required before offering the applicant the job. If a test is administered after the applicant accepts employment, it would be very difficult, based on statues, to revoke the offer of a job if the test indicated any violent tendencies.

While ADA laws allow an employer to exclude employees who pose a "direct threat" to the health and safety of the individual or others, the speculative nature of these screening tests does not meet the stringent requirements of ADA standards to establish the employee is, in fact, a "direct threat."

Another part of the screening process should involve, as an element of the background investigation, verification of any prior criminal convictions. In most states you may ask if the applicant has been convicted of felony or misdemeanor charges. You may not, in most instances, ask if there have been any arrests that did not lead to conviction. It is critical that the person charged with conducting the background investigation be familiar with the terms of the Revised Fair Credit Reporting Act

It may not be a reasonable policy to automatically exclude all applicants with convictions. The best course of action may be a system to fairly and consistently evaluate each case individually and weigh the potential liability. The best advice on this issue will come from your legal counsel. Many companies are tempted to lessen the screening and background investigation requirements for lower level, entry positions. This decision, often based on expense and expediency, could well be a costly mistake. Not fully screening a certain class of applicant could expose the firm to a bad hiring decision and result in a tragic incident. Only with an effective program can the likelihood of hiring the potentially violent employee be reduced.

Equally as important is the termination process. The single biggest trigger of rampage-type attacks in the workplace by employees is termination. How the firing is done can make the difference between a routine event and a crisis.

Two critical issues become clear from reviewing past incidents. First the employee being fired must believe that there is a future for him. Losing this job cannot be seen as the end of his employment road.

Some companies have found that offering out-placement assistance goes a long way to reduce the stress facing a fired worker. Also agreeing in advance with the terminated worker to a statement of separation that details what will be told to prospective employers further reduces stress and pressure.

Employees who feel they have lost control will sometimes seek to regain that control; in their mind, using a weapon will more than level the playing field. Getting the terminated employee involved in the process and allowing them to maintain the greatest degree of a sense of control as possible will dramatically reduce the potential for a revenge attack.

Properly disciplining and documenting the unwanted behavior exhibited by the employee will allow a legal foundation for the termination to be laid, and, in addition, allow the employee to realize the consequences for his behavior, so that the firing is not seen as a surprise.

DOWNSIZING

During the latter part of the 1980's and the first part of the 1990's, thousands of public and private organizations underwent major downsizing, re-engineering, right sizing, or whatever they may have called a drastic reduction in personnel. The stated reasons were to be more competitive in a global marketplace and to enhance profits for shareholders. Large numbers of employees were losing their jobs. In fact, during this period, 85 percent of the Fortune 1000 companies had reduced their workforces through downsizing. While this activity has not stopped, it has been reduced dramatically. However, corporate acquisitions and mergers have reached a new high and are causing large numbers of employees to lose their jobs.

Recent studies found that the number of workers who frequently worry about being laid-off has decreased somewhat from an all-time high in 1995. Still, those who believed that working hard meant job security continued to drop. In addition, organizational loyalty has reached new lows, particularly in the ranks of lower paid, unskilled workers. These conditions continue to create high levels of stress that could translate into higher potential for workplace violence.

In situations where large numbers of employees are laid off or terminated, there are strategies to reduce the impact of such actions on the employees. They include:

1. The availability and involvement of senior company leadership
2. The attention paid to those remaining, as well as those being terminated
3. Communication with employees, giving out straight facts in a timely manner, reducing the rumor mill

4. Involvement of employees in the design and implementation of the reductions
5. In case of downsizing, the reduction in personnel is just one aspect to a planned strategy to achieve the goals the company is seeking.

A reduction-in-force for whatever reason also places pressure on those workers who remain. Frequently, these employees are called on to perform the same work load as the previous full strength staff. Additional stress comes from wondering who will be cut in the next round of lay-offs. The work environment for both those with and without jobs is stressful.

PHYSICAL SECURITY AND HARDWARE

Despite the fact that most workplace violence is internal, it still makes sense to include security systems and physical security measures as part of the complete, integrated approach to combating workplace violence.

There has been a dramatic increase in security related technology available to make the workplace more secure. The myriad of technologies available have driven an approach to system design commonly known as integration. Integration allows distinct systems such as access control, alarms, closed circuit television and other security related sub-systems to function as a cohesive whole.

For example, an employee who has been terminated but failed to surrender his ID badge might pose a threat to the workplace. The badge might allow this person to gain access to sensitive areas or into the building, posing a danger to workers.

With an integrated system, if the worker presents his card to an electronic reader, the card that was canceled when the employee was terminated will generate an alarm, indicating that an unauthorized person attempted to gain access. The system could also display a stored photo image of the employee to the on-site guard and even print out a copy for distribution.

In addition, when the alarm is registered, a nearby closed circuit TV camera is automatically positioned to view the door, giving further information to security personnel.

While most companies wish to create and maintain a safe working environment, the reality is that most firms can neither afford nor wish to build what could be perceived as a fortress. The control of workplace vulnerabilities, risks and potential losses requires sound and efficient integration of both electronic and physical security elements with an effective program of prevention and employee-care programs.

The first step in including technological improvements to the security program is an assessment of threats, risks and needs. The major shortfall of ineffective programs is poor planning and failure to define the system parameters.

In addition to electronic and physical boundaries, many companies rely on security personnel, either proprietary or contract security officers. Again, failure to define the goals to be accomplished by the use of security personnel is the major reason for security inadequacies.

In planning to include electronic systems and security personnel, it is vital that a cohesive group representing the primary areas within the company be involved in determining the best combination of devices and people. This ensures that the program design meets the security needs in a cost-effective way, in a manner that blends with the corporate culture of the company.

PLANNING FOR THE CRISIS TO REDUCE ITS IMPACT

Despite all the best planning, use of policies and practices, dealing fairly with all employees and otherwise having a model prevention program, an incident could happen. To ensure that the responses are correct and the incident is managed properly, a Crisis Response Plan, a.k.a. Incident Response Plan, a.k.a. Crisis Management Plan is needed.

Such a plan details the steps that will be followed should the unthinkable happen. Not only is this plan effective for workplace violence, but also for other man-made or natural disasters. The same plan can minimize damage following a chemical spill at a company facility or an earthquake.

The plan should detail the positions responsible for the many duties required to properly respond to a crisis. An effective plan involves most departments within a company.

Many organizations find that establishing a Crisis Management Team (CMT) and in larger firms, one or more Crisis Response Teams (CRT) is effective for handling potential incidents of workplace violence. The CMT is typically comprised of senior representatives of human resources, legal, security, risk management, unions and other departments.

The CMT duties often include developing the prevention program, assessing reports of potential violence, guiding CRT members in the required response to incident, and other supervisory roles. In smaller organizations, the Crisis Management Team may also be the Crisis Response Team.

In organizations with multiple locations it is common that each distant facility have a CRT that provides on-site services under the direction of the CMT. The CRT obtains information, assesses options and exposures, and confers with the CMT to ensure that the proper actions are taken.

The CMT has the ongoing responsibility to keep the workplace violence response plan current and to ensure that it is periodically tested at both the CMT level and also with CRT members. It is suggested that twice a year, the Crisis Management Team meet for half to one full day. The first item on the agenda is a review of policies and procedures to ensure that they are still current. Replacement team members are introduced and acquainted with the program. The next item is an exchange of information regarding incidents that occurred during the preceding six months. Finally, the team participates in simulation exercises which are prepared by alternating team members or an outside consultant. These exercises are invaluable in preparing the team to respond correctly if and when a real incident occurs.

Only plans that are exercised, revised and remain fluid are effective. A plan that is written, put in a binder and never removed from the shelf until an incident happens is dangerous because it creates a false sense of protection. Write the plan, test it and then continue to test it.

PART TWO: WHEN TRAGEDY STRIKES AT WORK

Imagine that you, as a manager, are busy with your daily responsibilities, when tragedy strikes:

☐ You hear a commotion down the hall, respond, and discover that an employee has swallowed a lethal dose of drugs in the presence of his coworkers.

☐ An irate individual storms into your section's work area and shoots an employee while you and other employee look on, shocked and helpless to intervene.

☐ A dazed-looking employee walks into the work area, bruised and disheveled, collapses at her desk, and reports that she was attacked while conducting a routine business call.

Initially, your responses will probably be almost automatic. You will notify the proper authorities and take whatever steps are necessary to preserve life and safety.

After the paramedics and the investigators leave, the hard questions begin for you, as a manager:

☐ How do you help your employees recover from this event, so their personal well-being and professional effectiveness will not suffer long-term effects as a result of trauma?

☐ How do you get your staff moving again after employees have suffered from injury, bereavement, or emotional trauma?

GENERAL GUIDELINES

As you would expect, there are no easy answers, and each situation presents its own set of challenges. However, here are some general guidelines to help you in most situations: Stay firmly in charge. Let all employees know that you are concerned and doing all you can to help them. You represent the organization to your employees, and your caring presence can mean a great deal in helping them feel supported. You don't have to say anything profound; just be there, do your best to manage, and let your employees know you are concerned about them. Be visible to your subordinates, and take time to ask them how they are doing. Try to keep investigations and other official business from pulling you out of your work area for long periods of time.

Ask for support from higher management. Relief from deadlines and practical helps such as a temporary employee to lighten your burden of administrative work, can make it easier for you to focus on helping your employees and your organization return to normal functioning.

Don't "keep a stiff upper lip" or advise anybody else to do so. Let people know, in whatever way is natural for you, that you are feeling fear, grief, shock, anger, or whatever your natural reaction to the situation may be. This shows your employees you care about them. Since you also can function rationally in spite of your strong feelings, they know that they can do likewise.

Share information with your employees as soon as you have it available. Don't be afraid to say, *"I don't know."* Particularly in the first few hours after a tragedy, information will be scarce and much in demand. If you can be an advocate in obtaining it, you will show your employees you care and help lessen anxiety.

Ask for support from your Employee Assistance Program (EAP). The EAP is available to offer professional counseling to those who wish it, and to provide debriefings to groups affected by trauma. Encourage your employees to take advantage of the EAP as a way of preserving health, not as a sign of sickness.

Encourage employees to talk about their painful experiences. This is hard to do, but eases healing as people express their painful thoughts and feelings in a safe environment, and come to realize that their reactions are normal and shared by others. You may want to have a mental health professional come in to facilitate a special meeting for this purpose. Or your group may prefer to discuss the situation among themselves. Don't be afraid to participate, and to set a positive example by discussing your own feelings openly. Your example says more than your words.

Build on the strengths of the group. Encourage employees to take care of one another through such simple measures as listening to those in distress, offering practical help, visiting the hospitalized, or going with an employee on the first visit to a feared site. The more you have done to build a cohesive work group, and to foster self-confidence in your employees, the better your staff can help one another in a crisis.

Build on your work group's prior planning. If you have talked together about how you, as a group, would handle a hypothetical crises, it will help prepare all employees, mentally and practically, to deal with a real one. Knowing employees' strengths and experience, having an established plan for communication in emergencies, and being familiar with EAP procedures can help you "hit the ground running" when a crisis actually strikes.

Be aware of the healing value of work. Getting back to the daily routine can be a comforting experience, and most people can work productively while still dealing with grief and trauma. However, the process of getting a staff back to work is one which must be approached with great care and sensitivity. In particular, if anyone has died or been seriously injured, the process must be handled in a way that shows appropriate respect for them.

HOW TO LISTEN TO SOMEONE WHO IS HURTING

Whenever people face bereavement, injury, or other kinds of trauma, they need to talk about it in order to heal. To talk, they need willing listeners. Unfortunately, many of us shrink from listening to people in pain. We may feel like we have enough troubles of our own, or be afraid of making matters worse by saying the wrong thing.

Sometimes we excuse ourselves by assuming that listening to people who are hurting is strictly a matter for professionals, such as psychotherapists or members of the clergy. It is true that professional people can help in special ways, and provide the suffering individual with insights that most of us aren't able to offer. However, their assistance, although valuable, is no substitute for the caring interest of supervisors, coworkers, friends, and others from the person's normal daily life.

It is natural to feel reluctant or even afraid of facing another person's painful feelings. But it is important not to let this fear prevent us from doing what we can to help someone who is suffering.

Though each situation is unique, some guidelines can help make the process easier:

☐ The most important thing to do is simply to be there and listen and show you care.

☐ Find a private setting where you won't be overheard or interrupted. Arrange things so that there are no large objects, such as a desk, between you and the person.

☐ Ask questions which show your interest and encourage the person to keep talking, for example:
"What happened next?"
"What was that like?"

☐ Give verbal and non-verbal messages of caring and support. Facial expressions and body posture go a long way toward showing your interest. Don't hesitate to interject your own feelings as appropriate, for example:
"How terrible."
"I'm so sorry."

☐ Let people know that it's OK to cry. Some people are embarrassed if they cry in front of others. Handing over a box of tissues in a matter-of-fact way can help show that tears are normal and appropriate. It's also OK if you get a bit teary yourself.

☐ Don't be distressed by differences in the way people respond. One person may react very calmly to an event that leaves another completely devastated. One person may have an immediate emotional response; another may be "numb" at first and respond emotionally later. Emotions are rarely simple; people who are suffering loss often feel anger along with grief. Unless you see signs of actual danger, simply accept the feelings as that person's natural response at the moment. If a person is normally rational and sensible, those qualities will return once their painful feelings are expressed.

☐ Don't offer unsolicited advice. People usually will ask for advice later if they need it; initially it just gets in the way of talking things out.

☐ Don't turn the conversation into a forum for your own experiences. If you have had a similar experience, you may want to mention that briefly when the moment seems right. But do not say, *"I know exactly how you feel,"* because everybody is different.

☐ It's natural to worry about saying the "wrong thing." The following is a brief but helpful list of three other things **not** to say to someone who is suffering:
Do not say:

Anything critical of the person.
"You shouldn't take it so hard."
"Do you think your husband would have left you if you had been more sensitive to his needs?"
Anything which tries to minimize the person's pain.

"It could be a lot worse."

"You're young; you'll get over it."

Anything which asks the person to disguise or reject his/her feelings.

"You have to pull yourself together."

"You need to be strong for your children's sake."

These are helpful guidelines, but the most important thing is to be there and listen in a caring way. People will understand if you say something awkward in a difficult situation.

Once you have finished talking, it may be appropriate to offer simple forms of help. Check about basic things like eating and sleeping. Sharing a meal may help the person find an appetite. Giving a ride to someone too upset to drive may mean a lot. Ask what else you can do to be of assistance.

After you have talked to someone who is hurting, you may feel as if you have absorbed some of their pain. Take care of yourself by talking to a friend, taking a walk, or doing whatever helps restore your own spirits. Congratulate yourself on having had the moral courage to help someone in need when it wasn't easy.

RECOVERING FROM THE DEATH OF A COWORKER

The death of a coworker is a painful experience under any circumstances, and all the more difficult if it is unexpected.

Recovery of individuals and of your work group itself depends to a great extent on the effectiveness of the grief leadership provided by you—the group's manager. Effective grief leadership guides members of the work group as they mourn and memorialize the dead, help the deceased's family, and return to effective performance of their duties. The following guidelines have proved helpful.

Provide a private area were coworkers can mourn without public scrutiny. Initially, close friends and associates will feel shock and intense grief. If the loss is to be resolved, it is essential for all affected employees to spend time talking about the deceased person, sharing memories, and discussing the loss. This "grief work," which is essential for recovery, is intensely painful when done alone, but much less so when it can be shared with friends. Providing a private area where coworkers can talk together and shed tears without public scrutiny will ease this process.

Share information. Employees will feel a particularly strong need for information at this time. Managers can show their concern by making a concerned effort to get that information, and share it in a timely manner. Until you get the information, simply admitting honestly that you don't know is more comforting to employees than not being told anything.

Contact employees who are temporarily away from the office. Ordinarily, people in a small work group are aware of friendship patterns, and will take steps to ensure that those in particular need of comfort are given support. Therefore, problems may occur if key people are on leave or traveling. The manager and group members may need to reach out to those temporarily away from the office.

Serve as a role model. Managers need to serve as role models for appropriate grieving. If you show that you are actively grieving, but still able to function effectively, other employees will realize that they can also be sad without losing their ability to perform their duties rationally. You should avoid hiding your own feelings, as this often leads employees to misperceive you as not caring.

Consider offering a "debriefing." Often, a cohesive work group can go through the grief process without help. However, if members do not know each other well, or for whatever reason have difficulty talking, a professional person may need to come in and facilitate a "debriefing," or meeting in which grief is discussed.

Consider holding a memorial service, especially if coworkers cannot attend the funeral. A memorial service can be very helpful and is often a turning point in restoring a work group to normal productivity. This is not to imply that the deceased is forgotten; rather people find after a point that they can continue to work while grieving. Consider the following points in planning a memorial service:

☐ The memorial service should honor the deceased and provide an opportunity to say goodbye. Unlike a funeral, a memorial is not a religious service, and should be suitable for employees of all faiths. Friends may speak about the qualities they admired in the deceased, the person's contributions to the work and the morale of the group. Poetry or music reminiscent of the deceased might be shared.

☐ The most common mistake in planning memorials is to plan them at too high a level. Senior officials may want to take charge, to show that they care, and to assure a polished product. This approach usually "backfires," for example, *"The managers don't care about Sam; they just want to put on a show for the executives."*

☐ Memorial services are most effective when the closest associates of the deceased are given key roles in planning and carrying them out. Including the "right" people (i.e., the best friends of the deceased) make the service more comforting for everyone. If the best friends are too upset to speak, they can take non-verbal roles such as handing out programs.

Reach out to family members. Reaching out to the family of the deceased can be comforting for both employees and family members. Attending the funeral service, sending cards, visiting the bereaved family and offering various forms of help are all positive healing activities.

Support informal rituals. Informal rituals in the office can ease healing. A group of friends might join together to clean out the deceased person's desk, or organize a campaign for contributions to an appropriate charity. Sometimes employees may want to leave a particular work station or piece of equipment unused for a time in memory of the deceased. If possible, this wish should be honored.

Get back to the work routine in a way that shows respect for the deceased. Returning to the work routine can facilitate healing if the work group makes an effort to uphold values held by the deceased and strive toward goals that he or she particularly valued, for example: *"I want to show the customers I care, because Sam was such a caring person."*

Don't treat a new employee like a "replacement" for the employee who died. It is important that new employees not be made to feel like "replacements" for employees who have died. Reorganizing responsibilities and moving furniture can help spare the new employee and others the painful experience of having somebody new at "Sam's desk" doing "Sam's job."

Remind employees about the services of the Employee Assistance Program. Group members should be reminded that normal grieving can produce upsetting responses, such as sleeplessness, diminished appetite, and intrusive thoughts of the deceased. Ordinarily, these will subside with time, particularly if the individual receives strong group support. However, some individuals may find these reactions especially troubling or long lasting, and may need to turn to the Employee Assistance Program for professional help in getting over the experience.

SUPERVISING AN EMPLOYEE WITH SUICIDAL CONCERNS

Suicide is a significant cause of death among Americans, and personnel are not exempt from the problem. Though there are differences in suicide rates based on such factors as age, gender, and ethnicity, a person from any background can commit suicide, or go through a period of seriously contemplating it.

People considering suicide often have been "worn down" by many stresses and problems. Actual or expected loss, especially a love relationship, is often a contributing factor. The suicidal person is frequently lonely and without a solid support system. Sometimes this is a long-term characteristic of the person; in other cases a geographic move, death, or a divorce may deprive an individual of personal ties that were formerly supportive.

Listen carefully to what your employees say—people thinking about suicide often give hints about their intentions. Talking about not being present in the future, giving away prized possessions, and making funeral plans are examples of possible hints of suicidal intent. If you hear such talk, question it, kindly but firmly. You won't make the situation worse by clarifying it, and an open conversation with you may be the person's first step toward getting well.

Be alert to changes in behavior. A deterioration in job performance, personal appearance, punctuality, or other habits can be a sign of many problems, including suicidal concerns.

If an employee admits thinking about suicide:

- First offer your own personal concern and support. Let the person know you care—the employee is both a unique human being and a valued member of your team.
- Show understanding of the employee's pain and despair, but offer hope that, with appropriate help, solutions can be found for the problems that are leading the person to feel so desperate.
- Ask whether any of the employee's problems are work related, and, if so, take the initiative in attacking those problems. For example, the employee may feel improperly trained for key responsibilities, or may be having difficulties without making you aware of it. If you can act as an advocate in remedying some of these problems, you will help in three ways—removing one source of pain, showing concretely that someone cares, and offering hope that other problems can also be solved.

- Do not question the employee about personal problems, as the individual may wish to keep them out of the workplace, but listen with empathy if the employee chooses to share them.
- Do not offer advice, but acknowledge that the problems are real and painful.
- Protect the employee's privacy with regard to other employees. This will require thought and planning, as questions are sure to arise. When dealing with higher management, you need to think clearly about what they actually need to know, i.e., that the employee is temporarily working a reduced schedule on medical advice—as opposed to what they don't need to know, i.e., intimate personal information that the employee may have confided in you as the immediate supervisor.
- Without hovering over the employee, show your continued support and interest. Make it clear that the individual is an important part of the team, and plays a key role in mission accomplishment.
- Get help. As a general rule, anyone feeling enough pain to be considering suicide should be referred to a mental health professional, at least for evaluation. Make it clear that you want the employee to get the best possible help, and that some types of assistance are outside your own area of competence.
- Normally, the Employee Assistance Program (EAP) is the referral source for mental health assistance. If the employee consents, call the EAP yourself, emphasizing that the situation is serious and needs timely attention.
- If for some reason the EAP is not immediately available, turn to your community's Crisis Intervention or Suicide Prevention resource. These are normally listed with other emergency numbers in the telephone book, and available on a 24 hour basis.
- Follow up. Once your employee is involved in a treatment program, try to stay in touch with the program. This does **not** mean that you should involve yourself with specific personal problems that the employee is discussing with a therapist. What you do need to know, however, is how you can work with the treatment program and not at cross purposes to it. Does the employee need to adjust work hours to participate in therapy? Has the employee been prescribed medications which have side effects that could affect job performance? Should you challenge the employee as you normally do, or temporarily reassign the person to less demanding duties?

This kind of communication will occur only if the employee permits it, since mental health professionals will not, for ethical reasons, release information without the employee's consent. If you make it clear to the employee and treatment team what your goals are—to support them, not to delve into the employee's private concerns—you will probably have no difficulty getting cooperation. A meeting involving you, the employee, and the counselor can be particularly helpful in clarifying relevant issues and assuring that your supervisory approach is consistent with the employee's treatment.

Take care of yourself. Working with a suicidal person is highly stressful, and you should take positive steps to preserve your own mental health while you help your employee. You should not hesitate to get support for yourself, either from your own supervisor or from the EAP.

HELPING AN EMPLOYEE RECOVER FROM AN ASSAULT

Being assaulted on the job can lead not only to physical injury, but also to emotional distress. Recovery with return to job effectiveness requires not only the assistance of professional experts, such as physicians and psychotherapists, but also the enlightened support of supervisors and coworkers.

The role of the immediate supervisor is especially important, because that person most powerfully represents the organization to the employee. The supervisor needs to convey personal concern for the employee as well as the concern of the organization, and a sense of the employee's unique importance to the work group and its mission. The following guidelines have proved helpful in these situations.

If the employee is hospitalized, visit, send cards, and convey other expressions of concern. It is important that the employee not feel abandoned. The nursing staff can advise you of the length and type of interaction most appropriate. If the person is quite ill, a very brief visit and a few words of concern may be enough. As recovery continues, sharing news from the office will help the person continue to feel a part of the organization.

Encourage coworkers to show support. At some point the employee will need to tell the story of the assault, probably more than once, and may find it easier to discuss this with coworkers who are familiar with the work setting and may have had similar experiences. Coworkers can help significantly by listening in a caring way, showing support and avoiding any second guessing of the situation. Being assaulted is not only physically painful; it can make the world feel like a cold, frightening place. Simple expressions of kindness from friends and coworkers—a visit, a card game, a funny book, a favorite magazine—can help the person regain a sense of safety.

Help the employee's family. If the employee has a family, they may need support as well. If the situation has received media attention, the family may need assistance in screening phone calls and mail. Other kinds of help, such as caring for children while a spouse visits the hospital, can go a long way in showing that the work group cares for its members.

Plan the employee's return to work. The supervisor, employee, employee/labor relations specialist, and health care providers need to work together to plan the employee's return to work. Here are some important points to consider:

- There is truth in the old saying about "getting back on the horse that just threw you," and it can be helpful to get back to the crucial place or activity in a timely manner. The sooner the employee can return, the easier it will be to rejoin the group, and the employee will have missed out on less of the current information needed for effective job performance. However, it is important not to expose the employee to too much stress at once. A flexible approach, for example, part-time work, a different assignment at first, or assignment of a coworker for support, can often help the employee overcome anxiety and recover self-confidence and may allow the employee to return to work sooner than would otherwise be possible.

• The employee's physical needs must be clarified with health care providers, i.e., the supervisor and employee should understand precisely what is meant by phrases such as "light work." If the employee looks different, from wearing a cast or having visible scars, it is helpful to prepare other employees for this in advance. Advance thought needs to be given to any new environmental needs the employee may have, such as wheelchair access or a place to lie down during the day.

• Working out a flexible plan for a recovering employee may take time and energy in the short run, but that effort will be repaid in the long run by retaining an experienced employee as an integral part of the work group.

Offer counseling. Counseling services should be offered through the Employee Assistance Program (EAP), and with the attitude that it is perfectly natural to use such professional resources in the aftermath of a traumatic experience. Supervisors and EAP personnel should work together to make the experience as convenient and non-bureaucratic as possible. However, individual preferences and differences should be respected. Some employees find that they can recover from the effects of the experience with the help of their friends, family, and coworkers. Others may not feel the need for counseling until weeks have passed and they realize that they are not recovering as well as they would like.

Make career counseling and other forms of assistance available if the employee decides to change jobs. Even with excellent support, employees who have been assaulted sometimes feel "It just isn't worth it," and decide to transfer to a safer occupation. The employee should be encouraged not to make such an important decision in haste, but career counseling and other forms of assistance should be made available. Supervisors and coworkers who have tried to help the employee may need reassurance that their efforts contributed to the individual's recovery, and that the decision is not a rejection of them

MANAGING AFTER A DISASTER

A disaster such as an earthquake or hurricane creates unusual challenges for management. You and your staff may yourselves be suffering from its effects. Emotional stress, physical injury, bereavement, loss of property, and disruption of normal routines may limit the availability and energy of your work group. At the same time, the group may face new responsibilities—caring for its own members, and facilitating community recovery. Besides meeting customers' special needs for assistance following a disaster, agency personnel are often called on to support other Federal agencies in providing a wide range of community services.

Plan ahead. You and your work group should be familiar with any disaster plan that affects you, and should have your own plans, however informal, for how you might function in a disaster. Involving employees in planning helps give them a sense of empowerment, and can improve the quality of your plan by assuring that everyone's experience and skills are brought into play.

Despite the magnitude of the challenges, Federal Government agencies have a proud history of responding effectively to disasters. The following suggestions are general principles that can help you structure your disaster response (they are no substitute for a comprehensive disaster plan).

Take care of your own people first. You need to locate your staff and assure that they and their families have necessary medical care, housing, food, and other necessities before they can be effective in serving the public.

Consider setting up a relief center. Particularly if traditional disaster relief agencies are slow to mobilize, you may need to set up a relief center for your own employees, and provide food and other essential items to those in need. If necessary, assign a group of employees, preferably volunteers, to internal disaster relief, and relieve them temporarily of other duties. Their tasks might include staffing the relief center, taking inventory of unmet needs of affected employees, and locating resources to fit the needs.

Consider compiling resource information. Those most affected by the disaster are least likely to have functioning telephones, and may not be able to call around to locate a new apartment, a child care provider, a rental truck, a place to board the dog, or any of the many goods and services they need to begin normalizing their lives. Compiling information in a booklet or card file can be very helpful, and can result in a document that is helpful to the public as well as employees.

Modify office rules and procedures that are counterproductive after a disaster. Dress codes, rules about children in the office, and restrictions on using telephones for personal business, for example, may need to be temporarily adjusted in the post-disaster period. Agencies have the authority to grant administrative leave to employees who need time off to normalize their home and family situations.

Take steps to prevent accidents and illness. Much of the human suffering associated with a disaster happens after the event itself, and can be prevented through good management. It is particularly important to prevent the overwork and exhaustion that tend to occur as people throw themselves into disaster recovery operations. Post-disaster environments are often less safe and sanitary than normal ones, so people living and working in them need to exercise special care. Exhaustion can lower resistance to disease, decrease alertness, impair judgment, and make people less careful about health precautions and more vulnerable to accidents. There are several strategies for assuring that people do not exhaust themselves:

- After an initial crisis period, during which overwork may be necessary, develop procedures to assure that employees do not work too many hours without rest.
- Be sure to provide adequate staffing for all new responsibilities created after the disaster, such as internal relief operations.
- Set limits on work hours, if necessary, and train managers to monitor their subordinates and check for signs of exhaustion.
- Since leaders are especially prone to overwork, monitor each other and set a positive example for subordinates.
- Take care to assure that no employee has an essential task that no one else knows how to do, or that person will surely be overworked.

Communicate clear priorities for work. Since some normal operations may be suspended and new ones undertaken, this must be done carefully and consistently. Understanding priorities will not only help prevent overwork, but will also empower employees to make decisions about how to use their time most appropriately.

Provide opportunities for employees to talk about their stressful experiences. To recover from severe stress, people need to talk about what they have gone through, and to compare their reactions with those of others. Consider the following suggestions:

- Provide a group meeting organized by an Employee Assistance Program (EAP) counselor or other mental health professional.
- Remind employees of procedures for scheduling individual EAP appointments, since some employees may need more personal assistance in resolving problems arising from the disaster.
- Offer opportunities for employees to share their experience informally, for example, by providing a break area with coffee or other refreshments.

MANAGING WHEN THE STRESS DOES NOT GO AWAY

Previously chapters have focused mainly on traumatic events that overwhelm us with their suddenness. We are shocked and shaken by the enormity of the event and its unexpected nature.

Sometimes, though, long term stress can assume traumatic proportions. Carl Dudley and Melvin Schoonover, who interviewed clergy members in South Florida about six months after Hurricane Andrew, report, "They all agreed that surviving the storm was easy compared with surviving afterward." According to one pastor, "Stress-related deaths continue to haunt our congregation long after the storm—some people simply cannot get their lives together in this constant uncertainty."

Disasters are not the only source of long term stress. Threats of violence, whether from individuals outside the agency or from fellow employees, can lead to severe stress situations which go on for weeks, and affect many people. Harassment campaigns directed against employees can be nerve-wracking even when there is no apparent physical danger. The prospect of losing a group member to a slowly debilitating illness can produce a long period of stress for everyone involved. Organizational change can produce severe stress if employees feel uncertain and worried for long periods.

Getting the job done and taking care of employees under conditions of severe, long lasting stress can be one of the most difficult challenges a manager may face. It's not easy to take charge, develop innovative approaches, and be sensitive to the needs of others when you're at least as uncomfortable as your subordinates. There are, however, some management approaches that have proved helpful in these situations.

Take concrete steps to see that everything possible is being done to lessen the sources of stress. If danger is a problem, call law enforcement immediately, and get all the advice and concrete support you can for them. If employees are overwhelmed by competing demands in the aftermath of a large scale emergency, set clear priorities and make sure they are consistently followed. You probably can't "fix" the entire situation, but you can improve it. Your employees will feel better if they know you are working on their behalf.

Keep open lines of communication with your employees. This is always important, but even more so when everyone is under long term stress. In most stressful situations, one source of anxiety is a sense of being out of control. Your employees will feel better if they have up-to-date information and permission to approach you with their questions. Depending on the circumstances, you may want to adopt new communications strategies, such as having frequent meetings, publishing an informal newsletter, and keeping an updated notice board in a central place. Consider that

- Employees will have a greater sense of control if you are careful to listen to them with an open mind before making decisions that affect them. Even if your decision turns out not be the one they would have wished for, they will feel less powerless if they believe that their ideas and preferences were given serious consideration.
- Communicating with employees may be difficult for you if your own tendency, when under stress, is to withdraw from other people, or to become less flexible than you normally are. Both are common stress reactions, and can interfere with your leadership if you don't monitor yourself.

Encourage teamwork and cooperation. Under long term stress, there is no substitute for a supportive, caring work group. Employees will find the situation, whatever it is, less painful if they are surrounded by coworkers who care about them, and will listen if they need to talk, or lend a hand if they need help. A group accustomed to teamwork rather than internal competition will usually be able to cover for members who are temporarily unable to function at 100 percent effectiveness.

Ideally, your group has always been strong and cohesive. If not, do what you can to help it pull together under stress. Encourage and validate teamwork and cooperation. Avoid any appearance of favoritism and make it clear that there is opportunity for everyone to achieve and receive recognition.

Set clear work standards. Doing good work is always essential, but even more so in times of high stress, since success can bolster self esteem and group morale. Keep your standards high, but allow as much flexibility as possible in how the work gets done. If you set clear standards, but give employees some freedom in working out ways to meet them, they will probably be able to develop approaches that fit the contingencies of the stress situation. Check on how much flexibility you have with regard to such conditions as work hours, administrative leave, alternate work sites, etc. It's natural to assume that the way we have always done things is the only way, but you and your employees may have options that you haven't considered.

Make it clear that this is a difficult period, and it's OK to share feelings of anxiety, fatigue, or frustration. If you set the example by letting people know you can do a good job even though you are not feeling your best, you set a positive example. Define the situation in a way that emphasizes the strength of the group while acknowledging the challenges it faces. The tone should not be, "Poor us," but rather, "This is hard, but we're going to hang together and get through it."

Acknowledge the value of professional counseling, and encourage your employees to get whatever help they need. Long term stress can wear down the coping resources of the strongest person, and it makes sense to get extra support in order to preserve mental and physical health. One strategy is to bring in an Employee Assistance Program (EAP) counselor to talk to the group about stress management. Besides learning from the presentation, your employees will develop a personal contact which can make it easier to turn to the EAP if they need it.

Don't underestimate the impact of stress on you as an individual. Attend to your own stress management program, and use your resources for professional consultation and counseling. You will find it easier to take care of your work group if you also take care of yourself.

BUT IT COULD HAPPEN HERE . . .

While some industries and occupations seem more predisposed to workplace violence, no work environment is immune. Incidents have occurred in three-person businesses as well as those employing thousands of workers.

No one can absolutely prevent workplace violence, but with proper planning and an effective program, the chances of it occurring can be reduced dramatically.

The information contained in this chapter is meant solely as a guide to address the very real problem of workplace violence. Once completed, the entire program should be reviewed by an experienced labor law attorney to ensure that none of the policies and procedures are in conflict with any labor or other laws and/or regulations. Further information can be obtained from the resources listed next.

RESOURCES

The Workplace Violence Research Institute
1281 North Gene Autry Trail, Suite G
Palm Springs, CA 92262
(800) 230-7302

Consulting services, assistance in designing prevention programs, training for employees, evaluation of existing programs, and seminars on workplace violence. A wide variety of publications and training tools available.

American Society for Industrial Security
1655 North Fort Myer Drive
Suite 1200
Arlington, VA 22209
(703) 522-5800

A number of publications are available for purchase by non-members on the subject, in addition to the members-only O.P. Norton Information Resources Center, a comprehensive library of security publications.

National Institute for Occupational Safety and Health (NIOSH)
Centers for Disease Control
4676 Columbia Parkway
Cincinnati, OH 45226-1998
(800) 356-4674

A variety of information is available, including *Fatal Injuries to Workers in the United States, 1980-1989: A Decade of Surveillance and Violence in the Workplace-Risk Factors and Prevention Strategies.*

CAL/OSHA
455 Golden Gate Avenue, Room 5202
San Francisco, CA 94102
(415) 703-4341

Developed the Model Injury & Illness Prevention Program and the *CAL/OSHA Guidelines for Workplace Security;* both are available at no cost.

National Criminal Justice Reference Service
P.O. Box 6000
Rockville, MD 20850
(800) 851-3420

General information and comprehensive statistics on a wide range of criminal justice topics, including workplace violence, domestic violence and stalking.

Center for the Study and Prevention of Violence
University of Colorado at Boulder
Institute of Behavioral Science
Campus Box 442
Boulder, CO 80309-0442
(303) 492-1032

Listings of violence prevention and treatment programs. Provides topical database searches.

Center for Crisis Management
Graduate School of Business
University of Southern California
Bridge Hall 200
Los Angeles, CA 90084-1421
(213) 740-8504

Conducts national research on workplace violence, has a summary report available on a national survey it conducted on occupational violence.

Chapter 25

Private Security Faces High-Technology Crimes

Sanford Sherizen

I have saved this chapter featuring computers *for last, but not because it is of lessor importance than the first 24 chapters, quite the contrary. I have been emphasizing, up until now, how important it is in this day of computers to have a good working knowledge of the* basic *techniques of prevention, deterrence, and the other strategies, which lead to the development of an effective security program. The computer has not yet been developed that can modify an action by adding a judgment factor based on compassion and human behavior—those elements which, in the author's opinion, are vitally important in our professional dealings with the people with whom we come in contact on a daily basis.*

Obviously, because of the limited authority we have, enforcement methods are also necessary along with the accepted, and necessary, command presence *posture utilized by law enforcement personnel; but the firmness necessary should be structured and contrived. It must be controlled, otherwise the security officer creates the image of the "badge heavy" authoritarian who, in turn, creates fear, animosity, ill-will, and poor relationships with those whose cooperation he ultimately must have. Security officers are, without question,* public relations *people. Whenever assigned to a post in a company, whether as an "in house" or "contract" officer, he or she is often in contact with that company's customers and employees, and many times can be the first contact a customer or guest has with that company. He then* becomes *the company, as its representative. Thus, it is also important to understand the ethical and philosophical aspects of the security profession.*

As mentioned earlier in this book, the author was involved in the very early development of a computerized access control system and also worked closely with credit reporting agencies utilizing early computer technology. Within both of those functions, conditions arose where the computer was "down." For the period of time during which the computer was not functioning, the personnel whose training had been exclusively with the computer failed to respond to the emergency conditions in an effective manner due to their lack of knowledge of the basic elements of the job they were performing. That is the author's concern! That the "basics," including the ethics and philosophy, should be lost—without any resource for recovering that knowledge and information, other than the computer, which may be down at that moment.

The realistic approach, however, is that computer technology is here to stay. It is the most sophisticated tool ever presented to the security industry and it can do nothing more but to continue to develop, creating even more wonderful techniques to be utilized by our industry in every aspect of our everyday performance. It has significantly enhanced our profession and given it a level of dignity unequaled in the history of our craft. It will force the industry to educate and retain a much higher level of security officer, capable of understanding and controlling the technology, along with adopting it to new endeavors. But along with the protective functions come brand new criminals and heretofore unheard of crimes, as you will be reading in this chapter, with which today's security officer will have to contend.

When it became clear that computers *would be taking a starring roll in* Industrial Security's *second edition, the authors selection of a guest author was a forgone conclusion. Although we only met recently through our joint membership in IAPSC (International Association of Professional Security Consultants), Dr. Sanford Sherizen has long been identified as the foremost authority in the field.*

Dr. Sherizen currently is president of Data Security Systems, Inc., in Natick, Massachusetts. He is a criminologist and is considered a leading expert on developing management strategies for maximizing information protection and liability prevention. Along with a Ph.D. received from Northwestern University, he is a certified information systems security professional (CISSP).

Dr. Sherizen has had extensive public speaking experience before a variety of technical and business groups. He is a frequent conference speaker and has led a variety of information security seminars and courses. He has been widely quoted in the media and has been an invited guest on Nightline *and National Public Radio, London Broadcasting System, and Canadian Broadcasting Corporation shows to discuss information security and privacy matters. Additionally, he has been an expert witness before the U.S. Senate and Massachusetts legislative committees and has prepared reports for the U.S. Congress's Office of Technology Assessment (OTA)*

Dr. Sherizen has been a professor at Boston University, Northeastern University, and the University of Illinois (Chicago) and has taught courses at Harvard University, MIT, and Northwestern University. He has written more than 50 articles and is the author or co-author of four books, including Information Security in Financial Institutions *and* How to Reduce the Risk of Computer Crime. *He was presented the Outstanding Paper Award at the 17th National Computer Security Conference for his analysis on how deterrence can be applied to computer criminals.*

It is now my great pleasure and honor to present my guest author, Dr. Sanford Sherizen.

—David L. Berger

INTRODUCTION

Asset protection is an ongoing, never-ending series of challenges. As new security protections are put into operation, almost immediately they are reviewed and tested by criminals. Criminals then attempt to develop new crime methods to counter the protections, in the process often uncovering new vulnerabilities. As a result of these exposures, new and improved safeguards are needed in order to continue to protect assets.

Donald Cressey, the noted criminologist, notes these factors in his brief history of how those who guard banks and those who rob banks are in a constantly evolving battle:[1]

> Seventy-five years ago, the safe was locked with a key. Full-time safe burglars learned to pick the locks, and the combination lock was invented. The criminals rigged a lever by means of which the whole spindle of the combination lock would be pulled out and the safe opened. When correction was made to prevent this, the burglars drilled holes in the safe and inserted gunpowder or dynamite. Then the manufacturers made the safe "drill proof," and the burglars secured harder drills with more powerful leverage. When the manufacturers used harder materials, the clever burglars turned to nitroglycerine, which could be inserted in minute crevices around the door where powder and dynamite would not enter. The safemakers developed doors that fitted so perfectly that nitroglycerine could not be inserted in the cracks. The burglars then adopted the oxyacetylene torch, and the manufacturers devised a compound which was proof against the torch.
>
> Somewhere in this progression the burglars began to kidnap bankers and compel them to open the safe, and to prevent this the time lock was invented. Also, when the manufacturers made the safes difficult to open, the burglars hauled the safes away and opened them at their leisure. The manufacturers countered by making the safes too heavy to move, and further, banks installed night depositories so businesses would not have to leave much money in their own small safes. The safemakers experimented with safes which would release gas when disturbed, and burglars went equipped with gas masks.

Today, private security professionals are facing an ongoing battle with criminals who are quite different than those we have met before. In many ways, these new criminals have the advantage. They not only have a chance to pick the best opportunity to strike but, with readily available crime tools now including high-technology apparatus, an ability to attack faster, more successfully and more safely (for them). Technology, particularly computers, allows these criminals an ability to commit efficient and effective crimes.

For the private security field, the bottom line is clear. Private security must become more technical in improving security operations and in the manner by which it faces the many traditional crimes that have become computerized. If information technology (IT) is not used to its fullest, the private security field will become less relevant to the business world and our society's ability to fight newer forms of crime may be threatened.

Based on over fifteen years of information security consulting and writing, this chapter will stress the growing opportunities for applying high technology to improving critical security functions. The discussion will continue with an examination of the nature of computer crime and abuse, which causes serious problems for private security departments. The chapter will end with a number of action items for private security professionals to become technically aware and Internet involved.

HIGH TECHNOLOGY AND PRIVATE SECURITY

In the Electronic Age, the security profession has expanded its definition of assets that need to be protected. Among the most important assets for an organization is information. Traditional security approaches, which have been based on physical property protection, have necessarily undergone change as new means of creating and distributing information (fax, teleconferencing, e-mail) required new access control measures.

Much of what has been standard practice in the field of private security has been changed by technology. From risk management decisions to parking lot protection, the computer and other technological advances have created new and (sometimes) better ways of performing the security function. What was science fiction just a few years ago is now available in the local computer store or on the Internet.

Yet, this technology has been greeted within the private security field with very mixed results. In some cases, security departments are among the least computerized departments in an organization, indicating a lack of appreciation of the security role by some business executives as well as resistance from some security professionals when it comes to computers. On the other hand, not only are some security offices taking full advantage of computers but they now have many choices of new security products based on technological advances.

One example of the technical changes in private security is access control products. The traditional ways to control the movement of people and property included locks, alarms and guards. While there have been advances with these controls, the explosion of more sophisticated products came about with the development of computer chip technology, personal computers and computer linkages to communication systems, such as the Internet. Until some twenty years ago, the access control system products most commonly used were digital electronic locks and early versions of barium ferrite cards. With low priced microprocessors available, access control products progressed in speed, capacity and cost reduction.[2]

Today, the newer forms of access control continue to provide what have been the primary purposes of physical or other security, the so-called five D's, i.e., to deter, detect, delay, deny and/or destroy.[3] However, access control now is built upon, and to an increasing degree, built within computer applications. Just as there are now physical security protections at building entrances and exits, so there are physical as well as logical (hardware and software) tools to restrict access to computers and computer-based information. The 5 D's now operate through new products which allow an increased degree of coverage, integration of security and safety functions, minimal false alarms and the collection of large amounts of audit trail information in the event of investigations.

This "technologizing" of traditional security approaches creates opportunities as well as challenges for the private security field. The opportunities are composed of the new ways by which we can protect, detect and investigate. Identification and authentication are much easier to establish for individuals and for property. Data can be collected for long periods of time with databases allowing instant retrieval of information. Sensitive materials can be protected on a need-to-know basis by electronic restrictions on access. Encryption can be used to allow only authorized users opportunities to review classified information. Security management across widely distributed locations is possible.

The challenges of technology create serious problems for our profession. The law, for one, has not kept up with technical changes. Specific determinations regarding privacy, trade secret protections, Internet usage, software patents and similar corporate issues are still relatively undefined by the courts. Security professionals are expected to protect assets in an appropriate fashion while what is defined as appropriate is undergoing review by judicial officials.

Liabilities are growing for security managers as well as other managers related to how well they can show that they have made a "good faith effort" to protect information. In some instances, contradictory requirements are in place, such as the need to ensure proper background checks of potential employees while, at the same time, accepting the privacy rights of those individuals. Similarly, there are needs to secure information at the same time that the information is crossing national borders which have different legal requirements as to what are acceptable detection mechanisms.

Thus, technology and private security are intimately intertwined. Our work has become more complicated than ever before at the same time that the technology allows us to do our work in more effective ways.

COMPUTER CRIMES AND OTHER TECHNICAL CHANGES IN CRIME

Computer crimes are the perfect crimes for the 1990's. A person who would not use a weapon to hold someone up on the street might be quite willing to commit a computer crime. After all, the victim is usually an organization and not a person, no blood flows, the act only involves hitting some computer keys, the organization should have better protected itself, corporate downsizing is unjustified and revenge is appropriate, the company was very profitable last year, etc. It is possible that with these characteristics, people who would not commit other types of crimes may be willing to commit a computer crime.

Computer crimes are often loosely defined as those illegal acts where the computer is the object of the attack or is used as a tool in the attack. This view is of limited help to many non-computer security people, for it tends to concentrate on the computer aspects rather than on the crime aspects of the activity. It is misleading since computer crime is better understood and better responded to as a computerization of well known economic, financial, white collar crimes, such as fraud and embezzlement. Old crime methods have been translated into new crimes.

For private security practitioners, computer crimes add several important ingredients to make it a unique type of crime. These crimes are unique since they involve new crimes, new criminals, new losses and new liabilities.

New Crimes

Computer crimes are really "information crimes" and, as such, often involve intangible property, such as intellectual property. There are major legal differences in prosecuting someone who steals a physical computer and someone who steals some information off the computer. Another example would be with the setting off of a computer virus on a computer system, proof would have to be shown that a particular person was the only one who could have set off the virus and that the act occurred at a particular time, place, etc. and that nobody else could have had electronic access to that particular system.

There are computer crime laws in forty-nine of the fifty states in the United States in 1998 (Vermont is the holdout) but most of these laws have serious limitations. The result is that a majority of computer-related crimes are prosecuted under traditional wire and mail fraud charges rather than the computer crime laws. Further, it is not always clear who will have jurisdiction over a criminal case when more than one state or, even worse, more than one country is involved with an incident.

New Criminals

Further, computer crimes involve new criminals. While the majority of early computer criminals were those who had technical knowledge of the system, today's computer criminal is someone who may or may not be technically sophisticated. User-friendly computer systems have become abuser-friendly. As "Wintel" (Windows and Intel) has become the standard found in the majority of computers, well known vulnerabilities have become available to those who want to penetrate systems. Even those who may not know how to program are able to find on the Internet or from other readily available sources "do-it-yourself" tool kits and programs for creating a sophisticated virus.

While outside hackers (or more correctly crackers who are more willing to destroy information) continue to be a serious problem, the greater problem is found on the inside of organizations. The insider problem is that authorized individuals may commit unauthorized acts. Just as there are a variety of reasons why people committed other crimes, so the computer criminal may do it for money, challenge, revenge, control, political ideology and other similar reasons. A significant majority of computer criminals, at least to date, are people who would not commit more tangible crimes against property or person, as mentioned in the beginning of this section. Increasingly, managers and others who can authorize others to undertake a particular transaction to be followed with a later authorized activity to destroy the evidence of the transaction are in a position to gain from a computer crime.

New Losses

Computer crimes also are unique because they lead to new types of losses. Like other crimes, the losses can include money, reputation of an organization, customer loyalty and the sharing of trade secrets with competitors. Similarly, a computer crime can lead to those losses but at a much higher scale. The damages may be much more severe, up to and including a business going bankrupt. A computer crime could occur when someone copied some sensitive information and the loss might be considered under existing inadequate law as the cost of the diskette and the electricity to run the computer, since the original information was still in the hands of the organization. A computer virus which gets into the system can destroy data and cause losses of several years of a worker's information, creating havoc for an organization that is dependent upon computer availability. An organization which is the victim of a computer crime can lose customers and market share, even if the organization did nothing wrong other than being attacked. Computer crimes can cost an organization millions of dollars loss.

New Liabilities

Lastly, computer crimes lead to new liabilities. Due to changes in the laws, societal values and business procedures, information is a strategic asset and information security has become a strategic requirement. Information-related liabilities are increasingly among the most serious problems faced by business executives. These executives now "own" the information security problem. Fulfilling their due diligence requirements is dependent upon the confidentiality, availability and integrity of critical business information. In several recent cases involving the Security and Exchange Commission, executives have lost their position and even been banned from serving on Wall Street due to inadequate supervision of employees who were able to manipulate large amounts of money. Under the federal sentencing guidelines, organizations which do not have adequate controls over prevention, detection and timely reporting of crime incidents can be sued up to $290 million and be placed under corporate probation, where a federal probation officer will run the organization until it is in compliance.

As if all of those factors were not serious enough, computer crime is a growing threat to the survivability of society. Information warfare is the term that is used to describe the battlefield of the near future if not tomorrow. As societies become highly dependent upon information and their infrastructures operate by means of computerized controls, basic institutions in a society become exposed. In a recent study by the President's Commission on Critical Infrastructure Protection (www.pccip.gov), serious vulnerabilities were found in the nation's infrastructure, including information and communications, transportation, oil and gas, water supply, emergency services, government services, banking and finance and electrical power. One example of our nation's vulnerability would be if purposeful attacks by nation states or smaller political groups on power grids cause a crippling of the U.S. To counter these threats, efforts to increase Government and private sector cooperation and to improve intelligence collection are now underway .

Two key points can summarize the comments that have been made on the uniqueness of computer crime. Security professionals have to face a new and more difficult world of protection work. Technology is no longer a choice but a requirement for being able to do security tasks today.

The private security professional should not only be more technically aware but also be involved in learning how to use high technology to better protect people and property. That means that you have to find ways to become more computer literate and to find resources that will help with that effort. That is the purpose of the next section.

ACTION ITEMS FOR THE SECURITY PROFESSIONAL

Here are several suggestions to assist you in maximizing the use of technology. You personally do not have to become a security guru. Learn what needs to be learned and hire those who have particular computer skills.

Learn Computers

There are many ways to become computer literate. Even those who are most afraid of computers will find very user-friendly equipment and courses readily available in most of the U.S. Take an introductory course at a local computer vendor, an adult learning center at a local high school or community center or even through the good graces of your children. As prices have come down, a powerful computer is available at a relatively inexpensive price. Learn by playing with the computer. In any way possible, try to overcome the shyness or fear of becoming computer literate.

Determine Computer Needs

Realize the limits to what you need to know about computers technically. Decide what are the essential aspects of computers that are most directly involved in improving your security operations. Find out about the many free security sources now available on the Internet. While there is a need for highly technical people in the field of security, particularly in computer security and computer fraud investigations, the majority of private security practitioners only need to learn basic applications such as word processing, electronic mailing, information retrieval on the Internet and other work-related activities.

Find Allies

There are many others in your organization who have an interest in protecting assets. They include legal, auditors, information security, MIS, human resources, contingency planning/business continuity and insurance/risk management. These professionals have different concerns about assets than you do but there is a shared interest in protecting the organization, its employees and shareholders. Given their particular concerns about protection as well as the fact that they are at different levels in the organization with different degrees of political power, they can become powerful allies in supplementing your efforts. Consider sending them information about your security efforts and networking with them to maximize your work. Create a mailing list and send your allies periodical information on crime cases, legal changes, new liability problems and other materials of potential interest. Find out their particular concerns and network with them to provide useful information.

Stress Your Contributions

Information security has begun to recognize the importance of early detection of crimes and incident response capabilities. Private security professionals have important working knowledge that can be critical in detection and incident responses. Let your allies know that you have contacts with law enforcement and that security is filled with important decisions that have financial and liability consequences. For example, you know when and how to call upon law enforcement in order not to lose a case. Call them in too early and the result may be a loss of control over the situation and that the rules of evidence are more stringent for official investigations than if the organization is investigating. Call them in too late and there is a possibility, sometimes a certainty, that evidence can be compromised and guilty parties escape punishment. Indicate to your allies your knowledge of investigatory procedures and the problems that can occur if there is an inappropriate pointing of fingers at perpetrators, either before the evidence clearly suggests them or not in a manner following due process, which can create countersuits. Indicate the important role that physical security plays in protecting informational assets. In a phrase, become a key player in information protection strategies.

Understand Technology's Impact

While hardware and software are important ingredients in preventing high-tech crime, "peopleware" must also be considered. It is important for security personnel to realize how technology has changed critical aspects of our daily lives. Question what the impacts of technology are as it affects how organizations function, how work is changed and how behaviors are altered. Realize that there are serious concerns about how technology has led to loss of jobs and violations of privacy. Consider the ways that work is now organized in your organization and see how computerization has affected worker satisfaction. Seek out the view of employees as to what they see as the strengths and weaknesses of security. Read public opinion polls on where citizens draw their lines in accepting certain computer uses for consumer purposes. Find out what are the new limitations that technology provides you in carrying out your security work.

These action items have been presented to give you specific ways to become involved with computers. No matter your lack of experience with computers. No matter how un-technical you are. No matter that typing on a computer seems beneath you. You have to become more of a computer user in order to become more of a security professional.

A SELECTED LIST OF INFORMATION SECURITY RESOURCES

In order to gather further interest on issues raised in this chapter, several important sources of information will be listed. Some of these require you to use a computer while others can help you learn how to become information security literate.

- ASIS, www.asisonline.org
- Computer Emergency Response Team (CERT), www.cert.org
- Computer Operations, Audit & Security Technology (COAST), www.cs.purdue.edu/coast
- FBI, www.fbi.gov/
- International Information Systems Security Certification Consortium (ISC2), www.isc2.org
- MIS Training Institute, www.misti.com
- National Computer Security Association (ICSA), www.nsca.com
- President's Commission on Critical Infrastructure Protection, www.pccip.gov.

NOTES

1. D. R. Cressey, *Criminal Organization* (New York: Harper and Row, 1972), pp. 94-95.
2. Stan Wand, "Twenty Years of Access Control Advances," *Access Control & Security Systems Integration* (January 1998).
3. Clifford E. Simonsen, *Private Security in America: An Introduction* (Upper Saddle River, NJ: Prentice Hall, 1998), p. 244.

Appendix

Industrial Security Survey Checklist

Although the following checklist is reasonably comprehensive, it is of necessity general in nature. Every facility will have its own particular peculiarities and needs, and this Survey Checklist should be considered only as the starting point for a more detailed and specific examination. It is suggested that reference be made to individual chapters in this book for more definitive coverage of each subject, and of the possibilities available in the selection of hardware or procedures to provide the desired security protection.

A. General Environment and Operations
1. Obtain and examine plot plans and floor plans for the facility. Supplement with diagrams, drawings, and photos as necessary.
2. Examine the size and extent of the physical facility, number and location of buildings, exterior access roads, railroads or waterways, etc.
3. Are there any areas of new construction? Do these require specific temporary security measures? Is removable fencing available or in place?
4. What effects do the immediate neighborhoods have on facility security needs? Is it a high-crime area? Urban or suburban?
5. What adjacent structures exist? How close to the facility perimeter? Are there common walls?
B. Perimeter Security
1. Is there a perimeter fence, wall or other barrier? How high is the barrier?
2. Does the perimeter barrier enclose the entire facility? Should it?
3. Is the perimeter patrolled?
4. Are valuable materials or products stored in the open near the perimeter?
5. What openings exist in the perimeter? How are they controlled? Do the gates work? Are unused gates kept locked? Are locks in place and in good condition? Who is responsible for opening and closing gates? If in an office building or a single stand-alone structure, are doors locked, in good condition, or controlled the same as the above gates?

6. Is the perimeter fence maintained? Is there a cleared area inside and outside of the barrier? Are there any washouts? Shrubbery and other growth near the fence? Materials stored close to the fence?

7. Are perimeter intrusion alarms used? Should they be?

C. Exterior Security

1. Are outside areas maintained free of undergrowth, debris, and salvage? If office building, are hallways clear?

2. Are outside storage areas orderly and well defined?

3. Is the employee parking lot separated from work areas? How? Can employees go directly to their automobiles with goods? Is there a pedestrian gate between the facility and the parking lot? Is the lot fenced? Consider condition and accessibility of shared or community parking areas in office buildings and stores.

4. Is there a separate visitor parking area? Can visitors have direct contact with employees?

5. Are outside areas patrolled? When?

D. Security Lighting

1. What type of lighting is used in outside areas?

2. Is the perimeter barrier lighted? Does lighting extend beyond the perimeter?

3. Are there enough fixtures to provide overlapping coverage?

4. Are lights protected against vandalism or other attack?

5. Is lighting planned to reduce or eliminate shadows?

6. Is backup power or emergency lighting available?

7. Are all perimeter openings, gates, and doors provided with increased area lighting?

8. Do valuable storage areas and critical installations have special lighting?

9. Are parking lots and truck parks well lighted?

10. Are shipping and receiving docks well lighted?

11. Lighting maintenance is important and often neglected. Who is responsible for maintenance? Are light fixtures easy to service? Are lighting outages promptly reported and corrected?

E. Building Security

1. What type of construction? Multi-story or single story? Are walls or roofs easily penetrated? Are windows accessible from the outside?

2. Examine all doors and entrances. Is the physical condition of doors satisfactory? Are locks functioning? Hinges secure? Are hinge pins accessible from the outside? Is door frame as strong as the door and lock? Are all doors necessary?

3. Do emergency exit doors have panic hardware on the inside? Is outside hardware removed? Are doors alarmed to notify central control when used? Are there sealed doors in compliance with fire ordinances? Is there a functioning access control system, either manual, electronic, or computerized?

4. Are emergency exits clearly posted? Are they kept closed and secured when not in use?

5. Are all windows lower than 18 feet above ground protected in some way? How? Are there screens or grilles in place? Do grilles violate fire regulations? Are accessible windows alarmed during nonoperational hours?

6. Are all other openings 96 square inches or larger secured? Examine hatches, vents, duct openings, sewers, utility tunnels, skylights.

F. Locks, Key and Access Control

1. What types of standard locks are used (spring locks, deadbolt, padlocks)?

2. Are there specialized locks? Examine the use or desirability of combination locks, automated card-key locks, remote locks requiring attendant supervision. Is a computerized access control system utilized?

3. Are existing locks and latches regularly inspected?

4. Who has control of keys and access codes? What records are maintained? Does anyone other than security have perimeter entry keys or access codes? Is there a secure key control cabinet and issuance procedures?

5. Are there submaster and master keys? Who has them? Are they necessary?

6. What procedures exist for cylinder or combination changes?

G. Employee and Visitor Control

1. What kind of personnel screening is used in employee hiring? Are references checked? Are background investigations made for employees handling money or merchandise? Does security conduct these investigations?

2. Are polygraph, written honesty tests, or psychological evaluations used in hiring?

3. Examine the employee ID and pass system in effect. Are badges color-coded or sensitized for different area access? What system of ID issuance and recovery is used?

4. Is a badge system in effect for visitors? For outside contractors?

5. How is movement of visitors controlled? Consider the use of visitor lists and sign-in-and-out logs. Are escorts used for visitors?

6. Examine the number, location, and controls for employee entrances and exits. Are entry and exit points kept to the minimum necessary? Are controls adequate?

7. Are routes within the facility clearly marked? Are signs posted to direct visitors, vendors, and others through the facility? Are the signs easily seen and read? Are color-coded painted directional stripes used?

8. Are restricted areas clearly identified? Examine entry controls, posted signs, printed regulations.

9. Are all doors clearly labeled?

10. Is a package control system in effect?

11. Are employee lockers separated from work areas?

12. Is the company cafeteria separated from work areas? Are the eating facilities off premises?

13. How is vehicle access controlled? Consider visitors, vendors, outside contractors, truck drivers, and railroad personnel.

14. Can unauthorized vehicles drive up to the loading dock? Is there valet parking, free parking, or charged parking in the building?

15. Do outsiders, such as drivers, mingle freely with employees in shipping and receiving areas? Can drivers gain entry to storage areas to use the telephone, rest rooms, or vending machines? Are docks monitored by personnel? By CCTV? Are shipping and receiving areas well lighted for observation of activity?

H. The Security Guard Force

1. Consider the number of security personnel required. Consider all working shifts on an independent basis, depending on how many company personnel are working during each shift and the amount of coverage required to secure the premises. Are in-house or contract security officers retained on the premises?

2. Establish stationary guard posts, facility patrol routes, and frequencies.

3. Consider the selection of uniforms and equipment, including equipment normally carried and that available in emergencies. Are officers armed or unarmed? Under what conditions?

4. Examine the manual of operations. Does it spell out policy, general instructions, specific details of post orders, and patrol procedures? Is emergency planning covered in detail (disasters, evacuation, first aid, fire response)? Does the manual cover schedules, emergency phone numbers?

5. Examine logs and forms used by security. Include daily operations log, incident report forms, phone logs, sign-in-and-out registers, other forms necessary for record keeping.

6. Examine the security filing system.

7. Does a training program exist for security personnel? Are armed guards trained in weapons use? Are they qualified periodically? If contract officers are utilized, are their credentials and certifications inspected periodically?

8. What criteria are used in hiring security personnel? Do job descriptions exist for each promotional level?

9. Examine guard facilities and security office. Are facilities provided for training, lounge, lockers, equipment storage? Support personnel and equipment?

10. Examine procedures for incident investigation. Are investigation forms provided? Is investigative force separate from guard force? Is there an undercover operations capability?

I. Alarm Systems

1. Determine areas within the facility which should be secured by alarm. Are they? What kind of alarm should be used in each area to be secured?

2. Where might contact, sonic, ultrasonic, and microwave intrusion alarms be used?

3. What environmental alarm detection should be provided (temperature variance, humidity control, pressure, water flow)?

4. Are emergency exits alarmed? (See Building Security, E.3)

5. What system of fire warning is used? Is it satisfactory?

6. What type of alarm monitoring is used? Contract alarm company? In-house (proprietary) system? Under either system, is there provision for line integrity to notify the monitor if circuit is broken or disrupted intentionally or accidentally?

7. Where is the central control located? Examine wiring sequence to the control station. Is wiring vulnerable to attack?
8. Where is the alarm system control panel located at the site? Can it be reached and defeated easily?

J. Surveillance Systems (CCTV)
1. Is a CCTV system appropriate? Is it necessary for maximum security coverage? Will it save man-hours for guard coverage? Are there sufficient areas of coverage? Is it compatible with, or coordinated with other systems?
2. Examine areas for television cameras, coverage required, viewing angles.
3. Select proper cameras and housings. Are cameras in tamperproof containers? Are they weatherproof? Are pan, tilt, and zoom features necessary at each location? Examine lens selection, resolution required, lighting needed at each location.
4. How is surveillance system monitored? Where is the central control station located? What types of monitors are used? Consider size of screen(s), configuration of console, timed changing view, or constant view programming. Is the CCTV system coordinated with the computerized access control system utilized?
5. Are videotape capabilities necessary? If so, where?
6. Examine availability and cost of proper equipment. Is a service contract provided? Does manufacturer or supplier make regular service calls? Are standby units, or loaners, available when equipment has to be repaired?

K. Communications
1. Is a two-way radio system required and in use?
2. Where is the base station located? Consider selection of proper frequency depending on facility construction and environment.
3. Consider power of units. How many mobile units are needed? How many walkie-talkies?
4. Is proper radio procedure followed—codes, conduct, etc.? Examine provisions for telephones, fax, cellular telephones, etc.
5. What paging systems are provided? Loudspeaker? Individual "beepers"? Examine intercom placement between stations.
6. Are provisions made for voice integrity in communications? (Consider codes, scramblers, monitors to detect voltage variance indicating wiretapping.)

L. Fire and Emergency Planning
1. Examine the fire alarm system. (See Alarm Systems I.3-6)
2. Are fire extinguishers provided? What types? Where are they located? Do signs clearly indicate location of extinguishers and their use (type)? Are personnel instructed in the use of extinguishers?
3. What type of sprinkler system is used? How often is it inspected?
4. Is training in fire and emergency response provided for security personnel? For all company personnel?
5. Are fire brigades part of the company fire response?
6. Examine fire exits. Are they labeled according to fire code? Are signs and coded striping used to identify emergency exits? Is panic hardware used on appropriate exits?

7. What evacuation procedures are used (total or limited)? Who is responsible?
8. Is liaison established with local fire departments? Other governmental emergency response agencies?
9. Does an emergency plan exist for specific emergencies (flood, earthquake, windstorm, etc.)?
10. What provisions are made for power disruption? How are personnel notified? Are there emergency generators?
11. Who is responsible for safety? Is there a program of safety and hazard inspection? Do security personnel report fire and safety hazards discovered on patrol?
12. What provisions are made for first aid and emergency medical care? Are there local facilities in each work area? A central first aid or medical treatment room? Do adequate first-aid supplies exist?
13. Is there a company nurse? Doctor? Personnel trained in first aid? Has liaison been established with local medical facilities (doctors, hospitals, paramedics, ambulance service, Red Cross)?
14. Are records and reports of fire, accident, and medical emergencies maintained?
15. What provisions are made for accident investigation and follow-up?

M. Procedural Controls (vary with individual facility)
1. Accounting records and controls.
2. Materiel controls.
3. Shipping and receiving records. Are these responsibilities separated?
4. Sales records.
5. Purchasing records and controls. Provisions for handling cash and valuables.
6. Visitor sign-in sheets maintained?

N. Miscellaneous
1. Statistical charts and records.
2. Public relations.
3. Employee relations.
4. Management relations and liaison. What reporting procedures to management are in effect?
5. Liaison with company attorneys.
6. Liaison with local law enforcement agencies.
7. Liaison with local civic groups.
8. Budget planning.

Selected Bibliography

American Polygraph Association. *Polygraph: Issues and Answers.* Linthicum Heights, MD: American Polygraph Association, 1996.

American Society for Industrial Security. *A Guide to Security Investigations.* Washington, DC: American Society for Industrial Security, 1970.

American Society for Industrial Security. *Violence in the Workplace: A Survey of Published Literature 1989-1994.* Washington, DC: American Society for Industrial Security, 1994.

Astor, Saul D. *Loss Prevention: Controls and Concepts.* Los Angeles: Security World Publishing Co., 1978.

Barefoot, J. Kirk and David Maxwell. *Corporate Security Administration and Management.* Boston: Butterworth–Heinemann, 1987.

Barefoot, J. Kirk. *Employee Theft Investigation.* 2d ed. Boston: Butterworth–Heinemann, 1990.

Barefoot, J. Kirk, ed. *The Polygraph Story.* Linthicum Heights, MD: American Polygraph Association, 1974.

Berger, David. "Watch It!" *Buildings, The Construction and Building Management Journal.* September 1968, p. 87.

Burstein, Harvey. *Industrial Security Management.* 2d ed. Westport, CT: Greenwood Publishing Group, 1986.

Carroll, John M. *Confidential Information Sources: Public and Private.* 2d ed. Boston: Butterworth–Heinemann, 1991.

Carson, Charles R. *Managing Employee Honesty.* Los Angeles: Security World Publishing Co., 1977.

Chamber of Commerce of the United States. *Handbook on White Collar Crime.* Washington, DC: Chamber of Commerce of the United States, 1974.

Cole, Richard B. *The Application of Security Systems and Hardware.* Springfield, IL: Charles C. Thomas, 1970.

Cunningham, William C. *Private Security Trends, 1970-2000: The Hallcrest Report II.* Boston: Butterworth–Heinemann, 1990.

Davis, John Richelieu. *Industrial Plant Protection.* Springfield, IL: Charles C. Thomas, 1957.

_____. "A $40-Billion Crime Wave Swamps American Business." *U.S. News & World Report,* February 21, 1977, pp. 47-48.

Dey, Suresh C. *Industrial Security Management.* South Asia Books, 1987.

Fennelly, Lawrence J., ed. *Effective Physical Security.* 2d ed. Boston: Butterworth–Heinemann, 1997.

Gorrill, B. E. *Effective Personnel Security Procedures.* Homewood, IL: Dow Jones-Irwin, Inc., 1974.

Green, Gion, and Raymond C. Farber. *Introduction to Security.* rev.ed. Los Angeles: Security World Publishing Co., 1978.

Hamilton, Peter. *Espionage and Subversion in an Industrial Society.* London, England: Hutchinson & Co., 1969.

Healy, Richard J. *Design for Security.* New York: John Wiley and Sons, 1968.

Healy, Richard J., and Timothy J. Walsh. *Industrial Security Management.* New York: American Management Association, 1971.

Healy, Richard J., and Timothy J. Walsh. *Protecting Your Business against Espionage.* New York: Amacom, 1973.

Hemphill, Charles F., Jr. *Security for Business and Industry.* Homewood, IL: Dow Jones-Irwin, 1971.

Institute for Local Self-Government. *Private Security and the Public Interest.* Berkeley, CA: Institute for Local Self-Government, 1974.

Jeffery, C. Ray. *Crime Prevention through Environmental Design.* Beverly Hills, CA: Sage Publications, 1971.

Kakalik, J. S., and Sorrel Wildhorn. *The RAND Reports.* Washington, DC: U.S. Government Printing Office, 1972.

Kenley and James H. Meidl. *Flammable Hazardous Material.* 3d ed. Englewood Cliffs, NJ: Prentice Hall, 1995.

Kingsbury, Arthur A. *Introduction to Security and Crime Prevention Surveys.* Springfield, IL: Charles C. Thomas, 1973.

Knowles, Graham. *Bomb Security Guide.* Los Angeles: Security World Publishing Co., 1976.

Lack, Richard W. *Accident Prevention for Business and Industry: Security Management.* National Safety Council, 1997.

Leininger, Sheryl, ed. *Internal Theft: Investigation and Control.* Los Angeles: Security World Publishing Co., 1975.

Lipman, Ira A., ed. *The Private Security Industry: Issues and Trends.* Beverly Hills, CA: Sage Publications, 1988.

Mandelbaum, Albert J. *Fundamentals of Protective Systems.* Springfield, IL: Charles C. Thomas, 1973.

Mandell, Mel. *Handbook of Business and Industrial Security and Protection.* Englewood Cliffs, NJ: Prentice-Hall, 1973.

Momboisse, Raymond M. *Industrial Security for Strikes, Riots and Disasters.* Springfield, IL: Charles C. Thomas, 1969.

National Advisory Committee on Criminal Justice Standards and Goals. *Private Security: Report of the Task Force on Private Security.* Washington, DC, 1976.

National Crime Prevention Institute Staff and Timothy D. Crowe. *Crime Prevention through Environmental Design.* Boston: Butterworth–Heinemann, 1991.

National Fire Protection Association. *Guide on Hazardous Materials.* 3d ed. Boston: National Fire Protection Association, 1969.

National Fire Protection Association. *Handbook of Fire Protection.* Boston: National Fire Protection Association.

National Industrial Conference Board. *Release No. 2488.* New York: National Industrial Conference Board, August 16, 1971.

National Safety Council. *Accident Prevention Manual for Industrial Operations.* 7th ed. Chicago: National Safety Council, 1974.

Newman, Oscar. *Defensible Space.* New York: The Macmillan Company, 1972.

Paine, David. *Basic Principles of Industrial Security.* Madison, WI: Oak Security Publications Division, 1972.

Private Security Advisory Council to the U.S. Department of Justice, Law Enforcement Assistance Administration. "Law Enforcement and Private Security: Sources and Areas of Conflict." August 1976.

Private Security Task Force to the National Advisory Committee on Criminal Justice Standards and Goals. "Survey of Law Enforcement Relationships with the Private Security Industry." October 1975.

Security Management. Published monthly by the American Society for Industrial Security, 2000 K St., N.W., Suite 651, Washington, DC 20006.

Security World. Published monthly by Security World Publishing Co., Inc., 2639 South La Cienega Blvd., Los Angeles, CA 90034.

Sennewald, Charles A. *Effective Security Management.* 3d ed. Boston: Butterworth–Heinemann, 1998.

Simonsen, Clifford E. *Introduction to Security, Loss Prevention, and Assets Protection.* Englewood Cliffs, NJ: Prentice Hall, 1998.

Strobl, Walter M. *Security.* New York: Industrial Press, 1973.

Ursic, Henry S., and Leroy E. Pagano. *Security Management Systems.* Springfield, IL: Charles C. Thomas, 1974.

U.S. Department of Commerce. *Security Lighting for Nuclear Weapons Storage Sites.* NBS Special Publication 480-27, Washington, DC, November 1977.

U.S. Department of Justice. Law Enforcement Assistance Administration. National Private Security Advisory Council. *Scope of Legal Authority of Private Security Personnel.* Washington, DC, 1976.

U.S. Department of Justice. National Institute of Law Enforcement and Criminal Justice. Law Enforcement Assistance Administration. *Private Security: A Selected Bibliography.* Rockville, MD: National Criminal Justice Reference Service, 1978.

U.S. Department of Labor. *OSHA Handbook for Small Businesses.* OSHA 2209, Washington, DC, 1977.

Weber, Thad L. *Alarm Systems and Theft Prevention.* Los Angeles: Security World Publishing Co., 1973.

Woodruff, R. S. *Industrial Security Techniques.* Columbus, OH: Charles E. Merrill, 1974.

Index

A

Abuse, alcohol, 196–97
Access control, 81–90
  automatic, 229–33
    combination locks, 231
    digital systems, 231
    key lock entry identification, 231
    magnetic card entry, 230
    remote locks, 231–32
    sophisticated computerized ID entry
      systems, 232–33
  card-key control, 85
  combination locks, 84
  guard stations, 88–89
  identification cards, 85–86
  identification systems, 85
  key control systems, 81–82
  locks and keys, 81
  master key systems, 84
  posted signs, 86–88
  types of locks, 82–83
Access limitations, 107–8
Accident/injury reports, 52
Accidents, work, 128–29
Accounting departments, 149
Activators, pressure-sensitive, 220
Activity logs, 43
ADA (Americans with Disabilities Act), 258
Addiction, drug, 196
Agencies
  credit reporting, 10
  liaison with outside, 75–77
    emergency care facilities, 76–77
    relations with local fire departments, 76
    relations with local police, 75–76

personnel clearance, 10
  private detective, 11–12
  private investigation, 11–12
  undercover, 10–11
Aid, first, 133–34
Aids, VCRs training, 207–8
Alarm companies, central, 9–10
Alarm notification, off-premise, 223–24
Alarms, 131–32, 217–27
  applications, 225–26
  capacitance, 222
  installation and service, 226–27
  off-premise alarm notification, 223–24
  perimeter protection, 164–65
  proprietary systems, 224
  responses, 226
  security consoles, 224–25
  systems
    basics of, 217–18
    ultrasonic, 221
  telephone dialers, 223
  transmission and response systems, 222–23
  types of intrusion sensors, 218–21
Alcohol, 196–97
  abuse, 196–97
American Red Cross, 69
Applicant's rights, protection of, 96–97
Applications, verifying information on,
    98–99
Apprehension and arrest, theory of, 240–42
Arrests
  citizen's, 239–40
  practical approach to, 242–43
  private person's, 239
  theory of, 240–42

Violence, preventing workplace, 249–75
  developing prevention programs, 254–55
  downsizing, 259–60
  general guidelines, 262–63
  helping employees recover from assaults,
    269–70
  hiring and termination, 257–59
  information collection, 256–57
  introduction, 250–51
  it could happen anywhere, 274
  legal issues of workplace violence, 253–54
  listening to people who are hurting, 263–65
  managing after disasters, 270–72
  managing when stress does not go away,
    272–74
  miscellaneous threats in workplace, 252–53
  physical security and hardware, 260–61
  planning for crisis to reduce its impact, 261
  policies, 256–57
  recovering from deaths of coworkers,
    265–67
  resources, 274–75
  training, 256–57
  when tragedy strikes at work, 262
  workplace violence committee, 255–56
Visitors logs, 43

W

Walkie-talkies, 212
Walls
  building, 163
  masonry, 162
Warning
  signs, 87
  systems, 131–32
Water extinguishers, 113–14
Weapons, 38
Windstorms, 128

Wiretaps and bugs, 194
Work; *See also* Jobs
  accidents, 128–29
  when tragedy strikes at, 262
Workers; *See* Employees
Workplace, miscellaneous threats in, 252–53
Workplace violence
  committee, 255–56
  legal issues of, 253–54
Workplace violence, preventing, 249–75
  developing prevention programs, 254–55
  downsizing, 259–60
  general guidelines, 262–63
  helping employees recover from assaults,
    269–70
  hiring and termination, 257–59
  information collection, 256–57
  introduction, 250–51
  it could happen anywhere, 274
  listening to people who are hurting, 263–65
  managing after disasters, 270–72
  managing when stress does not go away,
    272–74
  physical security and hardware, 260–61
  planning for crisis to reduce its impact, 261
  policies, 256–57
  recovering from deaths of coworkers,
    265–67
  resources, 274–75
  seriousness of problems, 251–52
  supervising employees with suicidal
    concerns, 267–69
  training, 256–57
  when tragedy strikes at work, 262
Writing, report, 45

Z

Zones, clear, 162–63